JOHN REDMOND AND IRISH PARLIAMENTARY TRADITIONS

JOHN REDMOND AND IRISH PARLIAMENTARY TRADITIONS

edited by

MARTIN O'DONOGHUE AND EMER PURCELL

UNIVERSITY COLLEGE DUBLIN PRESS
PREAS CHOLÁISTE OLLSCOILE BHAILE ÁTHA CLIATH
2024

NUI CENTENARY PUBLICATION

First published 2024
by University College Dublin Press
UCD Humanities Institute, Room H103,
Belfield,
Dublin 4

www.ucdpress.ie

Text and notes © the editors, 2024

ISBN 978-17-3-90863-05

All rights reserved. No part of this publication may be reproduced, stored in a retrieval system, or transmitted in any form or by any means, electronic, photocopying, recording or otherwise without the prior permission of the publisher.

CIP data available from the British Library

The right of the editors to be identified as the editors of this work has been asserted by them

Typeset in Dublin by Gough Typesetting Limited
Text design by Lyn Davies
Printed in England on acid-free paper by
CPI Antony Rowe, Chippenham, Wiltshire.

Contents

	Abbreviations	vii
	Tables	ix
	Contributor Biographies	xi
	Acknowledgements	xv
	Foreword	xvii
	Introduction *Martin O'Donoghue and Emer Purcell*	1
1	John Redmond, Irish Pasts, and Imperial Actualities: Contexts of and Constraints on his Battle for Home Rule *Margaret O'Callaghan*	11
2	Isaac Butt's Legacy: The Irish Parliamentary Party, 1879–1918 *Colin W. Reid*	20
3	The Chairman and the Chief: John Redmond and Charles Stewart Parnell *Pauric Travers*	32
4	John Redmond & Edward Carson: Bloodshed, Borders, and the Union State *Alvin Jackson*	44
5	The Irish Party: Recruitment and the Great War, c.1914–1915 *Michael Wheatley*	53
6	Women's Suffrage, John Redmond, and the Irish Parliamentary Party *Margaret Ward*	62
7	The Irish Parliamentary Party and its Successors *Martin O'Donoghue*	74
8	The Parliamentary Career of Bridget Redmond TD, 1933–52: A Gendered Analysis *Claire McGing*	88
9	The Contradictions of Redmondism *Paul Bew*	105
	Notes	114
	Select Bibliography	137
	Index	141

Abbreviations

ACA: Army Comrades' Association
AFIL: All-for-Ireland League
AOH: Ancient Order of Hibernians (Board of Erin)
BMH: Bureau of Military History
CSO: Chief Secretary's Office (Ireland)
DFA: Department of Foreign Affairs (Ireland)
DIB: Dictionary of Irish Biography
DIFP: Documents on Irish Foreign Policy
DMP: Dublin Metropolitan Police
IBIS: Institute for British-Irish Studies
IFU: Irish Farmers' Union
IHS: Irish Historical Studies
IMC: Irish Manuscripts Commission
IPP: Irish Parliamentary Party
IRA: Irish Republican Army
IRB: Irish Republican Brotherhood
IWFL: Irish Women's Franchise League
MAI: Military Archives, Ireland
MP: Member of Parliament
NAI: National Archives, Ireland
NLI: National Library of Ireland
NLS: National Library of Scotland
NUI: National University of Ireland
ODNB: Oxford Dictionary of National Biography
QUB: Queen's University Belfast
PMLA: Proceedings of the Modern Language Association
PRIA: Proceedings of the Royal Irish Academy
PRONI: Public Record Office of Northern Ireland
RHS: Royal Historical Society
RIA: Royal Irish Academy
RIC: Royal Irish Constabulary
SDLP: Social Democratic and Labour Party
TCD: Trinity College Dublin
TD: Teachta Dála (a member of Dáil Éireann, the lower house of the Oireachtas [the Irish Parliament])
TNA: The National Archives (UK)
UCD: University College Dublin
UIL: United Irish League
WSPU: Women's Social and Political Union

Tables

Table 1: Bridget Redmond's electoral record in Waterford, 1933–52

Contributor Biographies

Paul Bew is Professor Emeritus of Politics and International Studies, School of Anthropology, Philosophy and Politics, Queen's University Belfast. Formerly a historical adviser to the Bloody Sunday Tribunals, he is a crossbench peer. His publications include *Land and the National Question in Ireland, 1858–82* (1979); *The State in Northern Ireland, 1921–72: Political Forces and Social Class* (1979); *C.S. Parnell* (1980); *Conflict and Conciliation in Ireland, 1890–1910: Parnellites and Radical Agrarians* (1987); *Ideology and the Irish Question: Ulster Unionism and Irish Nationalism, 1912–1916* (1994); *John Redmond* (1996); *Northern Ireland: A Chronology of the Troubles, 1968–99* (1999) (with Gordon Gillespie); *The Making and Remaking of the Good Friday Agreement* (2007); *Ireland: The Politics of Enmity 1789–2006* (2007); *Enigma: A New Life of Charles Stewart Parnell* (2011); *Churchill and Ireland* (2016), and most recently *Ancestral Voices: Judging Dillon and Parnell* (2023).

Alvin Jackson is Sir Richard Lodge Professor of History at the University of Edinburgh. He was educated at Corpus Christi College and Nuffield College, Oxford. He has taught at University College Dublin, and, as Professor of Modern Irish History, at Queen's University Belfast. He has been John Burns Visiting Professor at Boston College. He is the author of eight books, including *United Kingdoms: Multinational Union States in Europe and Beyond* (2023), and has edited *The Oxford Handbook of Modern Irish History* (2014). He is a Fellow of the Royal Society of Edinburgh, a Member of the Academia Europaea, and an honorary Member of the Royal Irish Academy. He also holds an honorary doctorate from University College Dublin.

Claire McGing is Equality, Diversity and Inclusion (EDI) Manager at the Dún Laoghaire Institute of Art, Design and Technology (IADT), County Dublin. She is actively engaged with EDI efforts in the higher education sector in Ireland and Europe. Claire's primary research focuses on women's political representation in historical and contemporary Ireland. She has published widely in this area, including journal articles, book chapters, media contributions, and policy reports for the National Women's Council and Women for Election. Additionally, she contributes to research projects on EDI in higher education and the creative and cultural industries. Claire was formerly a John and Pat Hume Scholar and Irish Research Council Scholar at Maynooth University.

Margaret O'Callaghan is Professor of History and Politics at the School of History, Anthropology, Philosophy and Politics at Queen's University Belfast. She is the author of many articles on aspects of British high politics and the state apparatus in Ireland from the late nineteenth century to the revolution, including the monograph, *British High Politics and a Nationalist Ireland: Criminality, Land and the Law under Forster and Balfour* (1994). She also wrote the section on the political position of women in independent Ireland for the *Field Day Anthology of Irish Writing*, Vol 5. With Mary E. Daly, she edited *1916 in 1966: Commemorating the Easter Rising* (2007) while her most recent publications are on the politics of commemorating the 1916 Rising in the 1970s, on Roger Casement, British imperial policy, and the First World War. She is currently working on the Irish historian Alice Stopford Green and the writing of Irish history.

Martin O'Donoghue is a Research Fellow at the Max Planck Institute for Legal History and Legal Theory in Frankfurt where his research examines the Westminster legacy and the establishment of parliamentary democracy in India and Ireland. He was awarded his PhD from the University of Galway in 2017 and has subsequently taught history at the University of Sheffield, Northumbria University, and the University of Limerick. He was the National Library of Ireland Studentship holder in 2017/18 and has been awarded visiting fellowships at the Humanities Institute, University College Dublin and the Arts and Humanities Institute, Maynooth University. His first book, *The Legacy of the Irish Parliamentary Party in Independent Ireland, 1922–1949*, was awarded the NUI Publication Prize in Irish History.

Emer Purcell is Publications Manager at the National University of Ireland. She is responsible for NUI's Decade of Centenaries programme of events and publications. She was previously a part-time lecturer in the School of History, University College Cork. She is the general editor of *Clerics, Kings, and Vikings* (2015), a collection of 44 essays in honour of Donnchadh Ó Corráin. She is co-editor with Carrie Griffin of *Text, Transmission, and Transformation in the European Middle Ages, c.1000–1500* (2018), and co-editor with Conor Mulvagh of *Eoin MacNeill: The Pen and the Sword* (2022); the second book in the series of NUI's Decade of Centenaries programme of publications.

Colin W. Reid is a Senior Lecturer in British and Irish History at the University of Sheffield. He is the author of *The Lost Ireland of Stephen Gwynn: Irish Constitutional Nationalism and Cultural Politics, 1864–1950* (2011, pb. 2015) and a number of articles on aspects of political thought in Ireland in the nineteenth and twentieth centuries.

Pauric Travers is a graduate of the National University of Ireland and the Australian National University. A former President of St Patrick's College, Drumcondra, he is Professor Emeritus at Dublin City University. He was the founding academic director of the Parnell Summer School and is currently Chairperson of the Parnell Society. His publications include *Donegal: The Irish Revolution 1912–23* (2022) and, with Donal McCartney, *Parnell Reconsidered* (2013) and *The Ivy Leaf: The Parnells Remembered* (2006).

Margaret Ward is Honorary Senior Lecturer in History at Queen's University, Belfast. She has a PhD from the University of the West of England and an Honorary Doctor of Laws from the University of Ulster, for her contribution to advancing women's equality. Her many publications include *Unmanageable Revolutionaries: Women and Irish Nationalism*, and republished in a revised edition in 2021; *Fearless Woman: Hanna Sheehy Skeffington, Feminism and the Irish Revolution* (2017); 'Gendered Memories and Belfast Cumann na mBan 1917–1922', in Linda Connolly (ed.), *Women and the Irish Revolution: Feminism, Activism, Violence* (2020) and 'Irish suffrage: remembrance, commemoration and memorialisation', in Oona Frawley (ed.), *Women and the Decade of Commemorations* (2021). Margaret's forthcoming book examines the activities and afterlives of republican women in Belfast and County Antrim in the years 1914–24.

Michael Wheatley is an independent researcher and writes on early twentieth-century Irish history. His main publications are *Nationalism and the Irish Party: Provincial Ireland 1910–1916* (2005) and, with Timothy Bowman and William Butler, *The Disparity of Sacrifice: Irish Recruitment to the British Armed Forces, 1914–1918* (2020).

Acknowledgements

This collection of essays is born of a symposium held on 6 March 2018 to mark the centenary of John Redmond's death. The State commemoration was organised by the Department of Tourism, Culture, Arts, Gaeltacht, Sport and Media and the National University of Ireland, in collaboration with the School of History, University College Dublin, and the Royal Irish Academy.

Seven of the papers delivered that day along with the addition of two invited essays form the structure and the themes of this book. Six years on, as editors we would like to express our sincere thanks to the eight scholars who have contributed to this volume. Each chapter presented here has helped realise our aim to produce an analysis that would present new perspectives on John Redmond, the Irish Parliamentary Party, and parliamentary traditions.

We are very grateful to the Parliamentary Archives, UK, and the National Library of Ireland for their permission to reproduce the images used on the front and back covers of this book. We would also like to thank the staff of the libraries and repositories that facilitated the research for each of the chapters: Military Archives, Ireland; National Archives of Ireland; National Library of Ireland; Parliamentary Archives, Public Record Office of Northern Ireland, House of Lords, UK; UCD Archives; and United Kingdom National Archives. We also acknowledge the institutional support of NUI as well as Northumbria University, the University of Sheffield, and the Max Planck Institute for Legal History and Legal Theory where colleagues supported the project through drafting, editing and, finally, publication.

We would also like to thank: Attracta Halpin (former Registrar of NUI), Patrick O'Leary (Registrar of NUI), and Maurice Manning as both Chancellor of NUI and as Chairman of the Expert Group on Centenary Commemorations, for their support and assistance with this project. For many helpful discussions on Redmond and the Home Rule movement, Brian Hanley, Conor Mulvagh, and James McConnel.

We acknowledge with thanks the subvention received from Department of Tourism, Culture, Arts, Gaeltacht, Sport and Media and the grant received from the NUI Publications Committee, towards the cost of the publication that has allowed UCD Press to offer the book at a very reasonable price. A rarity for academic books in the current climate.

It remains to record our sincere gratitude to the two readers who reviewed the text as part of the UCD Press peer review process. They both made invaluable suggestions which have greatly enhanced the book; in particular, their close reading of the text and suggestions for framing and layout of the manuscript. We are also very grateful to UCD Press for the guidance and advice we received from Noelle Moran in bringing this volume to publication. A final thanks to the wider UCD Press team including Orla Carr, Fiachra McCarthy, Shane Gough, Nigel Carre and Deirdre Roberts.

Martin O'Donoghue and Emer Purcell
Frankfurt and Dublin, May 2024

Foreword

'John Redmond and the Irish Parliamentary Party: A Centenary Symposium' was held in the National Gallery of Ireland on 6 March 2018. The symposium was organised by the Department of Tourism, Culture, Arts, Gaeltacht, Sport and Media and the National University of Ireland, in collaboration with the Royal Irish Academy, and the School of History, University College Dublin, as part of the John Redmond State commemorative programme. The symposium set out to reassess John Redmond and the achievements of the Irish Parliamentary Party under his leadership. The Decade of Centenaries provided the opportunity to consider issues and events relevant to the Irish Parliamentary Party (IPP) such as Home Rule, First World War, women's suffrage, and parliamentary democracy.

The Redmond symposium also formed a central part of NUI's ambitious and broad-based commemorative programme for the Decade of Centenaries. From the outset it was decided that, as part of the programme, the university would honour figures associated with NUI who had made significant contributions to the building of the new Irish state such as Douglas Hyde, Eoin MacNeill, Éamon de Valera and Patrick McGilligan. The NUI commemoration programme began in 2013 with a seminar 'Douglas Hyde: The professor who became president of Ireland', and the proceedings were published in 2016. In 2013, NUI published a facsimile reproduction of *Lia Fáil: Irisleabhar Gaeilge Ollscoil na hÉireann* launched by President Michael D. Higgins. In 2018, the inaugural Hyde lecture/Léacht de hÍde (in partnership with the School of Irish, Celtic Studies and Folklore, UCD) took place when a paper 'The legacy of Douglas Hyde' was delivered by President Higgins in UCD. The second Hyde lecture, 'Douglas Hyde's American tour 1905–06', was delivered by Professor Liam Mac Mathúna in UCD in 2019.

In 2016, two additional travelling scholarships in Mathematics were offered to honour Éamon de Valera, the second chancellor of the university who presided over its affairs from his election in 1921 until his death in 1975. In that year a specially commissioned Éamon de Valera medal was also presented to each of the 2016 NUI award winners. As 2021 marked the centenary of de Valera's election as chancellor, a lecture series, 'DevTalks: Towards an assessment of his legacy', was jointly hosted by NUI and Dublin Institute of Advanced Studies.

Given his strong personal, and continuing family, connections with NUI, the university felt it particularly appropriate to honour Eoin MacNeill. To mark the centenary of the publication of MacNeill's article, 'The North began', HistoryHub.ie, UCD's public history website, produced an eight-part online series, 'Eoin MacNeill: Revolutionary and scholar' in November 2013. In 2016, NUI held a seminar 'Eoin MacNeill: A reassessment of the scholar revolutionary'. The two programmes combined provided a ready-made framework for a publication that, with the addition of invited contributions, formed a fresh re-evaluation of MacNeill's contribution to the shaping of modern Ireland and Irish academia: *Eoin MacNeill: The Pen and the Sword* edited by Conor Mulvagh and Emer Purcell was published in 2022.

In July 2022, NUI held a seminar that examined the contribution of Patrick McGilligan who succeeded MacNeill as TD for NUI in 1923. He also served on the NUI Senate. McGilligan was a key player in two of the major developments of the 1920s: the establishment of the ESB and the constitutional developments in the British Commonwealth that led to the Statute of Westminster in 1931.

NUI's Decade of Centenary programme was determined to acknowledge and foreground the contribution of Irish women and NUI graduates to the formation of the state. In December 2018, in collaboration with Maynooth University, NUI marked the centenary of women's suffrage with a symposium, 'Political voices: The participation of women in Irish public life, 1918–2018.' The proceedings of which will be published in due course. Publication is also at an advanced stage of the *National University of Ireland First World War Honour Roll: Centenary Edition and Essays*, a reproduction of the original 1919 list accompanied by a collection of essays, one of which also examines the contribution of NUI women to the war effort.

This present collection also follows through on that commitment; Margaret Ward critically examines Redmond's and the Irish Party's relationship with the suffrage movement. While Claire McGing explores the extraordinary career of Bridget Redmond and demonstrates her capabilities as a TD who represented not just the Redmond family tradition, but more importantly her constituents.

Margaret O'Callaghan's chapter opens this volume with a wonderful exposition on the Redmond tradition and how it sits within the many 'pasts' Ireland's historical narrative has created for itself. The volume closes with Paul Bew's contextualisation of the relevance of the issues at the heart of the Irish Parliamentary Party: Ireland, and its relationship with the United Kingdom in the early years of the twentieth century. Bew's comments, delivered just two years after the United Kingdom passed the referendum to withdraw from the European Union in 2016, hold true today, four years after the withdrawal has happened, demonstrating the still complex relations between Ireland and the UK a century later.

Michael Wheatley's chapter demonstrates that no analysis of Redmond and the Irish Party would be complete without a discussion of the First World War, the position Redmond adopted and how that position has been presented and interpreted in subsequent history. The chapters in this volume by Colin Reid and Pauric Travers discuss Redmond in comparison to previous leaders such as Isaac Butt and Charles Stewart Parnell, while his relationship with Edward Carson is analysed by Alvin Jackson. Martin O'Donoghue looks at Redmond and the Irish Party's successors, presenting a comprehensive context within which to situate Redmond and to see him anew at this the end of the Decade of Centenaries.

Redmond and the Irish Party were a central part of Irish politics at the start of 1910. By the end of the decade 1920, they were seen as largely irrelevant. That is a harsh fact, but a fact, nonetheless. But it is also a fact that obscures the very substantial and enduring contribution of Redmond and his predecessors as leaders of the Irish Party – Butt, Parnell, and later John Dillon – and of course the Irish Party itself, to the development of our modern State.

This volume, so superbly edited by Dr Martin O'Donoghue and Dr Emer Purcell, is a hugely important and timely contribution to our understanding of the legacy of John Redmond and the Irish Parliamentary Party.

Maurice Manning
Chancellor of the National University of Ireland
Chairman of the Expert Advisory Group on Centenary Commemorations
January 2024

Introduction

Martin O'Donoghue and Emer Purcell

> There were new problems and new forces whose nature [John] Redmond did not wholly comprehend. Yet at the last, one comes back simply to this. Redmond was faced with a problem which has not yet been solved. Self-government and unity has not yet come to Ireland. His successors using very different means have achieved a greater independence than Redmond aspired to and a partition he refused to contemplate in any lasting form. Not all problems after all are susceptible at a given moment of a happy solution.[1]

Debates about John Redmond and the late Irish Parliamentary Party have quite a long history in Irish politics, and, almost as long an origin story. That debates, centred on Redmond, would last a century after his death would not necessarily have been apparent when he died on 6 March 1918. Narratives of his funeral all emphasise the passing of Redmond from a changed Ireland that had rejected him as leader. Historians have noted the decision to hold a funeral in his native Wexford rather than Dublin for fear of 'hostile demonstration'.[2] While the level of mourning should not be understated even then, especially in the south-east, in a country where political funerals have often carried the power of remarkable political import,[3] this was not an event to turn a political tide or a moment apparently to be nurtured for later generations of Irish nationalists. Yet, it was one that was soon commemorated.[4] As Nicholas Mansergh reminded us in 1960, Redmond entered politics, following his father, who was a supporter of Isaac Butt, the intellectual father of Home Rule. John E. Redmond himself would then spend the first half of his career a follower of the next major home rule leader, Charles Stewart Parnell.[5] When Redmond passed away in 1918, his son succeeded him in the parliamentary seat, and the term 'Redmondite' – for good or for ill – has never fully disappeared from the Irish political lexicon through war, democratisation, independence, partition, the creation and renewal of new political movements, and even centenary commemoration. The story of Redmond and the Irish Parliamentary Party therefore calls us to examine a range of important questions about modern Ireland stretching from the 1870s right up to today.

Redmond was born in Dublin on 1 September 1856, the third child of William Archer Redmond and Mary (*née* Hoey) Redmond. His mother Mary was from a Protestant and unionist family from County Wicklow, and his father from a Catholic land-holding family from County Wexford. His father was MP for Wexford between 1872 and 1880; prior to that, the seat had been held by his great-uncle John Edward Redmond (1859–65). When William Archer died in 1880, his son did not inherit his seat as he had wanted; Parnell nominated Tim Healy instead, but in 1881 John Edward Redmond won a seat for New

Ross and his career in Westminster began. He was famously loyal to Parnell when the IPP split after revelations of Parnell's adulterous affair with Katharine O'Shea. In 1891, when Parnell died, Redmond took his seat in Waterford and led the Parnellite faction until the party reunited in 1900.

The Decade of Centenaries sparked renewed interest in Redmond and the Parliamentary Party, with the 100th anniversary of his death on 6 March 2018 providing stimulus for a range of events and publications. State commemoration of the anniversary of his death was marked by a symposium organised by the National University of Ireland and the Department of Tourism, Culture, Arts, Gaeltacht, Sport and Media, in collaboration with the School of History, University College Dublin, and the Royal Irish Academy. The papers delivered at the symposium, and the Royal Irish Academy discourse given by Alvin Jackson later that evening, form the basis of this collection, along with some invited contributions, and thus present a more complete analysis both of Redmond, the party, and its legacy. The collection brings together scholars from different disciplines, offering a range of new perspectives on Redmond and the IPP.

In this volume, Redmond's career and the IPP are situated within the many contexts of the politics of the nineteenth and early twentieth centuries: the British Empire, Home Rule, Nationalism, Unionism, the First World War and the 1916 Rising. More broadly, Anglo-Irish relations are considered across an extended timeframe, encompassing the twenty-first century context of Brexit and its implications for both islands where questions of sovereignty, diplomacy, and nationality were again contested and reassessed. The contributors are interested in analysing the core political principles of Redmond and the party (as well as their predecessors and successors) and how they have been viewed in historiography and popular memory.

The chapters utilise numerous sources, including contemporary newspapers, memoirs and other publications, private papers of politicians, and the archives of political parties and nationalist organisations. They reflect on aspects of Redmond and the party that have not always been to the fore in previous analyses and public debates – scrutinising how he related to Isaac Butt and Charles Stewart Parnell and how he viewed the crucial question of suffrage in the pre-war years.[6] They also assess how the party coped with the political tumults of those years, its role in developing political traditions on the island of Ireland, and the relationship of the old party with the politics of independent Ireland. This book provides a vibrant contemporary overview of Redmond and his party following the centenary of the party's stunning defeat at the end of the First World War. It also marks the 150th anniversary of the 1874 General Election where the Home Rule League, founded the previous year by Isaac Butt, first emerged as a distinct third parliamentary bloc in the House of Commons. Winning 60 seats, the 'home rulers' of the Irish Parliamentary Party became a major player at Westminster for the next 44 years. The final chapters reflect on the legacy of Redmond and the party – examining the home rule movement in broader context by analysing the continuities and discontinuities between the IPP and the parties which succeeded it.

Offering new insights into the Irish Parliamentary Party's relationship with the women's suffrage movement and gender, Margaret Ward's contribution emphasises how Redmond's opposition to suffrage was more than mere political expediency and reflected longer term doubts about granting women the vote. The place of women in parliament and Irish party politics emerges as a theme throughout the volume. The IPP was perhaps the least progressive party of its era in terms of suffrage; yet ironically, Bridget Redmond, emerged as a representative of the Redmondite tradition in Waterford and became the longest serving female TD up to that point. Gender, representation, and politics are still as relevant today as the 33rd Dáil elected in 2020 had less than 23 per cent representation of women.[7]

While the initial rationale for the collection was a critical reassessment of Redmond and the IPP, this book is more than that, as it centres on a number of debates that resonate in contemporary Ireland. The most obvious themes are Anglo-Irish relations, nationalism, and unionism, in all their myriad forms as they emerged from the Home Rule debate, the 1916 Rising and the impact of the First World War. In addition, the parties and the leaders who represented these views and movements are analysed. New insights into political party formation and styles of political leadership are offered, including consideration of not just Redmond, Parnell, Butt, and Edward Carson, but also Conservative and Liberal leaders such as William Gladstone, Arthur Balfour, and H. H. Asquith. The electoral process, the extension of the vote and the granting of suffrage to women are exemplified in the importance of the 1918 Election. The legacies of the political parties that succeeded after that election and in independent Ireland such as Sinn Féin, Cumann na nGaedheal, Fianna Fáil, and Fine Gael echo through to current affairs.

THE LEADERS AND 'THEIR' PARTIES? REDMOND AND THE IRISH PARTY IN CONTEXT

The Irish Parliamentary Party and the period covered in this volume have of course been the subject of serious scholarship with renewed interest in the period of Redmond's leadership in recent decades in particular.[8] The earlier Irish Party and the significance of the Land League, the New Departure and subsequent land legislation also attracted much academic debate, especially in the 1970s and 1980s.[9] However, despite the scale of the Home Rule movement and its pre-eminence in nationalist politics for almost half a century, no study of the party and its leaders has encompassed the period from Isaac Butt's proposals for federalism to the legacy of Redmondism in the 1940s and 1950s.[10] While Alvin Jackson's *Home Rule: An Irish History* provided a fascinating longue durée account of home rule as concept and a form of devolution, this volume draws attention to the parliamentary party specifically and the complicated role of Redmond in modern Irish history, memory, and commemoration.[11]

Writing of the 1898 centenary commemorations of the 1798 Rebellion, Senia Paŝeta remarked:

> When required, [John] Redmond could wrap himself in a revolutionary cloak by virtue of his support for Parnell and his good relations with many Fenians, thus linking himself with Ireland's radical past.[12]

As Reid points out in this volume, Redmond's first experience of parliament was visiting his father and hearing Isaac Butt address the Commons. He was also often portrayed as less forceful or inspirational in comparison to his daring predecessor in Parnell, yet Redmond was after all the Parnellite leader in the 1890s – a time when he moved in much more radical circles than was the case in the 1910s. Many Irish Party MPs had Fenian roots and, as Gerard MacAtasney has written, Redmond visited Tom Clarke, one of the architects of the 1916 Rising, 'eight or nine times' in prison in the 1890s.[13] Redmond and Dillon even wrote references for Clarke when he applied for a role as clerk with Rathdown Poor Law Union after his release.[14] The later Redmond cast himself in a different light, especially in London and throughout the empire. However, as late as 4 September 1907, Redmond spoke at the Mansion House, declaring that the Act of Union was 'a great criminal act of usurpation' and had 'no binding, moral or legal force'. Adding that he had expressed similar sentiments in the House of Commons, Redmond reiterated that physical force 'would be absolutely justifiable if it were possible'.[15] After becoming leader of the reunited party after 1900, he moved closer to an imperially tinged nationalism even if the activities of the Ancient Order of the Hibernians sometimes displayed a violent side to their constitutionalist image, as William O'Brien among others found out.[16] As Jackson suggests there were perhaps overlaps in Redmond's thinking 'with Catholic – Thomist and other – teaching on the notion of the just war. One aspect of his reasoning certainly related to the overwhelming strength of British firepower, the impracticality of any Irish assault – and the inevitability of bloody Irish defeat'.[17] As the contributors to this volume highlight, there are various ambiguities to interrogate when considering the ideas and tactics of Redmond as parliamentary leader.

In 1973, Brian Farrell's collection, *The Irish Parliamentary Tradition*, placed the IPP in a constitutional chain of succession with F. S. L. Lyons writing a chapter on the party after Parnell. The previous leader earned a chapter all to himself.[18] Sixteen years earlier, Conor Cruise O'Brien's famous study of the 1880s Irish Party referred to 'Parnell and his party' and the question may legitimately be asked – to what extent has the latter-day party ever really been characterised as 'Redmond's party'?[19] Yet, Redmond can be seen in many contexts, and so too can the Irish Party. Redmond is also very much part of scholarly debates. No biography appeared between Denis Gwynn's 1932 study and work by Bew in 1996,[20] but the number of publications on Redmond in the period since is at least a match for scholarship on Parnell, or even Daniel O'Connell, the first great Irish constitutional nationalist leader of the nineteenth century in the era before the IPP developed the template for the modern, disciplined parliamentary party.[21] Despite the IPP's reverence for the restoration of an Irish parliament at the College Green location associated with the eighteenth-century leader, Henry Grattan, he has been the subject of only one biography by R. B. McDowell in the last 30 years.[22]

The parliamentary tradition in the era of Redmond (and its afterlife) is, by contrast, the subject of renewed focus. Since Bew's biography, Joseph Finnan published *John Redmond and Irish Unity* while Dermot Meleady published his major two-volume biography and a collection of Redmond's letters. Jackson's dual biography of Carson and Redmond further enriches discussions of the period and the contexts in which Redmond carved out his political career.[23] Amid renewed debate about the applicability of a colonial framework for the analysis of Irish history, the attitudes of Redmond and the Party to the United Kingdom and the wider empire are also noteworthy, as O'Callaghan reminds us in this volume.[24] Redmond of course spent much of his political life at Westminster, and as recent research has shown, his destiny was shaped (perhaps circumscribed) by the context of pre-war British politics.[25] George Dangerfield famously proposed that British politics was rocked at the time by the suffrage movement and the conflict with the Lords as much as Irish politics.[26] Yet, as Eugenio Biagini and Patricia Jalland have shown, the fates of Irish nationalism and British liberalism had been interwoven before Redmond assumed the party chairmanship, and Westminster was a context Redmond in many ways mastered.[27] By the 1900s, the IPP was 'part of the furniture at Westminster'.[28] As O'Callaghan reminds us, Redmond, 'particularly after the fall of Parnell in 1891, lived in a sphere of narrow choices; he lacked significant agency over the question of Home Rule for most of his political career.'[29] He was an impressive Commons performer who earned the respect of those in all parties but it is not the only context in which Redmond operated or in which we should consider him.

John Redmond, like his brother Willie, married an Australian woman and appeared as happy visiting parts of the empire as he did in Britain or the United States representing the Party. Paul Townend has recently argued that we should view the period of Parnell's leadership as a moment of anti-imperial awakening, pointing to the IPP leader's condemnation of British actions in Afghanistan (1877–8), South Africa (1881), Egypt (1882) and Sudan (1884–5).[30] By contrast, the federalist Butt, with his view of Ireland's possible role in a United Kingdom and empire did not see Ireland as colonised when he made the claim that India belonged to Ireland just as much as it did to England at a Home Rule conference in 1873.[31] Butt was also interested in the usefulness of the Canadian settlement for bringing about a new constitutional arrangement in Ireland. By the time Redmond became leader of the reunited party, his affinity to some form of imperial identity became clear despite his earlier (and even sometimes later) rhetoric. Mansergh suggested he could have been an 'Irish Botha' if circumstances had allowed.[32] In his preface to Michael MacDonagh's *The Irish at the Front* in 1916, Redmond praised the martial manhood of the soldiers and even recounted firing a gun on the battlefield himself.[33] However, as Wheatley has shown, the imperial aspect of his political thought could not be mapped onto grassroots Home Rule supporters.[34] The Irish Party's wider relationship with empire therefore reflects something of the complexities of Irish experience generally, and as O'Callaghan notes here, the denouement of Home Rule and Redmond's political career were in important ways shaped by imperial concerns and contexts.[35]

That Redmond saw an imperial context for Irish affairs after the achievement of Home Rule or that he was an adept operator in a British context did not do much to endear him to what is now often called the 'Rising generation'. This point has been made numerous by times by historians even when emphasising the effects of circumstances beyond Redmond's control.[36] Nor did Redmond or the Party do the movement's previous claim to be 'essentially a Labour party' any favours when it stood aside during the 1913 Dublin strike and lockout.[37] The Party retained some working-class support even by 1918, but new forms of trade union activism brought a different kind of class politics to the party's previous 'Labour-Nationalist' wing of 'rather mild sort of rebel'(s) like J. P. Nannetti.[38] While McDermott and McCarthy have drawn attention to the staunch fidelity of Waterford and Wexford to the IPP leader, the rich tableau of county studies produced in recent decades have told stories often diverse but near uniform in their narration of a rejection of Redmond for the vibrant Sinn Féin political movement in the aftermath of 1916.[39]

If, as O'Callaghan suggests in this volume, 'John Redmond's career cannot bear the weight of the battles that contemporary polemicists place upon him and it', then this is perhaps explained by the fact that Redmond and the party he led have been chiefly remembered for the years commemorated by the Decade of Centenaries.[40] A memory of Redmond and the party that focuses on the years 1912–23 will ultimately remember them in opposition to the revolution, in opposition to the 'victors', and even worse, as somehow, unfairly, on the other side to independence.[41] While in discussing the memory and legacy of Redmond and the Party, this volume thus contributes to a range of stimulating works on memory and commemoration in recent years, it does so by approaching a topic encased in layers of political debate and historicised in very particular ways.[42]

Introduction to chapters

In order to understand Redmond and 'his party', one must look much further back in history than merely 1912. While Redmond has inevitably been viewed in the context of the Irish revolution in public debate (particularly during the Decade of Centenaries), O'Callaghan's chapter invokes different versions of the Irish past to illuminate how we might view his career from a number of perspectives. O'Callaghan analyses Redmond's place in the context of the party which preceded him as well as the leader's own relationship with Irish history stretching back to 1798. As she shows, neither the republican denunciations of Redmond informed by the revolution nor the counter-factual defences of Redmond which condemn the Easter Rising engage with the Redmond of the 1880s, 1890s or 1900s. Situating Redmond in British, Irish, and imperial contexts, O'Callaghan considers the democratisation of the 1880s and its relationship with political polarisation over the Home Rule question. In a discussion with relevance to contemporary politics, she explores the different political realities that developed between the 1884 Reform Act and the Third Home Rule Crisis – as nationalists anticipated the 'imminent' delivery of Home Rule and British elites remained convinced that Home Rule was simply 'unallowable'. Importantly, O'Callaghan reminds us of the need to consider agency – even in the assessment of political leaders. Redmond and 'his party' may be seen as a period following 'Parnell and his party', but Redmond, in particular, existed in contingent political circumstances that often restricted his choices before and after he assumed leadership of the reunited party.[43]

Sharing O'Callaghan's interest in considering Redmond outside of merely the familiar context of the revolutionary decade, Colin Reid's chapter frames the history of the Irish Party after 1879 as the legacy of Isaac Butt. While Butt has been called the 'father of home rule' and was a proponent of land reform, he is understandably viewed in very different terms to Parnell, Michael Davitt, or even Redmond. As Reid shows, this is because his political ideas have been often misunderstood or subjected to insufficient analysis. Federalism is a subject of increasing scholarly interest in many contexts and Butt's interest in it as a political solution for Ireland is key to understanding the first Home Rule leader.[44] Where O'Connellite repealers may have looked back at the 1782 model of legislative independence in the era of Grattan, Butt's original vision was one of 'shared sovereignty' between Britain and Ireland, with a Dublin chamber that would have some influence over imperial concerns as well as domestic affairs. Recovering Butt from relative obscurity in comparison to O'Connell, Parnell and Redmond, Reid demonstrates the fluidity of Irish political thought in the second half of the nineteenth century as well as the enduring influence of Buttite ideas on Redmond in relation to Irish self-government. Reid's analysis of political language highlights how proposals that have subsequently been seen as 'moderate' could in subtle ways offer innovation and even implied threats to the stability of the British state. Furthermore, reflecting on the centenary of Butt's birth in 1913, this chapter underlines how Butt's federalist thought and imperial sympathies 'chimed' with Redmond's temperament and political aims as he faced into the Third Home Rule Crisis.

The past is one of the themes of the volume, but leadership and the party remain pivotal to understanding the political evolution of Redmond and 'Redmondism'. Pauric Travers compares the leadership of Parnell and Redmond. He examines the relationship between the two men: its development from their first encounters and its influence on the later political fortunes of Redmond. Travers, most importantly, notes that after Parnell's death, Redmond more than anyone was the keeper of the Parnell flame, and he provides a comprehensive reassessment of the contribution Redmond made to the shaping of Parnell's reputation after 1891. Addressing this reputation in 1975, Emmet Larkin provocatively argued that Parnell had created a 'de facto Irish state' between 1882 and 1885 in the form of himself, the Party and the Catholic Church.[45] When J. J. Lee subsequently challenged this thesis, he listed among his reasons the fall of the Irish Party and the failure of any later leader to match Parnell in terms of personal power, and the scholarly consensus on Redmond has, as Travers notes, certainly posited him as 'chairman' rather than 'chief'.[46] This profile of him as parliamentarian and leader, however, highlights his core political instincts through a long career which begun under Parnell's tutelage.

Redmond, unlike Parnell or Butt, was a Catholic, and as nationalist leader, he had to face to a greater extent than his predecessors the reality of how the association of politics and religious difference on the island might impact any Home Rule arrangement. This fact only underlines the significance of the next comparative analysis undertaken by Alvin Jackson in his examination of Redmond alongside Edward Carson and how the United Kingdom government broached the idea of partition. Though contemporaries routinely viewed Redmond and Carson together, and though they had a strong political and personal relationship, much modern Irish historical scholarship has precluded any systematic comparison. In fact, comparing Redmond and Carson provides important illumination on the central themes of their careers, as well as on the political cultures of the multi-national union state within which they each operated. Jackson's consideration of Redmond and Carson brings the discussion up to the present day, drawing important threads of comparison between proposals for exclusion of Ulster counties and different schemes for Home Rule and partition with the debates surrounding 'hard' and 'soft' borders in the context of Brexit. Such issues, as Bew's contribution also so skilfully demonstrates, will continue to remain relevant to all with an interest in Irish studies, Anglo-Irish relations, and British and European politics.

Partition and war of course loom large in all discussions of the late Irish Party led by Redmond. The work of Michael Wheatley takes up these themes. Wheatley's chapter re-examines the fate of the Party as conflict broke out in Europe. Wheatley challenges any notion that Irish Party decline was inevitable or that the Party, broad-based and often vibrant across Ireland, was simply a decrepit political organism ready to be swept aside by the tumult of the First World War. Pointing to the vitality of organisations like the Ancient Order of Hibernians and the Volunteers, Wheatley, however, distinguishes the most active arms of the Home Rule movement from the political project of the Party's leader prior to the war. He underlines both the political context for Redmond's policies and speeches in 1914, and also the grassroots and realpolitik considerations at play. While Wheatley draws attention to aspects of the Irish response to war with Germany, he argues that Home Rule remained the primary concern of Irish nationalists. Support for war did not necessarily equate to support for recruitment, either. Tracing the decline of Home Rule activism as war dragged on and electoral politics remained in wartime dormancy, Wheatley's clearly illustrates a 'policy impasse' brought on by the course of events in Ireland and Europe that threatened the Party's supremacy before the transformative effect of rebellion at Easter 1916. In so doing, Wheatley argues that the Party was already facing its own political mortality long before what has often been termed the 'deathblow' to the movement: the conscription crisis.

Margaret Ward's contribution demonstrates that studies of Redmond and the IPP have paid insufficient attention to the question of suffrage in the period it was debated, contested, and ultimately granted. This is despite the crucial enfranchisement of women aged 30 and over in 1918. Ward analyses the voting record of the IPP and the impact upon the suffrage campaign of the Party's determination to win Home Rule for Ireland. She argues that the grand narratives of Irish history and monographs covering aspects of these years disregard the gendered implications of a Home Rule settlement that omitted the female half of the population. In so doing, they ignore the misogyny that existed within the Irish Party. She constructs an alternative narrative that focuses on histories of the suffrage movement and suffrage newspapers in Ireland and Britain. Ward's narrative does justice to the feminist campaign, putting into context the anomaly of men doing their best to assure other men that Home Rule posed no threat to their political and cultural identity, while continuing to deny Irish women of any political persuasion the right to citizenship in the forthcoming constitutional arrangement. She concludes: 'When the chronology of events in the period 1909–12 is examined, it becomes clear that Redmond and many of his colleagues were opponents of women's suffrage long before they raised the pretext that Home Rule would be jeopardised if a women's suffrage measure was passed.'[47]

Claire McGing and Martin O'Donoghue analyse the tradition of Redmond and Redmondism beyond 1918 in chapters that examine gender and the development of party politics more broadly. O'Donoghue considers the legacies of the Party's tactics, organisations, and ideology, as well as the personal legacies of its members and followers. Examining the iterations of nationalist parties from 1918, he considers Sinn Féin, both sides of the Treaty split, and the Nationalist Party in Northern Ireland. Analysing each in turn as well as considering examples from among the Irish diaspora and other contexts, the chapter ultimately concludes that there was no true reincarnation of the IPP. The old Irish Party structures retained greater strength in Ulster in 1918, but the development of Northern Ireland and its politics left Joe Devlin and colleagues marginalised and demoralised. While they played leading roles in the Nationalist Party in Northern Ireland, it bore little resemblance to the Irish Party in either grassroots or parliamentary politics. Conversely, Sinn Féin, which learned much from its Home Rule predecessors, provided the foundation stone for 'civil war' politics – former Home Rulers who sought power in independent Ireland had to join with those with revolutionary heritage. In a broader sense, examination of the dilemmas and challenges that the Irish Party faced reveals important insights about political culture, electoral politics, Anglo-Irish relations, and the question of partition.

McGing examines the political career of Bridget Redmond through the lens of gender. Situating her in the male-dominated political culture of the Free State as well as bringing to the fore Redmond's input beyond simply the political organisation inherited from her husband, William Archer Redmond. McGing sheds new light on the contribution to public life of the last 'keeper of the Redmondite flame' in Waterford.[48] She analyses Redmond's role as a legislator and her political philosophy, with a focus on her contributions to women's issues and her remarkable record of electoral success. While her election to the Dáil took place within the context of enduring Redmondite loyalty in Waterford, McGing demonstrates that the TD first elected in 1933 was more than just a Redmond. Pointing to her work at constituency level, including her high-profile role in the Blueshirt movement in the south-east, as well as her parliamentary interventions, McGing highlights that Redmond was also more than merely a 'silent sister', despite a political and social context that did not easily facilitate women's participation in representative politics. Scrutinising Dáil debates, her examination of Redmond's career as TD reveals a more wide-ranging and significant career than has often been acknowledged in the past.

In the concluding chapter, Bew takes the long view, and explores what the politics of Redmondism can tell us in an age where the themes of unity and approaches to Anglo-Irish relations once more stimulate public debate. Examining the tone of Redmond's conciliation with Britain, Bew points out that Redmond's vision of Home Rule, that Irish MPs would remain at Westminster but have their own parliament in Ireland, is effectively devolution – the position of Scotland in the last decade or more. In addition, he suggests that:

> many have argued that Redmond failed on partition but, for a hundred years since, other traditions have taken over and they too have failed. So, that is not a killing point against Redmond. He was not offering a solution to partition; he was offering the best possible and most benign and fairest compromise to the rights that existed on all sides.[49]

This fundamental tension has continued to be at the heart of Anglo-Irish relations from the Government of Ireland Act 1920, the Boundary Commission through to the Anglo-Irish Agreement in 1985, and the Good Friday Agreement in 1998; and more recently the UK's post-Brexit relationship with the European Union which remained at risk due to the Northern Ireland Protocol. Indeed, Bew skilfully asks if contemporary defences of Redmondism may be impossible in the aftermath of Brexit, and if an independent Irish state that faces Europe rather than Britain is in fact the legacy of James Connolly and Roger Casement rather than John Redmond.

As the Decade of Centenaries draws to a close, it is fitting that this collection situates John Redmond and the Irish Parliamentary Party anew within more than just the context of the early twentieth century, viewed one hundred years on. Redmond's legacy has been traditionally interpreted based, in particular, on the years 1912–18, Home Rule, the First World War, the 1916 Rising and its fallout, suffrage, and the 1918 Election. The chapters here, beginning with O'Callaghan's contribution, show that in mediating these and other issues, he was, to varying degrees and at different times, hampered by the nature of politics and the Irish Parliamentary Party itself. To some extent, Redmond did develop a modus vivendi with other leading members within the Party, but as Bew remarks, 'he was never granted the authority and the prestige of true leadership by powerful colleagues such as John Dillon, William O'Brien, Tim Healy and Joe Devlin.'[50] While Redmond and the Party actually dominated the Irish political scene for decades, as the themes explored in this collection demonstrate, the complicated nature of Irish political developments and Anglo-Irish relations itself, also constrained Redmond, the Party and their successors in ways deserving of further consideration.

CHAPTER I

JOHN REDMOND, IRISH PASTS, AND IMPERIAL ACTUALITIES: CONTEXTS OF AND CONSTRAINTS ON HIS BATTLE FOR HOME RULE*

Margaret O'Callaghan

The Irish past can be a battle chest from which political opponents haul out stories, personages, and events to sharpen as weapons in contemporary political conflict. Frozen in an image from his corpulent late 50s on the eve of the First World War, the figure of John Redmond is a particularly potent totem to take out to battle on that ground where Irish historical memory and Irish politics lock. It has been John Redmond's unavoidable fate to be read through the 1916 Rising. Those who celebrate 1916 as the great event in modern Irish history paint Redmond as an obsolete, imperialist Home Ruler, a failed politician who brought a truncated form of limited Home Rule, suspended for the war, on to the statute books, too late, in 1914, and conceded some form of Ulster exclusion, prior to supporting the British war effort.

Those who loathe 'the cult of 1916' enlist Redmond as a wise and sagacious statesman, the supreme constitutionalist, who won the promised land of Home Rule first glimpsed under Parnell's leadership in 1886. Had 1916 never happened, according to this interpretation, Redmond's wise counsels would have prevailed and the end of the war would have seen a Home Rule Ireland, acquired without bloodshed, in power and status substantially the same as that which was acquired through the 1921 Treaty.[1] Those who adopt this view suggest that partition might never have happened, or at the least have never been consolidated in the 1920s in the form it then took and has since preserved.

Neither of these argumentative stances, for different reasons, have much interest in the younger Redmond of the 1880s and 1890s. Nor do they usually reflect on his formation and political action in the radically different politics of the decades of the 1880s, the 1890s and the 1900s.[2] From the perspective of those decades, John Redmond's career cannot bear the weight of the battles that contemporary polemicists place upon him and it. Redmond, particularly after the fall of Parnell in 1891, lived in a sphere of narrow choices; he lacked significant agency over the question of Home Rule for most of his political career.[3]

Like that of most nationalists and unionists of his political generation, Redmond's world was defined by the Parnellite conversion of William Gladstone to Home Rule in 1886. Despite Gladstone's failure to carry his own Liberal Party on the issue in 1886, despite the fact that he was on his last legs by the time he got it through the House of Commons in 1893, (and unlikely as he was in that decade or even the next one to get a Home Rule bill through the House of Lords), Gladstone's adoption of the nationalist demand made Home

Rule, together with the land question, the defining Irish political issues of the day. Home Rule seemed apparently tantalisingly close to achievement but was constantly stymied.

In the language of Charles Stewart Parnell, the Irish nation stood within sight of the Promised Land. But the Conservative Party decision to oppose Home Rule as a key and immoveable point of policy made the high game that Parnell had played for a brief moment impossible to bring forward – a sighting of the promised land was all it could be. Imminent Home Rule was in fact a millennial delusion after 1886. It had become an ideologically justified criminal anathema to all English and Irish Unionists by the end of the Special Commission in 1889, and ruled out of what Victorians called the sphere of practical politics by the time of the Parnell Split of 1891.[4] The Home Rule issue was, however, the forcing ground of Irish political democratisation,[5] the issue through which modern Irish nationalism and modern Irish unionism were constructed and defined.[6]

Jack Redmond (as John was known to family) was from that unusual formation: a Wexford Catholic gentry family.[7] As a clerk in the House of Commons, he was a second division figure in the high days of the early 1880s. A late entrant to the Bar Library, he had been principally occupied in New Tipperary legal cases arising out of the Plan of Campaign when the Parnell divorce case blew the Nationalist Liberal alliance temporarily apart in 1890. As leader of the Parnellites, the smallest faction of the splintered Irish Parliamentary Party from the death of Parnell to the reunification of the Irish Party in 1900, he was negotiating with disparate elements: hillside men as the old Fenians who had supported Parnell were called; amnesty campaigners; his own social class; and some agrarian campaigners.[8]

Redmond was romantically attached to the 1798 Rebellion: he celebrated the Fenian tradition, and along with his brother Willie, he engaged in high nationalist rhetorical hyperbole in these years. Parnell's movement had been constitutionally focused but through the New Departure of the early 1880s it encompassed a broad spectrum of nationalist opinion that ran from Buttite federalism, through agrarian radicalism, to Fenian activism. When Parnell was thrown over by the majority of the Parliamentary Party, Redmond and Edward Harrington were the significant MPs who stood with him. Parnell made rejection of Liberal dictation to Irish democracy the slightly false premise of his campaign for his political life, so brilliantly documented in Frank Callanan's *Parnell Split*.[9] It was however, not simply at Liberal dictation that the bulk of Catholic Ireland had thrown him over.

The 'Parnell spilt' and Parnell's death 'made all Platonic tolerance vain, and vain all Doric discipline'.[10] The Parnell funeral, with constitutionalists, GAA guards of honour, language societies and Fenian bearers, was the most powerful and evocative public display of Irish nationalist sentiment since the reinterment of Terence Bellew McManus decades earlier.[11] The anti-Parnellites, made up of competing factions of McCarthyites and Dillonites, followers of the viciously intelligent Tim Healy, with William O'Brien and Davitt on the edges, all clung after 1891 to aspects of the Liberal alliance.[12] The small Parnellite rump led by Redmond initially ditched the alliance, as Parnell had done, and inherited from Parnell's last year of fighting for his life the active IRB men who had stewarded and defended him on all of his last platforms. Thus, Redmond the Parnellite led a strange coalition, a broad church of Irish nationalism through the last decade of the nineteenth century.

On 27 September 1896 at a meeting in Tipperary to demand amnesty for the five remaining Fenian prisoners in British jails, John Redmond said of one of them

> Wilson is a man of whom no words of praise could be too high. I have learned in my many visits to Portland for five years to love, honour and respect Henry Wilson. I have seen day after day how his brave spirit was keeping him alive ... I have seen year after year the fading away of his physical strength.[13]

Henry Wilson was, as Dermot Meleady has pointed out in his biography of Redmond, the alias of Tom Clarke, perhaps the key figure in planning the 1916 Easter Rising.[14]

The Redmond of the 1890s relied on the support of the newly established *Irish Independent*, the Parnellite paper that was partly run and written by a Fenian cabal, including the maverick J. J. O' Kelly in London. The Dublin Metropolitan Police, and in particular the ubiquitous John Mallon,[15] were outraged at open Fenian business being done from the newspaper premises. Redmond himself lectured widely on 1798, spoke at amnesty meetings, and kept anti-clerical company while simultaneously developing a federalist line on Home Rule that celebrated Ireland's role in the British Empire. Supporting the empire did not preclude Redmond from both opposing the Boer War and giving homage to those Irish who had died in the British Army.

The 1798 Commemoration Committee had enlisted all nationalists in a campaign to erect a statue of Wolfe Tone at the Grafton Street corner of St Stephen's Green.[16] Nervous of the new alliances of his former IRB acquaintances who had been to some degree purged in preparation for the reunification of the Irish Party, Redmond put his energies into a Parnell monument instead.[17] Unconfined by the Liberal alliance, Redmond co-operated with Horace Plunkett and moderate unionists in the Recess Committee; he tried to ensure that the 1898 democratisation of local government did not mean that, as Healy wished, all landlord influence ended at his demesne gate. He co-operated with aspects of the Tory government's 'killing Home Rule by kindness'[18] policies because both tenants and landlords wanted land purchase and other benefits, even if not for Tory ideological reasons.[19] The past is another country, and Redmond's positions in the 1890s (to us contradictory) reflect the complex formation of the broad spectrum that was Irish nationalism at that time. Redmond tried to heal the split through negotiations with William O'Brien and other tactical moderates in the rupture.[20]

Commemorations may be dubious moments for some historians, but centenary commemorations give us one great gift: the ability to map a comparable duration from the past (in this case the 1880s to 1918), against the sense of a comparable period from our own time. For those of us who have lived through the Northern conflict we can see that, for us, from 1886 to 1918 is a similar or analogous timeframe as that from the Anglo-Irish Agreement of 1985 to Brexit. So, we can think of the period from Gladstone's First Home Rule Bill of 1886 to the Third Home Rule Bill of 1912 through 1916 to the death of Redmond on this date in 1918 as not perhaps so very long a period.

We can also perhaps recall that the 1880s were game changing in Britain and Ireland, because the 1884 and 1885 reforms of the franchise marked the democratisation of politics. This was a political revolution for all political parties as they entered uncharted territory in terms of how to deal with a mass electorate. For Albert Venn Dicey and for a host of other constitutional analysts this opened a new chapter in the British Constitution. The challenge for all political parties was to educate the new electorate into the mentality of the élite: to guide and control 'the protean masses' and attract their votes.[21] But that game-changing democratisation of politics was more fundamental in Ireland than elsewhere in the United Kingdom because of Ireland's demographic actualities, and because in Ireland the electoral system of 'first past the post' rendered local political and religious minorities representation less visible. In Ireland it meant the polarisation of politics, exacerbated as a consequence of Gladstone's conversion to Home Rule. Democratisation, the massively increased electorate, polarised popular politics on the ground through the elections of 1885 and 1886 and divided the country into pro and anti-Home Rule camps. It also divided the élites in Ireland and in the United Kingdom on the subject of Ireland; there was polarisation at the key moment of democratisation. This was not an accidental consequence of the democratisation of politics but its absolute corollary – a result of the historically laid down confessional and ideological geography of Ireland.[22]

As constitutional theorists of deeply divided societies Donald Horowitz and Arend Lijphart disagree on many things, but they agree on one indicator for successful consociationalism in the present, and that is the presence of cooperation between elites at the moment of mass democratisation.[23] That is precisely what did not happen in Ireland. Irish unionists of all social classes were enfolded within the pro-Union elite of both islands, while Irish nationalists were politically educated in Home Rule through the land question into a very different formation, an oppositional one. Eugenio Biagini has argued for Irish Home Rule as a kind of subset of British liberalism. There are some truths in this perspective, but it is a far from persuasive case.[24]

Sections of Irish nationalism worked closely with British liberalism; there was devout affection for Gladstone in Ireland as a kind of Home Rule enabler or deliverer. But effectively the process of democratisation unfolded very differently in Ireland compared to how it worked on the other island. The Home Rule to which Gladstone was converted was, however, primarily conceived by him as a means of stabilising the Union of Great Britain and Ireland in the light of a declension of what he perceived to be 'the Irish ills' of religion, land, and administration. The Home Rule that Gladstone saw himself as embracing was essentially the arrangement for local administration put forward by Isaac Butt. This had been the language of Jack Redmond's father's generation.[25]

But the language of the Land War of the 1880s, the rhetoric of agrarian resistance, declared not just class war but also a new sensibility of popular politics that was facilitated by *United Ireland*, an organ built out of Richard Pigott's earlier, motley collection of such organs.[26] That rhetoric was both new and old. It carried forward an amalgam of older rhetorics: Daniel O'Connell's extreme language designed to embolden the weak; T. D. Sullivan's ballads, the harder language of Fenian texts; and an older language from agrarian secret societies and rural regulatory actions. This became the idiom of Irish nationalist self-representation. Even during the 1880s, the speeches of Irish Nationalist MP beckoned to limitless Irish national patriotic vistas ahead – their own fields, their own land, their own territory.

The Conservative strike-back after 1886 was to represent this language as incitement to criminality.[27] For whole categories of Irish landowners, Irish unionists, English, Welsh and Scottish unionists, Home Rule became something quite simply unallowable. The tens of thousands of Irish Unionist Alliance and Property Defence Association pamphlets that flooded England were intended to explain to the English electorate that Ireland was a dangerous, savage, and brutal place.[28] Thinking teleologically through the Third Home Rule Bill and indeed the Fourth if you want to see the 1920 Government of Ireland Bill as such, might appear to suggest a gradual extending of the Home Rule project. Closer examination denies that view. What that perception also obscures is the extent to which for most Tories, and gradually after 1893, a very large number of Liberals, Home Rule was, it was hoped, a receding chimera.

In writing about the 1867 extension of the franchise, Maurice Cowling was at pains to point out that popular protests at the railings of Hyde Park were not the reason for the elite conceding that reform.[29] Even if we do not go the full distance with Cowling on 1867, or with A. B. Cooke and John Vincent in *The Governing Passion* on 1886,[30] we too need to remember that the connections between high and low politics are not straightforward but rather complex and refracting. Parliamentary Irish politics took place in at least two theatres, one of these being Westminster and the other, the hustings in Ireland. In the years after Parnell's death the fragmented Irish Parliamentary Party and after the new century, the reunited United Irish League continued to speak in a hard rhetoric of quasi-independence. As Meleady's biography shows Redmond's rhetoric in the 1890s, when he spoke on Fenian Amnesty platforms with Maud Gonne, the Dalys and others, was barely constitutional.[31] And while William O'Brien may have been the only Irish Parliamentary Party politician to see that the gap between what Home Rule promised and what the imperial state would allow was huge, Redmond was also sympathetic to O'Brien's attempts to cooperate with various forces in Irish society from the time of the reunification of the Irish Party in 1900.[32]

The leverage of Parnell in relation to getting Home Rule was gone before his fall. It was really gone from the irrevocable decision of the Conservative Party and its Liberal unionist allies to see Home Rule as a threat to empire and as such unallowable.[33] There is little in the public or private communications of any leading Tory politician in the succeeding two decades as far as I am aware that indicates otherwise. The threat and danger of Home Rule, furthermore, does some electoral service for Tories and liberal unionists as a subset of wider imperial jingoism.

'Killing Home Rule with kindness' may be a well-worn cliché. The purpose of the Tory and Liberal Unionist government in Ireland from 1895 to 1906 was initially to do nothing. But when prompted by Horace Plunkett and others to believe that they had one last chance to win Ireland for the Union they did attempt to change the nature of popular politics in Ireland by economic amelioration rather than the firm repression of a decade earlier. And that did appear to work.

The Irish Party, or sections of it, were successful at cooperating with both Tories and Liberals in bringing a range of quite dramatic economic, social, and agrarian improvements to Ireland in the years between 1895 and 1910. To look through the papers on their work on land purchase makes the scale of their engagement and the changes they effected seem quite remarkable. John Dillon's worries about the dangers of successful land purchase measures taking the fire out of the Home Rule cause were not really that misplaced. As Paul Bew has pointed out, the old age pensions further seemed to secure Ireland within existing arrangements.[34] So while Redmond could influence Liberal policy after they returned to power in 1906 in a variety of 'real' ways, he signally failed to get a Home Rule bill introduced. He did not actually have any political leverage until the power of the House of Lords was removed in 1910 for internal British political reasons, and the Party held the balance of power at Westminster, with the Liberal Party compelled to introduce a Home Rule bill in order to stay in power.

The Council Bill of 1907 represented the kind of Home Rule that Liberals were willing to offer, and that Tories might have accepted. But 1907 was also 21 years from 1886; the year when James Joyce amusingly called 'Home Rule Comes of Age'.[35] As Tom Garvin's work on the social backgrounds of those who later became revolutionaries makes clear, the respective generational cohorts who had grown up in the messianic language of imminent Home Rule continued to live in its frame.[36] Had the Council Bill gone through in 1908, things might have placated this generation but the collision of two sharply differentiated world views – those of the Irish nationalist and the British and Irish unionist – was lit up and exposed by the forcing ground of H. H. Asquith's unforeseen and imposed necessity of introducing some form of so-called Home Rule as a result of the fall out of the second great change in the British Constitution in these years: the Parliament Bill.[37]

The Parliament Act of 1911 similarly marked a revolution in governance, confirming the reality dimly visible in the 1880s of the House of Commons no longer being restrained or held back by the aristocratic interest of the House of Lords. A Home Rule bill pushed by Gladstone had passed the House of Commons as early as 1893 and had been blocked by the veto of the Lords.[38] The Parliament Act also gave Redmond the balance of power.[39] These changes marked specific types of revolutionary consequences for Ireland, but they were initiated with little primary consideration of what their differentiated results might be.

In a work published in 1929, T. P. O'Connor wrote that

> it has been seen that Ireland, under the urge of this movement had gradually possessed the mind of Gladstone and set him on with devotion to the idea of her emancipation, so that at the time this narrative approaches that he was to make the bold leap to Home Rule that took English people's breath away ... With the fact accomplished nowadays, all that hubbub may seem strange; but the younger generation who cannot understand these things have only to examine the literature and speeches of the time to see how Gladstone's decisive advance was regarded with horror; how to so many otherwise well-balanced minds dismemberment of the Empire should seem imminent; how the then Prince of Wales expressed the opinion that Gladstone's mind was going, and how the Queen was urging upon friends of his that he should retire from active leadership and go up to the Lords, where he would be impotent to carry forward these revolutionary proposals into which she read a menace to the very throne.[40]

It had seemed in 1886 that democratisation and the Liberal commitment to Home Rule had driven unionists in both islands and nationalists in Ireland into two different world views and simultaneously precipitated a breakdown in social relations between the upper echelons of the Liberal Party.[41] By the crisis years of 1912 to 1914, however, Tories and Liberals were not necessarily as polarised on Home Rule as they had been in 1886. From the Liberal leader Rosebery's (Archibald Primrose, Earl of Rosebery) predominant partner speech, and certainly from the new politics of the Boer War and the Committee on Imperial Defence, neither party had wanted to grant Home Rule to Ireland. That was the true meaning of the Irish Council Bill. It was a realistic attempt to offer what the British political elite could just about tolerate.[42]

Given the Liberals' desire to stay in power, the Third Home Rule Bill was an unintended consequence of the Parliament Bill. As Ronan Fanning has pointed out, Churchill and Lloyd George had tried to make some separate provision for Ulster before the Bill was introduced.[43] But Micawberesque hopings[44] drove the Liberal government on. The Home Rule bill was a fairly constrained affair in any case, but it was more than either of the two British parties had wanted to offer. The dusted down and renewed debates on a federal United Kingdom, hinted at by Asquith tentatively through his strange speech introducing the Home Rule bill, represented another map of a potential route of salvation away from Home Rule *tout court*; this came out of Alfred Milner's kindergarten in South Africa after the Boer War.

From 1912 onwards, Liberal politicians were just hoping for the best as the renewed public debate on Home Rule opened up the yawning chasm between what Irish nationalists expected, what Irish unionists dreaded, and what any British government, even a Liberal one, was prepared to give. Arthur Balfour, ever one to call a spade a shovel, pointed out in the summer of 1916 that the game had changed. Give Redmond something there and then – what had been denied for so long – or his and Dillon's life's work would be blown away. Sadly, Balfour could not succeed in saving them in 1916 because, as the documents published by Deirdre McMahon demonstrate, his Conservative and unionist followers had heard the beat of a different drum and the language of a different process of democratisation for too long.[45] This became painfully apparent to Redmond over the course of the deliberations and ensuing stasis of the Irish Convention.

The Irish Convention of 1917–18 was a political gathering of men in a room to discuss the future fate of the Home Rule project,[46] a project in circulation since Gladstone's first introduction of the bill for Home Rule in 1886. It was new, however, in two ways. In the first instance it was the first large quasi-representative gathering of exclusively Irish representatives whether nationalist, unionist or, in more recent times, Labour and others, and in the second, it contained no individuals with the power to make a political decision. In some degree it resembled, or sought to resemble, the Land Conference of 1903.[47] The latter had drawn up a blueprint for the settlement of the land issue between diverging Irish interests through the mediation of the then Chief Secretary, George Wyndham. It had also presented some shadowy reflection of what the limited assembly proposed in the Liberal Council Bill of 1907 might have looked like. The Council Bill had been Sir Antony McDonnell's attempt to push a Liberal government who wanted to do nothing on Ireland to do something.[48] The 'convention of representative Irishmen' summoned in 1917 by Lloyd George had, however, a far wider if nebulous brief. This was to 'solve', the so-called 'Irish question'. The prime minister assured them that such decisions as they made would be implemented.

Home Rule had been on the statute books in 1914. But being on the statute books and having political reality were not the same things. What was on the statute books – quite apart from the unresolved question of exclusion of four, six or nine northern counties – was a highly limited form of devolution within the empire. It was arguably less than what had been offered almost 30 years before in 1886.[49] This had also been the case with the offers of the summer of 1916 when both Redmond and Carson had initially agreed to an immediate but partitioned Home Rule, and the even odder offer to Redmond in 1917 of immediate Home Rule for a partitioned entity or alternatively for a Convention.[50] All were deeply unclear as to implementation or even strategy for their implementation. In all three 'Home Rule nearly there' cases whether at the start of the war, Lloyd George's attempt in the aftermath of Easter 1916 to put in place a quick fix Home Rule, or the offer immediately preceding the Irish Convention that Redmond rejected, the form of Home Rule on offer was profoundly limited.

The political landscape and Irish public opinions had changed in those 30 years since 1886. This happened initially through the polarising effects of democratisation, and then through the paramilitarisation of Ireland initiated by the Ulster Volunteers, and then more rapidly again by the start of the war, subsequently accelerated by government reaction to 1916.

The Convention has been described as one based on liberal precepts in a period when the lights of liberalism were extinguished.[51] But the Ulster Unionist representatives had clear instructions and intentions to maintain a partitionist line. That was the sole function of their presence. Redmond retained his consistent opposition to partition, something to which he had in fact already conceded. He focused instead on a deal with the southern unionists that perhaps unrealistically carried a hope of subverting partition. The addition of church representatives, William Martin Murphy, cranks, faddists of every description and others sealed the fate of the Irish Convention as a talking shop that was intended to be sold to the United States and elsewhere as serious evidence of the desire of Britain to deal with this Irish problem.

Who or what did the representatives at the Convention represent? Some were elected representatives; the parliamentary party had done well in a number of the earlier wartime by-elections. Count Plunkett and later Joe McGuinness, Éamon de Valera and then William T. Cosgrave were elected during the lifetime of the Convention, and the new Sinn Féin was, as Michael Laffan says, growing apace by the summer of 1917.[52] Timing was all, and the Convention trapped Redmond at a kind of stopped clock around which change happened. It was in retrospect a dangerous drawn-out hiatus during which other processes of change accelerated.

One of the first problems the Convention had was around the word 'representative'. Who, in particular, *was* representative of non-parliamentary party Irish nationalist interests? There was of course the parliamentary party and its nominees, but the party was affected by Dillon's distancing of himself from Redmond and by the collapse of American fund raising because of Redmond's passionate support for the war with a Germany with whom many of the American Irish fundraisers were affiliated. While American entry into the war in 1917 did not make the Irish question irrelevant for United States politics, the Convention provided Lloyd George and his Tory-dominated coalition with a ready answer to American queries; that they had passed the problem on to the interested parties, and it was now their problem to sort out.

Although the Convention made things worse for Redmond, it did have some interesting features. The heavy involvement of the proto-Round Table circle through Philip Kerr, later Lord Lothian, and Alfred Milner. Sir Bertram Windle of Cork and his son-in-law J. J. Horgan would with Stephen Gwynn, pull this Round Table strand into a key focus in Irish politics.[53] Through Lloyd George's war cabinet and his kitchen cabinet, the Milnerites and these new Commonwealth creators from the South African kindergarten shifted debate.

Federalism principally functioned as a ruse to block or limit or restrain the boundaries of what Home Rule could mean for Ireland.

The Convention secretariat provided another glimpse into the future in the person of W. G. S. Adams, Gladstone Professor of Political Theory and Institutions at the University of Oxford, a Home Ruler who had earlier worked with Horace Plunkett and through whom connection was established with his later student, the brilliant Nicholas Mansergh.[54] Erskine Childers, absent in Ireland since the Howth gun running of 1914, also made a rather mysterious return from British naval exploits.[55] The role of Conor Cruise O'Brien's father, Francis, the employee of Horace Plunkett and journalist with Æ [George Russell] on the *Irish Homestead*, however, remains obscure.[56]

In many ways the secretariat is the most interesting thing about the Convention. The choice of Horace Plunkett as chair, however, seems to have been an unfortunate one. Although a significant Irish political player for over two decades, his earlier publications hardly endeared him to most nationalists while he was long-winded, verbose, and unfocused, lacking almost any sense of the political.[57] In the face of a Sinn Féin boycott, meanwhile, Alice Stopford Green suggested George Russell, herself, Edward MacLysaght, and others to represent the 'advanced nationalist' position. They took her advice but excluded her.

Balfour's trip to the United States in March 1917 in an attempt to bring the US into the war revealed to him that even though Woodrow Wilson was himself deeply anti-Irish, the 'Irish thing' mattered there. At the start of the Convention, Ireland was restive, under quasi-martial law and in what Redmond's old nemesis Tim Healy saw was a period of radical change. Internee and prisoner releases at the *start* of the Convention were evidence of governmental good will, but the oddly trumped-up German Plot and the decision to introduce conscription shortly after Redmond's death were politically disastrous both for the Convention and for the Ireland for which Redmond had come to stand. The death throes of Redmond's Ireland were confirmed by the cabinet decision to let the Tory diehards, led by the intransigent Walter Long, steer all future government policy towards Ireland.

Easter 1916 had been an armed challenge not just to British rule but also to Redmond's Ireland. Its aftermath in time of global war, made Ireland's political future uncertain. The Irish Convention of 1917–18, to which Redmond devoted so much, was bookended by the threat of conscription, and by the new hard-line military policy in response. Frank Callanan cites a prescient observation made in 1918 by that most astute analyst of change, Tim Healy, which cuts to the essence both of the Redmondite party's predicament by the end of that year and to the obstacles to our understanding of the extent of the post-1886 determinants of Redmond's ultimate failure:[58]

Our view of Redmond today is framed both by the mentalities of the Irish past, the imperial determinants that frustrated his politics and his party, and by the perspectives of subsequent Irish history. We should perhaps have more compassion for those like him and indeed all others of the time who could not see into the future. This is a blindness which we all share.

CHAPTER 2

ISAAC BUTT'S LEGACY: THE IRISH PARLIAMENTARY PARTY, 1879–1918

Colin W. Reid

Isaac Butt may be regarded as the father of Home Rule, but his reputation has never achieved the exalted status of Irish constitutional leaders such as Daniel O'Connell or Charles Stewart Parnell. Even the historical recovery of John Redmond over the past few decades stands in stark contrast to Butt's lingering obscurity.[1] There is no Isaac Butt Summer School, nor national symposia in his name. There is no 'national' statue of Butt standing alongside O'Connell and Parnell in the heart of Dublin (although a fine bronze statue of Butt was unveiled in his native Stranorlar in 2012). Butt was not included as one of the four faces of constitutional nationalism that were (controversially) projected onto College Green during the Easter Rising Centenary events in 2016.[2] The only trace of the instigator of Home Rule in the capital's landscape is Butt Bridge, which was named shortly after his death in 1879. The Isaac Butt Bar on Store Street, near Connolly Station, was replaced in recent years by a quirky bar/cafe called The Good Bits, which in turn has closed down. As Butt was rather too fond of a tipple, the irony works on a number of levels.

Similarly, scholarly interest in Butt is patchy. There is no modern biography of the founder of the Home Rule movement, with the only book-length profile of his life, by Terence de Vere White, published as long ago as 1946.[3] Historians continue to rely on two works from the 1960s in understanding pre-Parnellite Home Rule political culture, namely Lawrence McCaffrey's long-form essay on federalism and David Thorney's study of Butt's leadership.[4] Both these works are limited in methodological scope and contain problematic assumptions. McCaffrey conceptualised federalism as a form of 'conservative nationalism' which was doomed to failure, while Thornley, who barely touched on the complexity of Butt's political thought before 1868, cast him as the personification of a 'curious imperial nationalism'.[5] More recent accounts have challenged the inference that the idea of self-government lay exclusively within the domain of nationalists, suggesting a great deal more fluidity within the Irish political spectrum than the binary unionist-nationalist paradigm implies.[6] But it remains the case that there is a dearth of new work on the era of Isaac Butt and early Home Rule, with little akin to recent innovative studies of the Redmondite Party, which have shed light on its leadership structures, grassroots activism, and the strangely alluring figure of Redmond himself.[7]

Butt's relative absence from the Irish historical consciousness can partly be explained by the stereotypical view of him, shared by contemporaries and later observers, as a political failure. Such a depiction of Butt stresses his noble intentions while condemning him as temperamentally unsuited to the cut-and-thrust of frontline politics. His perceived 'moderation', both of style and approach, was undermined by the brilliance of the Parnellite assault of the late 1870s and 1880s. As Alan O'Day vividly put it, the perception was that 'Parnell spoke for Ireland when Butt appeared to bow and scrape before the imperial lion'.[8] While Butt and Redmond appear on the surface to be temperamentally similar – the first biography of Redmond, written in 1910 by the Irish leader's nephew, tellingly claimed that Redmond 'has all the polished manners of Isaac Butt without any of his weaknesses' – a gulf remains in accounts of their respective 'success'.[9] The intellectual recovery of Redmond by historians over the last 20 years is founded on a belief that the promise of Home Rule was agonisingly close under his watch. No amount of revisionism of Butt can plausibly make the case that Home Rule was a possibility during the 1870s. It is, then, all too tempting to view Butt and his movement merely as a preface for the more dramatic events that followed, a narrative that – in the wonderful imagery conjured by Roy Foster – depicts Butt as the John the Baptist to Parnell's Messiah.[10]

It is not the case, however, that Butt was merely the witness to Parnell's light. Such a view ignores Butt's considerable intellectual prowess, which manifested itself politically in *argument* rather than *organisation*. The New Departure of the late 1870s, in which Butt's preferred scheme of federalism was dropped in favour of a more distinctively 'Irish' form of Home Rule, and agrarian radicalism was linked to the demand for self-government, represented in many ways the 'de-Buttification' of the Irish Party: Butt's ideas appear to have been jettisoned in favour of a more confrontational approach, with the blessing of the American Fenians. But while Butt and Parnell stand as the yin and yang of Irish constitutional politics – the former a cautious intellectual, seemingly out of his depth, the latter an aggressive and opportunistic politician – we should remember that Parnell entered politics as a follower of Butt. Parnell may have toppled Butt without remorse or mercy (or, as Paul Bew has put it, with 'an element of sadistic cruelty'),[11] but the Parnellite takeover of the Party did not usher in a new revolutionary year one in Irish constitutional politics. Indeed, Parnell's (and later, Redmond's) success was, in a way, built on the rationale for self-government and land reform that had been nurtured by Butt. Butt also enjoyed a warmer posthumous reputation within the Irish Party, particularly during the highpoint of Redmond's leadership on the eve of the First World War, than the strict Parnellite narrative would imply.

In this chapter, I want to frame the Irish Parliamentary Party after 1879 as the legacy of Isaac Butt. Butt died in 1879, but his thinking continued to shape ideas regarding agrarian radicalism and, at various moments during the leadership of John Redmond, federal definitions of Home Rule. Butt may seem 'moderate' in comparison to Parnell, but there was a distinctively radical tinge to his ideas that became integral to the Home Rule cause. There was, in other words, more continuity between Butt's outlook and a later generation of Home Rulers than meets the eye. The second thing I want to analyse is the rediscovery of Butt during the centenary of his birth in 1913. Falling on the apogee of Redmond's leadership, when Home Rule seemed unstoppable, the centenary of the Donegal-born Butt allowed the high command of the Irish Party to appropriate their political ancestor as an illustrious example of a patriotic, Protestant Ulsterman. In the context of the Ulster crisis, Butt, from a Redmondite perspective, represented an idealised form of northern Protestantism, the historical memory of whom stood in sharp contrast to the militantly anti-Home Rule stance of unionists in the north. The nationalist lament was obvious: if only Ulster unionism could see the error of their ways and rediscover the patriotism of their kinsman who founded the Home Rule movement.

I

Isaac Butt was *the* quintessential nineteenth-century Irish gentleman. A pioneer of political economy, novelist, editor, precocious lawyer, the heart of the early Home Rule movement, a man ruined by debt and surrounded in scandal, Butt's contribution to Ireland's political and intellectual life was as substantial as the space he inhabited in the bustling gossip trade of Dublin society. Butt is the case study *par excellence* for recovering the fluidity of pre-Parnellite Irish political culture, as he remained a champion of Ireland's British connection while agitating for a federalist form of self-government for the smaller island. Butt is often mistaken for a 'nationalist' by many historians, but it is more accurate to position him as a patriotic conservative who gave only conditional support to the Union between Ireland and Britain.[12] This explains the rationale of the federalist scheme that he propagated during the 1870s, the nuances of which were lost on most contemporaries.[13] From Butt's perspective as the leader of the nascent Home Rule movement, the Union, which centralised power in London, had failed to provide political stability and economic prosperity to Ireland. Through federalism and the enshrining of distinct constitutional rights for the component parts of the United Kingdom, Butt believed that equality between Ireland and Britain would be created politically and protected legally. More than any other issue, though, it was the land question that pushed Butt into this line of radical constitutional thought.

Butt emerged as one of the foremost advocates of land reform during the 1860s, and it is this issue which Butt's influence was most felt over the Parnellite Party. Through a string of key interventions, Butt's stance on land reform entered the Irish political canon. One of his parliamentary speeches on tenure nestled beside a philosophical lecture on his kinsman, Bishop Berkeley, in Charles Read and T. P. O'Connor's great anthology of Irish thought, *The Cabinet of Irish Literature*, from 1880.[14] Simply put, the legacy of Butt was instrumental in calibrating the aggressive tone of agrarianism under the leadership of Parnell. In *The Fall of Feudalism in Ireland*, Michael Davitt positioned Butt as the vital link between the post-Famine Tenant Right League and the radical activism of the Land League generation. Butt's writings on land from the 1860s became, in Davitt's words, 'text-books for Land League speakers and writers.'[15] Indeed, Butt's influence on the radical agrarianism of the Land League, particularly those members who agitated for the 'three Fs' – fair rent, fixity of tenure and free sale – remains hugely overlooked.

Davitt posited Butt as 'moderate precursor' to the Land League but suggested that James Fintan Lalor was the movement's 'prophet'. Certainly, Butt's core demand for fixity of tenure appears 'moderate' when compared to Lalor, who advocated land nationalisation during the 1840s, and the later agitation initiated by Davitt. Butt himself presented fixity of tenure as a 'conservative measure', which reconciled 'the rights of property with the right of the people to live upon their land'.[16] It is not necessarily the case, however, that Butt's contribution to political debate should be uncritically bracketed as 'moderate'. Taken on his own word in 1870, Butt's vision of federal Home Rule was a conservative and moderate measure. A. V. Dicey, the most influential constitutional lawyer of the day, however, argued that the federalist motion backed by Butt was the most radical proposal regarding the design of the state ever put before the British parliament.[17] While Butt's advocacy of tenant right might appear cautious, fixity of tenure involved the legislative weakening of the long-established property rights of landlords in Ireland, and was thus condemned by the landed interest as revolutionary. Despite their 'moderate' framing, Butt's ideas, concerning both land reform and the wider constitution, were dramatically divisive.

An underappreciated aspect of Butt's writings on land, especially from the 1860s, is its ferocity. His writings deployed language more akin to his revolutionary contemporaries, James Fintan Lalor or John Mitchel, rather than his fellow Tory travellers. Butt angrily denounced the Britain's Irish policy since the Acts of Union, framing the lack of legal rights by tenants as a continuation of the age-old conquest of Ireland. 'The whole system of landed property,' Butt affirmed, 'is regarded by the great mass of the people as an alien institution, all its rights are looked upon as enforced by conquest, and maintained only by a foreign force.'[18] After Butt was criticised by the landed interest for his vocal support for reform, he penned the stinging pamphlet, *The Irish People and the Irish Land* (1867), which pushed the conquest imagery further. 'The perpetual origin of misery and degradation,' he angrily proclaimed, 'has been the fact that the great mass of the people have been treated as belonging to a conquered race.'[19] The arbitrary power of eviction in Ireland was sanctioned by 'the sword of Oliver Cromwell'.[20] The 'old monster grievance of the Irish race' was landlordism, 'which embodies the policy and the passions of territorial conquest.'[21] The 'whole system of landed property in Ireland.' Butt lamented, was 'the creation of English conquest'.[22] Such lines written by Butt could have blended seamlessly into any of James Fintan Lalor's polemic essays written at the height of the Famine.[23]

So, the 'moderate' idea of land reform as advocated by Butt was articulated in an impassioned language that teetered at the edges of questioning the legitimacy of the British administration in Ireland. Butt's palpable anger during the 1860s was fuelled by disinterest of the state in enshrining tenant right in legislation but was also moulded by fear of a social revolution spearheaded by a resurgent Fenianism, guided by the radical principles of Mitchel and Lalor. The robustness of Butt's denouncement of British inertia in Ireland may have been an attempt to channel Fenian sentiment and push Irish radicalism towards constitutional agitation. While Butt instinctively remained a conservative proponent of the British Empire from the 1830s to the 1870s, there were definite shifts in how he imaged Ireland's relationship with Britain, and these were articulated in a language that increasingly highlighted Ireland's lack of legal, political, and economic parity with England. Butt, with great rhetorical skill, crafted a political argument using familiar metaphors that appealed to the national mind, such as 'conquest'. At the same time, while Butt's language regarding land remained bellicose, his proposed remedy for hardship on the countryside remained the legislative process, with legal rights awarded to tenants. This was constitutional struggle framed by the vocabulary of agrarian radicalism. It was exactly the kind of ambiguously aggressive approach that distinguished the Parnellite campaigns of the later 1870s and 1880s.

The failure of the state to intervene to 'solve' the land question accelerated Butt's move towards Home Rule. Only a parliament truly accountable to the Irish people, he surmised, could deliver full legal rights for the occupiers of the soil. In 1870, Butt emerged as the president of a small but significant society based in Dublin called the Home Government

Association, which advocated Irish self-government within a federal framework. This was the first body dedicated to Home Rule; and the makeup of this body was extraordinary, with landed and urban Tories aggrieved at the scale of the Liberal government's Irish reforms, most notably the disestablishment of the Church of Ireland in 1869, jostling for position alongside old Repealers and agrarian activists in making the case for a Dublin parliament.[24] To protect this uneasy alliance, land was deliberately kept off the agenda of the Home Government Association and its successor body, the Home Rule League. The first resolution adopted by the Home Government Association affirmed that the ultimate goal of the organisation was the achievement of a 'national parliament'. Crucially, this was followed by a second resolution making clear that this was the sole objective of the Association.[25] Home Rule, in Butt's imagination, was a genuinely national issue, and needed wide support from the Irish people, rural and urban, landed, and landless, Protestant and Catholic. Butt was all too aware of the divisiveness of the land question, and the levels of extreme hostility it provoked within rural society. Lord Lifford, for one, vehemently denounced Butt's writings on the question as 'communistic'.[26] From the perspective of 1870, it thus made sense to separate the land question from the pursuit of Home Rule, given the fragility of the fledgling Home Government Association. But retrospectively, the irony of this stance is obvious: the strength of the Parnellite machine rested on the melding of the national call for self-government *and* agrarian radicalism.[27] Perhaps we should view Parnellism as Butt's inadvertent creation: he armed the Parnellites with the idioms to assert land reform and Home Rule. It was the fusion of land and the national question that galvanised the Home Rule Party in the 1880s. The eulogy of Butt that appears in the writings of Michael Davitt, the leading light of the Land League, is, then, acutely germane.

II

The centenary of Butt's birth fell in 1913, in the midst of the constitutional crisis over the Third Home Rule Bill. A number of lectures were delivered on Butt's life and legacy, and his legal assistant (and, most likely, his illegitimate son), James Collins published an enjoyable character profile to coincide with the centenary. Collins emphasised Butt's kind-hearted and quirky nature – including a story about Butt's mishap with a bottle of dye, leaving him with green hair, and his attraction to 'a number of Catholic practices' – which gave his final years an even more tragic gloss.[28] Butt's versatility and intellectual range was the subject of a piece in the *Irish Book Lover* in 1913, which recalled his brilliant editorship of the *Dublin University Magazine* and later writings, especially (echoing Michael Davitt), relating to the land question.[29] Many national and provincial newspapers supportive of the nationalist cause ran short columns marking the centenary. These cast a sympathetic light on Butt's role in the struggle for Home Rule, which was, from the nationalist perspective in 1913, seemingly nearing its climax. 'Today we are about to reap the fruit of the movement which [Butt] inaugurated,' affirmed the *Irish Independent*, 'and we hope and trust that at this opportune moment Ireland will take some step to perpetuate the memory of that great and true-hearted patriot.'[30] To salute the 'founder of the Home Rule movement', nationalists in Donegal proposed the construction of the 'Isaac Butt Memorial Hall' in Ballybofey, near Butt's birthplace of Stranorlar.[31] The Hall opened in 1920, when the prospects for Home Rule looked rather different.[32]

It was not the case, however, that Butt was plucked from a decades-long obscurity in 1913. He emerged the hero of Frank Hugh O'Donnell's wonderfully eccentric two-volume *History of the Irish Parliamentary Party*, which was published in 1910. O'Donnell, a former Home Rule MP who served under both Butt and Parnell, was a cantankerous and divisive figure, alienating and falling out with a number of figures of note during his day. Among his notable targets were the Catholic Church (as he colourfully put it in 1908, 'I write exclusively against the domination of a political sacerdotalism'[33]) and the leading players behind the Irish literary revival, especially that 'Mystic Minor Poet', W. B. Yeats.[34] O'Donnell's *History of the Irish Parliamentary Party* was, unsurprisingly, not a straightforward 'history', but a contumelious denunciation of the direction that the Home Rule movement took under the leadership of Parnell (and, by extension, Redmond). In O'Donnell's reading, Parnellism's fundamental characteristic – its channelling of agrarian radicalism and Fenian sentiment into the Home Rule ideal – was fatally flawed, as it increased social and political tensions in Ireland. Coupled with Parnell's (and, again, Redmond's) pandering to the Anglophobia of wealthy Irish-American patrons, O'Donnell fiercely affirmed that Parnellism had destroyed Butt's inclusive conception of Irish self-government. 'The harsh yell of hate,' he colourfully argued, 'was to silence the voice of patriotism, while a flood-tide of imported money was to drown the scruples of vulgar consciences and stimulate the instincts of anarchy and greed.'[35] O'Donnell condemned Parnell and his followers for promoting a social civil war between the gentry and political nationalists, which culminated in the purging of the landed (and often Protestant) gentlemen from the Home Rule movement led by Butt.[36] The Parnellite campaign, lamented O'Donnell, merely entrenched agrarian and sectarian divisions in Ireland, which continued to blight Redmond's reign as party chair.[37] The rejection of Butt's vision of Home Rule, O'Donnell concluded, profoundly narrowed the class and religious base of the Irish national movement, thereby undermining its central rationale. As he put it,

> All the three religions in Ireland [Protestant, Catholic and Dissenter] were alike no bar to patriotism and self-government. It was a demonstration of Irish fraternity such as was to be never more possible after Parnellism and Davittism had driven alike the Catholic O'Conors [Denis O'Conor and his brother, the O'Conor Don] and the Protestant [Captain Richard] King Harmans, along with the whole mass of the classes which had much to lose, into the camp of the Unionist Party.[38]

It was a serious charge, but given the erratic nature of its source, the blow did not land. Even where O'Donnell's central argument found sympathy, as in the pages of the *Irish Times*, the book was denounced as 'exaggerated' and 'untrustworthy'.[39] It was only later, long after the Home Rule and independence struggles were over, that Butt's biographer, Terence de Vere White, endorsed his subject matter's ambition to wield together 'the diverse elements of Irish life into a national party', tacitly promoting O'Donnell's judgement.[40]

The distinctiveness of Butt's politics, then, was used to critique the Parnellite and Redmondite Irish Party. When O'Donnell's book was published in 1910, Home Rule seemed a distant and wistful hope, which fuelled this revision of Butt, who personified an elusive path not taken. Even the reviewer of the *History of the Irish Parliamentary Party* in the *Irish Times* could not resist quoting an unnamed Conservative minister who reputedly claimed that 'Butt would have got Home Rule, Parnell made it unlikely, and

John Redmond has made it impossible'.⁴¹ By 1913, the year of Butt's centenary, things, however, looked rather different. With the introduction of Home Rule legislation, the year before, the Irish Party, under Redmond's leadership, appeared on the cusp of success. This conditioned Irish Party moves to commemorate Butt, thereby incorporating him into a linear narrative of constitutional nationalist glory. At the St Patrick's Day banquet in London in 1913, John Redmond saluted Butt's invigoration of the national cause following the demoralising collapse of the Fenian conspiracy in 1867. 'I deny that Isaac Butt failed,' announced Redmond. 'He was a great link in the chain of success' that connected Daniel O'Connell to Parnell and the present day. Redmond also drew attention to the fact that Butt was the product of a marriage between a northern father and southern mother. Butt was, according to Redmond, 'the type of that union of north and south which we in this generation will never surrender.'⁴²

Other parliamentarians within the Irish Party used the centenary to 'claim' Butt and use him in similar ways. Joe Devlin delivered a lecture in Belfast towards the end of 1913 that appealed for Butt's place in the pantheon of constitutional nationalist leaders, praising him as the 'father of Home Rule'. After some 35 years after his death, 'Butt's Home Rule bill,' Devlin asserted, 'will pass into law next year.' Like Redmond, Devlin emphasised Butt's northern background, affirming that historically '[t]he cause of Irish nationality owed much to Ulster'.⁴³ Devlin reminded his audience (which contained many Catholic clergymen) that Butt, an Ulster Protestant, stood up for a patriotic vision of Ireland's future, just as the United Irish movement, which was founded in Belfast, had done during the 1790s. It went unspoken, but Devlin's implication was clear: Ulster Protestants had lost their way since the death of Butt, abandoning the patriotism of their forefathers and retreating into unconditional unionism and anti-democratic reaction.⁴⁴ This was a recasting of recent Irish history, not-so-subtly framing unionism as a false consciousness that would wither away once Home Rule was delivered. Ironically, in using 'the father of Home Rule' in this way, Butt's own *unionist* convictions were written out of his posthumous biography.⁴⁵

A similar interpretation of Butt was also found in the most thorough centenary reflection made by a member of the Edwardian Irish Party, which came in the form of an article in the *Fortnightly Review* by John Gordon Swift MacNeill, the MP for South Donegal. As a young man drawn to the idea of the restoration of an Irish parliament, MacNeill joined the Home Government Association and met Butt for the first time in 1873, leaving a vivid description in his memoir of the then 60-year old Home Rule chief: 'He was tall, and had a wealth of snow-white hair, with a broad forehead, homely but pleasing features, and dark eyes of dazzling brilliancy.'⁴⁶ MacNeill was precisely the kind of nationally-minded Protestant Tory that Butt hoped would rally to the Home Rule cause; but given MacNeill's standing in the Parnellite and Redmondite parties as one of a very small number from this background, the limitations of this inclusive vision in an increasingly polarised political culture after the 1870s are painfully obvious.⁴⁷ Nevertheless, MacNeill painted a sympathetic picture of his old mentor, positioning him as the 'father of Home Rule', the man who planted the seed that a later generation – Redmond's generation – would reap. The rhetorical image of Butt as the personification of the 'union of the North and South of Ireland' was conjured once again, with MacNeill plunging into Butt's family history, confirming that he came from 'a stock which gives him associations with every class and creed of Irishman'.⁴⁸

MacNeill also devoted space to Butt's particular significance in moving the national demand from Repeal of the Act of Union to Home Rule, suggesting this was more than a question of semantics. Repeal implied a return to the constitution of 1782, the so-called 'Grattan's Parliament', with an Irish parliament enjoying legislative independence, but an executive curtailed by the primacy of the British-appointed Lord Lieutenant and Chief Secretary for Ireland. A return to the pre-1800 conditions also suggested that Irish members could not continue to sit in Westminster. Butt found these scenarios unedifying, and thus developed a scheme for federalism, which ensured a full measure of self-government for Ireland (with, crucially, an Irish executive accountable to a Dublin parliament) and continuing representation in the London parliament. MacNeill believed that it was 'an unconscious tribute to the superior political genius of Butt' in formulating the federal scheme that the proviso of continued Irish representation in Westminster was written into the 1893 and 1912 Home Rule Bills.[49] Under a federal constitution, Butt believed that Ireland would have the best of both worlds: full control over the domestic sphere *and* a direct say over the affairs of the Empire. In his centenary appreciation, MacNeill moulded the design of latter-day Home Rule into a federal shape, with the effect of implying that Butt was a more influential figure than Parnell – who went largely unmentioned in the article – in asserting the appropriate framework for self-government. If federalism was the demand for 'an Irish Parliament with full control over our domestic affairs', as Butt posited, then Home Rule as understood by MacNeill was federal.[50] Devlin, too, in the course of his centenary lecture, declared that 'Butt's Home Rule scheme is the scheme of the Home Rule bill of today in all essentials'.[51] Despite the obstructionism controversy of the 1870s, the 'New Departure' and the ruthless overthrowing of Butt by the faction led by Parnell, it appeared that, within the late Edwardian party at least, the Buttite and Parnellite definitions of Home Rule were largely the same. The fundamental difference between federal and devolved Home Rule – the former implied an explicit division of sovereignty *between* the parliaments in London and Dublin, while the latter marked a conditional transfer of sovereignty *from* London *to* Dublin – was glossed over by party lieutenants. Like many of Butt's contemporaries during the 1870s, some in the Edwardian Irish Party seemingly did not grasp the nuances of federalism.[52]

The party chairman was, however, more attuned to the advantages of federalism. Throughout his career, John Redmond articulated a federal ideal as a solution to the Irish national question. While Redmond was a self-proclaimed Parnellite (he was, of course, the leader of the Parnellite faction after the split of 1891),[53] he was greatly attracted to Butt's vision of Home Rule. Federalist discourses were generally deployed to reconcile the need for meaningful self-government with imperial unity, traits which chimed with Redmond's political outlook.[54] Like Devlin and Swift MacNeill, Redmond praised Butt's contribution to the cause of self-government, suggesting that the Home Rule bill introduced in 1912 marked the realisation of his creative constitutional thinking. Butt's reconciliatory language, non-confrontational political instincts and imperial sympathies also chimed with Redmond's temperament; indeed, Redmond was on record in proclaiming that 'Isaac Butt was most undoubtedly one of the greatest men of our race'.[55] While it might be expected that Redmond, as the figurehead of the Home Rule movement, would mark the centenary of Butt's birth in 1913, this was not the first time that the chairman had advocated the virtues of federalism or name-dropped Butt positively.

Redmond had, of course, a direct link with the early Home Rule Party. His father, William Archer Redmond, had been a prominent member of Butt's parliamentary grouping, sitting as the MP for Wexford between 1872 and 1880. Redmond senior shared many of his leader's royalist and imperial sentiments.[56] In 1878, for example, in stark contrast to opportunistic anti-imperialism that animated the Parnellite faction of the Party during the contemporaneous Afghan and Zulu wars,[57] William Archer Redmond declared that he could not be 'indifferent to the fortunes and policy of an Empire of which Ireland formed an important part', words that might have been uttered by his son on the eve of the First World War.[58] Later in life, John recalled visiting parliament in 1876 (when he was 20-years-old) to observe his father at work, and being spellbound by a speech by Butt that brilliantly deployed quotations from *Macbeth*. In making the case for the creation of a select committee to examine the demand for Home Rule, Butt asserted that Irish social, economic, and political ailments had crossed a threshold of severity, and only a parliament in Dublin was able to cure them. 'In the words of Macbeth,' Butt flamboyantly asked the Commons,

> Canst thou not minister to a mind diseas'd
> Pluck from the memory a rooted sorrow
> Raze out the written troubles of the brain
> And with some sweet oblivious antidote
> Cleanse the stuff'd bosom of that perilous stuff
> Which weighs upon the heart?

Butt carried on, transforming *Macbeth* into an analogy for Home Rule:

> Parliament might say – We reply as the physician did in *Macbeth*, 'Therein the patient must minister to himself.' He believed she must minister to herself, and minister in a higher sense than that spoken of just now. He believed no good intentions on the part of that House or the Government could ever supply that knowledge – that instinctive knowledge – of the wants and wishes of the people of Ireland which was necessary in legislating for her, and which could never be acquired by learning, only by residence among, and acquaintance with, the people themselves.[59]

In his biography of John Redmond from 1919, recalling this moment, Stephen Gwynn endorsed the 'finely apposite Shakespearean quotation'.[60] Certainly, Butt's sense of dramatic oratory and literary incision left an indelible mark on the young John Redmond. He repeated the quotation during the parliamentary debate over the Home Rule Bill of 1893, adding powerfully that 'We say that Ireland's sole remaining hope is in herself. Ireland must bind up her own wounds and cure her own disorder'.[61] *Macbeth* might have provided solace for Home Rulers such as Redmond, but it is difficult to avoid retrospectively viewing the collapse of the Home Rule project in the aftermath of the First World War as possessing the qualities of a modern Shakespearean tragedy.

Posthumously, then, Butt's ideas continued to carry weight within elements of the Home Rule movement, despite the seeming rejection of his methods after 1879. Redmond referred glowingly to Butt in several keynote speeches during the 1880s, 1890s, and 1900s. What emerges from a reading of these speeches, not uncontroversially, is a heartfelt commitment to Butt's ambitious idea of federalism. In a lecture in Melbourne during the Redmond brothers' tour of Australia and New Zealand in 1883,[62] for example, John responded to criticism that the Irish Party were refusing to flesh out the details of what Home Rule would look like. After affirming that the details of self-government can wait until the principle has been conceded, Redmond went on to outline Butt's position, stressing that Home Rule would provide a full form of self-government for Ireland while leaving the United Kingdom constitutionally intact. He studded the lecture with quotations from Butt that suggested that a federal Home Rule parliament in Dublin 'would rank, act and rule as the parliament of an independent nation'.[63] Redmond followed up with an excerpt from Parnell, 'lest some people might say that I am quoting Mr Butt and not the present leaders of the movement for Home Rule', which suggested that the Irish goal remained domestic autonomy while retaining citizenship within the United Kingdom.[64] Parnell and Butt were, in Redmond's eyes, saying the same thing about Home Rule and Ireland's relationship with Britain and the wider empire.

Except that they were not. Butt's scheme, as set out in his pamphlet, *Irish Federalism*, was an elegant intervention that attempted to square many circles, reconciling Irish national demands for freedom with the structures of the British Empire, and Irish Tory suspicions of the direction of London politics with the more separatist sympathies of old Repealers and Fenians. Parnell, in contrast to Butt, did not commit himself to any one image of self-government, and instead responded reactively to events as he found them. Depending on his audience and the occasion, he oscillated from uncompromising separatism to something resembling devolution. He routinely name-dropped the constitution of 1782 (the so-called 'Grattan's Parliament') in speeches, particularly in the mid-1880s, but was ambiguous in his understanding of the historical concept. He spoke – incorrectly – of the constitution of 1782 as providing independence for Ireland.[65] Indeed, Parnell's most celebrated utterance, delivered in Cork in 1885, that 'no man has the right to fix the boundary of a nation', was prefaced by the claim that '[w]e cannot ask for anything less that the restitution of Grattan's Parliament'.[66] For Parnell, and many nationalists drawn to the historical allure of the age of Grattan and the Irish Volunteers, '1782' was equated with freedom.

Butt had explicitly rejected the constitution of 1782 because 'Grattan's Parliament' lacked an accountable executive. He posited a federal union, as such a structure would allow Ireland to 'exercise a greater influence than she did so, or ever could do, under the Constitution of 1782'.[67] Redmond agreed with this reading and displayed an awareness of the sharp differences in constitutional thought that separated Butt and Parnell, even if he attempted to rhetorically align them. On St Patrick's Day in 1892, some five months after the death of Parnell, Redmond addressed a gathering at the Rotunda in Dublin on the 'National Demand'. He announced that the dismissal of Butt's federalist scheme as too 'moderate' was an inaccurate reading of the recent past propagated by 'many badly informed people'. 'What Butt demanded,' clarified Redmond, was nothing less than 'absolute supremacy over Ireland in the management of Irish affairs.'[68] Redmond explicitly adopted a Buttite interpretation of 'Grattan's Parliament', which stood at odds with the popular Parnellite endorsement of '1782'. Citing the lack of an Irish executive, 'Grattan's Parliament,' Redmond proclaimed, 'though it was in name an Independent Parliament, [was] in reality a dependent parliament.' Federalism, as imagined by Butt, in contrast, proposed 'a Parliament which, in name, was dependent, but in reality was independent'.[69] Redmond understood the differences between the two visions of Irish self-government in the critical field of sovereignty: taken in a literal sense, '1782' did not appease the appetite for national self-reliance in Ireland, as the Irish parliament was dependent on an executive across the sea, whereas federalism offered 'absolute supreme power, free from any interference or control of the English Parliament, over exclusively Irish affairs'.[70] It was a quiet rebuke to the Parnellite infatuation with '1782'. Whatever Redmond saw in Parnell's leadership qualities, it was not his constitutional imagination.

Redmond thus believed that federalism was a glittering prize, even if other Irish nationalists did not see it this way. In 1910, he caused a minor political controversy when, during a tour of the US, he likened his vision for Irish Home Rule to American federalism, with Ireland, in this analogy, receiving the same powers as a state such as New Jersey. Rhetorically, this went down badly with Redmond's base, as he appeared to downplay Irish national and historical grievances. 'A federated United Kingdom supposes that English and Irish interests are identical', scolded Francis Cruise O'Brien in the *Leader*. 'History has something to say on the point.'[71] Rather mischievously, the *Daily Express* reported on Redmond's stance under the headline, 'The New Home Rule: Mr Redmond Comes Out as a British Patriot.'[72] Nevertheless, Redmond greeted the introduction of the Home Rule Bill in 1912 in the Commons as 'first step in a great system of federation', the realisation of Butt's vision for a wider federal United Kingdom:

> It is said that this measure cannot be final. In one sense it does not profess to be final. It was put forward by the Prime Minister as the first and necessary preliminary step in a great system of federation in which, when it is completed, the people of each component part of the United Kingdom will be enabled to transact their own local business for themselves.[73]

Like Butt, Redmond did not believe that the conditions for the creation of parliaments in the other constituent countries within the United Kingdom were in place, but this should not deter such constitutional planning. 'A beginning to federalism must be made', Redmond insisted, crucially adding that 'Ireland is entitled from her whole history to have the first place.'[74] This, despite the fact that the New Departure of the late 1870s, and the entire tenor of Parnellism at its most euphoric, supposedly consigned Butt's federalist vision of Home Rule to the dustbin of nationalist history.

III

Isaac Butt was one of the most influential figures of nineteenth-century Ireland, whose influence was felt in political, social, economic, intellectual, legal, and rhetorical spheres. In sharp contrast to the large body of historical work on the Parnellite and Redmondite Irish Parties, Butt and the party he led during the 1870s, continue to languish, unjustly, in relative obscurity. Butt has suffered from the looming shadows cast by those who followed after him. Yet, Butt's influence over the Irish Party did not terminate with his overthrow as leader by the more aggressive members of his parliamentary party or even his death in 1879. Butt's writings on the land question contributed to the vocabulary of the Land War, and the subsequent agrarian radicalism that was aligned to the Parnellite and Redmondite Irish Parties. He also provided the intellectual justification for Irish self-government. It was his hesitancy to combine these two impulses that left him marooned politically, allowing the initiative to be taken by his more opportunistic followers.

The centenary of Butt's birth in 1913, falling as it did during the seeming climax of the Home Rule struggle, marked an important watershed moment. Butt's legacy was warmly appraised by parliamentarians and newspaper editorials, largely for the first time since his death, and his Ulster Protestant background was emphasised as a demonstration of nationalist tolerance and unionist patriotic waywardness. But 1913 was not the year that John Redmond rediscovered Isaac Butt; Redmond had positioned himself as an advocate of Butt's federal ideas as early as the 1880s, even though federalism was abandoned as the favoured definition of Home Rule by Parnell. This is testament both to the richness of Butt's vision of Home Rule and the political open-mindedness of John Redmond. Redmond was as much a Buttite as a Parnellite.

Federalism remains the constitutional path not taken in 'these islands', although the idea has been taken up at various points by British imperial reformers, Irish unionists, neo-Redmondites and the Provisional IRA.[75] A federal solution continues to inform notions of British political reform in the ages of devolution and Brexit.[76] But as Redmond and Butt found to their chagrin, for all the potential of federalism to reimagine Ireland and its relations with Britain, its reputation is poor. Writing in 1880, Charles Gavan Duffy captured the essence of the problem when recalling the controversy caused after Daniel O'Connell flirted with federalism some 36 years before:

> Federalism as it was then commonly understood meant little more than the creation of a Legislative Council with fiscal powers somewhere in excess of a grand jury, but not authorised to deal with the greatest concerns of a nation – domestic and international trade, the land code, education, national defences, and the subsidies to religious denominations.[77]

Federalism may be ubiquitous in the history of constitutional ideas in Ireland, but it has struggled to shake off the notion that such an arrangement is a slight on Irish nationhood.

Redmond resembled Butt in many ways, not least their shared desire to dampen the Irish separatist passion within political discourse, preferring to view the 'Irish question' as a constitutional riddle rather than national dilemma. 'The demands of Ireland,' Redmond wrote in 1892, 'are moderate and constitutional.'[78] It was precisely the form of political language that angered and frustrated a young Parnell and his followers in Isaac Butt's Party, leading to the obstructionist campaign in parliament and, eventually, the Fenian-inspired New Departure. There is a bitter irony at play here. Classical humanism, personified by Aristotle, Cicero, and Machiavelli, believed that history unfolded in a series of recurring cycles.[79] In the end, Redmond, a follower of Parnell, fell and was replaced by more radical forces in a process that closely mirrored Butt's fate. In his memoir, Thomas McKnight, the editor of the Belfast-based *Northern Whig*, conjured an image of Butt towards the end of his life as 'the old man, [who] found himself virtually set aside by his rebellious children'. As so often, those 'rebellious children', in their maturity, became their parents, and in time suffered a similar inter-generational backlash.[80] Butt may have wryly appreciated the irony.

CHAPTER 3

THE CHAIRMAN AND THE CHIEF: JOHN REDMOND AND CHARLES STEWART PARNELL

Pauric Travers

> I now perform the proudest task of my life in unveiling this noble monument ... to the memory of the greatest son of Ireland since the days of Hugh O'Neill.[1]

John Redmond's speech at the unveiling of Augustus Saint-Gaudens' Parnell statue on O'Connell Street on 1 October 1911 reflects his long-standing loyalty to the dead chief and a justifiable satisfaction at the completion of an ill-fated project. Even the unionist *Irish Times*, which grudgingly conceded that Redmond was invariably impressive in his style of oratory acknowledged that he was notably so on this occasion.[2] They stood, Redmond declared, 'at the juncture between two eras'; the national cause was 'at long last was back at the point where Parnell had left it, sweeping to victory on a spring-tide of enthusiasm'. The protracted nature of the commemorative project – the statue was unveiled more than a decade after it was first announced and within a few days of the twentieth anniversary of the death of Parnell – at least had the advantage that its final completion coincided with what promised to be Redmond's greatest achievement. The passing of the Parliament Act ending the veto of the House of Lords six weeks earlier combined with the outcome of the two general elections of 1910, which gave the Irish Party the balance of power, made Home Rule for Ireland likely. Redmond was set fair to gain a prize that had eluded Parnell and, in doing so, would finally step out from the shadow of his former Chief and establish himself as a leader of equal or greater stature – or so it seemed.

The names of John Redmond and Charles Stewart Parnell are inextricably linked in the pages of Irish history. During the stormy years of the 1880s and in the Parnell split, Redmond was Parnell's most loyal lieutenant. After the Chief's death, notwithstanding Fenian and other claims to his legacy, Redmond emerged as the keeper of the Parnell flame.[3] This chapter examines the relationship between Redmond and Parnell, its development from their first encounters and its influence on the later political fortunes of Redmond. It examines the roots of Redmond's loyalty to Parnell and focuses particularly on the formative period of the Split which strained his loyalty almost to breaking point. Following consideration of Redmond's negotiation of Parnell's posthumous legacy, it concludes with some reflections on the post-1900 period. The chapter also compares the personalities and leadership styles of the two men, assesses their status as parliamentarians and leaders of the Irish Party and considers their views on the nature and meaning of Home Rule.

As early as 1910, Francis Cruise O'Brien noted that the negative comparison of John Redmond and Charles Stewart Parnell as political leaders was firmly established as a commonplace of political commentary.⁴ More than a century of historical analysis has, if anything, entrenched that perception. The comparison has tended to emphasise the differences between the two leaders in terms of religion, social background, and leadership style. Undoubtedly, their leadership styles were radically different: one was cautious and consultative while the other was imperious and remote. Redmond lacked the charisma, political instinct and daring of Parnell.⁵ Yet for all the contrasts between them, it is striking how much Redmond and Parnell had in common.⁶ Both were men of simple tastes and naturally reticent. Neither was gregarious nor sought the company of colleagues. In London, both shunned the club life beloved by many MPs of all parties. Redmond was content in his modest apartment in Kensington while Parnell sought the calm of Eltham or Brighton. In Ireland, both had a preference for country life and country pursuits. It is perhaps indicative that some of Redmond's happiest times in his later life were spent at Aghavannagh which had been Parnell's shooting lodge.⁷

Loyalty to Parnell as the leader of the Irish Party and to his memory after his death was a defining feature of the political career of John Redmond. That loyalty dated back to Redmond's initiation into the rough and tumble of Irish politics and was literally sealed in blood. In March 1880, while he was in Wexford supporting his father William Archer Redmond's campaign for Wexford borough, the 23-year-old Redmond attended a Parnellite meeting in Enniscorthy in the shadow of Vinegar Hill. Parnell, who had had just returned from America where he had addressed the House of Representatives, was in the county seeking to ensure the nomination of Parnellite candidates. He was met with a hostile crowd and prevented from speaking. Redmond recalled a man shouting that they would show Parnell that 'the blood of Vinegar Hill is still green':

> The priests were against Parnell. Parnell stood on the platform calm and self-possessed. There was no use in trying to talk. He faced the crowd, looking sad and sorrowful, but not at all angry; It was an awful picture of patience. A rotten egg was flung at him. It struck him on the beard and trickled down. He took no notice of it.⁸

Later Redmond was knocked down and cut in the face in a confrontation with an angry mob. When Parnell met him and was told what had happened, he said smiling, 'Well, you have shed your blood for us at all events.' Parnell's gratitude did not extend to supporting him for the nomination when his father William Archer died later that year. Redmond expressed an interest in taking his father's seat, but the nomination went instead to Tim Healy. Redmond undertook not to oppose the Parnellite nominee and, in return for his stepping aside, was promised by Parnell that his time would come.⁹ He did not have to wait long – less than three months later he was returned unopposed as the Home Rule MP for New Ross borough.

Although he was four years younger entering parliament than Parnell had been – Redmond was 24 when he entered Parliament; Parnell had been 28 – Redmond was altogether better prepared for the challenges he faced, having acted as his father's parliamentary assistant and as a clerk in the House of Commons. He was also from the outset a more comfortable and accomplished public speaker. Contemporaries who witnessed Parnell's debut on the political stage were singularly unimpressed. A. M. Sullivan recalled that in addressing a meeting in 1874 following his selection as candidate for Dublin, the young Parnell 'broke down utterly. He faltered, he paused, went on, got confused and, pale with intense but subdued nervous anxiety, caused everyone to feel deep sympathy for him'. T. W. Russell was struck by his 'extraordinary political ignorance and incapacity' while O'Connor Power concluded that 'he could not speak at all'. James Bryce recalled that 'so far from glittering with the florid rhetoric supposed to characterise Irish eloquence', Parnell's speeches were 'singularly plain, bare, and dry'. Parnell overcame these shortcomings and developed a style which was distinctive and effective. T. P. O'Connor considered that Parnell developed into 'one of the most potent parliamentary debaters in the House of Commons while Gladstone, who was often on the receiving end of his disconcerting directness, considered that the secret of Parnell's effectiveness as a speaker was that he had that rarest of qualities – measure.[10]

Redmond in contrast was an impressive speaker from the outset, even though he was naturally shy and reticent like Parnell. Inevitably when he first appeared on the political scene, he drew comparison with his father who had a reputation for being an able and polished public speaker. Justin McCarthy who observed both men closely concluded that the son had inherited his father's graceful manner of speaking but that he possessed a faculty of genuine eloquence not displayed by his elder. Several commentators remarked on the power, clarity and vibrancy of Redmond's voice which was to prove an invaluable asset in Parliament and on the hustings in speeches such as that at Woodenbridge in 1914. McCarthy who first heard him address a public meeting at Hyde Park corner was struck by the remarkable strength, volume, and variety of intonation. 'He had a magnificent voice, clear, resonant and thrilling which made itself heard all over the crowd without the slightest apparent effort on the part of the speaker.'[11]

This evident facility in addressing large crowds which Parnell conspicuously lacked led to Redmond being called upon to address Home Rule meetings in Britain and Ireland and further afield in America and Australia during the 1880s. He was a less frequent contributor to debates in the House of Commons in his early years in Parliament, remaining preoccupied with work behind the scenes as an effective party whip and behind the scenes manager. This is ironic as his somewhat florid style suited the House and he went on to be recognised as one of the outstanding parliamentary speakers of his generation. McCarthy considered him one of the few really eloquent speakers of his day, although he conceded that he was somewhat old fashioned in his preference for reason rather than emotion. Redmond was not populist in style and lacked Parnell's capacity to coin a memorable phrase. However, R. Barry O'Brien, Parnell's biographer, asserted in the introduction to his collection of Redmond's speeches published in 1910 that no one held a more distinguished place as an orator in the House of Commons than Redmond whose speeches were persuasive and dignified. A. G. Gardiner, editor of the *Daily News* was impressed by Redmond as an orator of the 'proud, full sail' while W. T. Stead, another distinguished newspaper editor in 1905 declared Redmond 'an admirable debater and the greatest of our parliamentarians'. J. J. Horgan considered Redmond 'the last great Irish orator in the classic tradition; his speeches were not emotional in content ... it was reason that reinforced and inspired his rhetoric; the emphasis placed on every phrase had been decided in advance. Differing from most great orators, he shrank from popular demonstrations of all kinds, accepting them rather as the necessary burdens of his position.'[12]

The contrast between Parnell and Redmond as speakers is well illustrated by their respective contributions to the parliamentary debate on the First Home Rule Bill in 1886 which stretched over 16 nights, and which were in the estimation of John Morley worthy of the occasion and the fame of the House of Commons. While several speakers showed themselves as masters of the higher arts of parliamentary discussion, only one held 'the magic secret of Demosthenic oratory'. According to Morley, Parnell

> made one of the most masterly speeches that ever fell from him ... As he dealt with Ulster, with finance, with the supremacy of Parliament, with the loyal minority, with the settlement of education in an Irish legislature, – soberly, steadily, deliberately ... the effect of Mr Parnell's speech was to make even able disputants on either side look little better than amateurs.[13]

Michael Davitt agreed that this was probably Parnell's finest parliamentary speech.[14] Redmond's speech was impressive too but in a more conventional style. He presented the case for self-government as an entitlement and mutually beneficial to Britain and Ireland and forensically addressed each and every objection which had been raised to Home Rule. Like Parnell, he indicated that he accepted the measure as a final settlement of the Irish question despite its limitations.[15]

Both Redmond and Parnell have been criticised by later historians for their failure to anticipate the seriousness of opposition to Home Rule among Ulster Protestants and to take steps to reassure unionists. In his speech on the second reading of the Home Rule Bill, Parnell had addressed this very question although his words have sometimes been misinterpreted as a statement of uncompromising irredentism. 'No Sir,' Parnell said, 'we cannot give up a single Irishman. We want the energy, the patriotism, the talent, and the works of every Irishman to make this great experiment – to ensure that this great experiment shall be successful. The best form of government for a country I believe to be one that requires that the government shall be the resultant of what forces are in that country.' He went on to refer to the fears of Ulster Protestants and to reassure them that all classes and creeds were wanted.[16] He returned to that theme at the height of the Split in a speech at the Ulster Hall in May 1891 in which he said that it was the duty of the majority 'to leave no stone unturned, no means unused, to conciliate the reasonable and unreasonable prejudices of the minority'. Ireland could never be united, he declared, 'so long as there was a minority who felt that Irish freedom meant harm or damage to them'.[17]

Redmond also addressed the Ulster question in his speech on the Home Rule Bill in 1886. He was a little more dismissive than Parnell, arguing that the opposition in Ulster was overstated and that a majority in the nine counties of the province supported Home Rule. However, in the main, his remarks echoed Parnell's in conciliatory tone. Theirs, he said, was a national and not a sectarian movement. He acknowledged the fears of Protestants and, although they considered these fears unfounded, they desired by every means to allay them. Hence their willingness to accept the First Order or Upper House provided for in the bill, even though it was considered undemocratic by some.[18] These comments fairly reflect Redmond's attitude throughout his career. On more than one occasion, Redmond cited Parnell's 'not a single Irishman' comment but most notably at the unveiling of the Parnell monument in 1911, when he reminded his audience that Parnell was a Protestant 'who had the blood of Ulster Presbyterians in his veins'. Quoting Parnell's dictum 'We cannot spare a single Irishman', Redmond suggested that it should be their watchword as they faced 'the future of construction and reconciliation and fulfilment'.[19]

In response to these comments, the Tory *Morning Post* pointed out that 20 years had passed since Parnell had died and a quarter century since he used these words and asked rhetorically what Redmond had done in the meantime to convince Ulster of the friendliness of the Home Rule movement.[20] In fairness to Redmond, he had consistently pursued a conciliatory policy in that period.[21] However, by 1911 Ulster opposition had become considerably more intense and the prospect of resistance more likely. For that reason, it might be argued that the criticism of underestimating the Ulster question can be more fairly laid at Redmond's door than Parnell's, but that perspective is undoubtedly influenced by later events.

Parnell and Redmond both made significant contributions to Parliament but in different ways. Parnell was disruptive, as he intended to be. His mastery of parliamentary procedure and strategy combined with his tight control of his own party enabled him to wield considerable power and influence. Barry O'Brien observed that in the House of Commons the speech was everything, but Parnell despised the speech – he wanted the verdict.[22] Redmond was more constructive: he was comfortable in the chamber and put more faith in its potential to advance his cause through reasoned argument. Another contemporary, the journalist Michael MacDonagh, considered that, while Parnell 'excelled in daunting a hostile House of Commons', Redmond's role was more often that of 'retaining and increasing the confidence of a friendly House'.[23] As leader of the reunited Irish Party from 1900, Redmond was an acknowledged, even by his opponents, as a leading parliamentarian. It has often been commented that he was more highly thought of in England than in Ireland. Indeed, the influential British journalist and editor W. T. Stead, in a portrait published November 1905, went so far as to suggest that Redmond had a better chance than most to be prime minister of the United Kingdom: 'he has the qualities for the post. He is a gentleman. He is the greatest of our parliamentarians. He is an admirable debater, a super leader, a man of dispassionate intellect, of sound sympathies and of splendid courage.'[24] That reputation helped bring him to the verge of the promise land by 1912–14 but was to prove a mixed blessing when the outbreak of the First World War transformed politics in both Britain and Ireland.

The split in the nationalist movement which followed the O'Shea divorce case strained the loyalty of Parnell's followers including Redmond. Like the Treaty Split 30 years later, there was no clear pattern to the division: people took sides for a variety of reasons, personal and political. Some like Healy who had long resented Parnell's dominance had been waiting in the long grass for their opportunity; some were ambitious for advancement while others had moral scruples or were influenced by the belated but unambiguous condemnation of Parnell by the Catholic Church. For most, the attitude of Gladstone and the pragmatic political calculation of what would best serve the cause of Home Rule weighed heavily. In Redmond's case, a conviction about the importance of the Irish Party remaining independent was joined with a strong personal loyalty. Paul Bew has suggested that there was also a social dimension to the loyalty of Redmond.[25]

The O'Shea divorce case with Parnell cited as co-respondent followed closely after the sudden death of Redmond's first wife, Johanna. This meant that he was isolated from political events in the following months. Parnell's assurances to his colleagues that he would be vindicated was enough to deter any move against his leadership. When, in November 1890, it emerged that Parnell would not contest the divorce petition, Redmond immediately told a friend that he intended to 'stick with Parnell'.[26] On the day after the verdict was announced, he chaired 'a large and representative' meeting of the central branch of the National League in Dublin. In a short but forceful speech, he nailed his colours unambiguously to the Parnellite mast. The Irish people, he said, 'had read with amusement, tempered only with disgust, the stupid prophecies and malicious rumours with reference to the political position of our leader, Mr Parnell.' Indirectly referring to the verdict of the divorce court he dismissed as 'the wildest and most grotesque absurdity' the suggestion in the anti-Irish press in England that Parnell's leadership was prejudiced by what had emerged.[27] A notable feature of Redmond's view of the leadership issue which was implicit in the speech was the assumption that it was a matter for Parnell to decide. That remained his position throughout the Split.

While the focus of Redmond's address to the National League was ostensibly a rebuttal of the Tory press, the speech was also in the nature of a pre-emptive strike, aimed at forestalling possible dissent within the ranks of the Irish Party and the nationalist movement itself. Linking personal loyalty and political allegiance, Redmond took the liberty of speaking on behalf of the members of the parliamentary party collectively:

> Mr Parnell's colleagues in the House of Commons are bound to him by the double tie of private friendship and political allegiance. For myself, I can say for ten years he has been my friend. Nothing that has happened can destroy or weaken the bonds of that friendship. [applause] On the contrary, it seems to us that when trouble has come upon a man, when a shadow has darkened or embittered his life, that then above all others is the time for those who claim to be his friends to draw closer and near him. [applause] But private friendship is one thing. Political allegiance is another. The Irish Party are bound to their leader by ties of absolute confidence and unquestioning loyalty. In this the Irish Party truthfully reflect the sentiment of the entire Irish people.[28]

Redmond's words had the desired effect as unanimous pledges of loyalty followed at the meeting and were repeated two days later at another meeting in Dublin attended by more than 20 MPs, including Healy. However, the tide began to turn when it became clear that the hostile reaction of Nonconformist opinion in Britain was calling the Liberal alliance into question.

Within a fortnight it became evident just how reliable were the ties of absolute confidence and unquestioning loyalty which bound the members of the Irish Party to their embattled leader. The infamous debates in Committee Room 15 from 1 to 5 December began with orderly argument and descended into bad-tempered and melodramatic farce. Based on the published accounts, Gladstone's biographer, John Morley, concluded that no case was ever better opened within the walls of Westminster than in the three speeches made on the first day by Thomas Sexton and Healy on one side and Redmond on the other.[29] Redmond's contribution in particular was notable for its gravity, dignity, and rationality. The *Freeman's Journal* correspondent noted that it was applauded for its 'impassioned eloquence and powerful reasoning. Mr Redmond has never made a better speech, and it evidently afforded extreme gratification to Mr Parnell himself.'[30] Parnell was not known for public expressions of tenderness or even emotion, but his reaction is corroborated by another source who recalled Parnell's 'proud and scornful eyes' softening momentarily as he acknowledged, 'My friend, Jack Redmond.'[31]

Redmond's speech combined praise of Parnell and expressions of personal loyalty with reasoned argument. Addressing Parnell directly, he repeated that he had been his friend and remained so: 'this was no time in which a man who has once been your friend should be against you.' He insisted, however, that his prime motivation was not personal but political. He appealed to his colleagues in biblical terms not to sell their leader or trade the independence of their Party for the Liberal alliance. In an ill-considered move, he concluded by undertaking to resign his seat if the Party came to a different conclusion, a promise quickly broken but not forgotten by his enemies.[32]

Parnell's belated appreciation for Redmond was undoubtedly genuine but it did not betoken a taking of Redmond into his closest confidence. Along with some other colleagues, Redmond had been shown Parnell's manifesto 'To the People of Ireland' before it appeared in the press on 29 November but he had not been consulted before it was written.[33] The logic of Redmond's position in supporting Parnell, despite an ultimatum from Gladstone that they must choose between Parnell and Home Rule, meant the abandonment of the Liberal alliance, for the moment at least, but the boldness of the manifesto in tone and content left him surprised and uneasy.[34] While Redmond championed the principle of an Irish nationalist movement unbeholden to English parties, he was less inclined to irrevocably burn his bridges. He remained steadfast in his support of Parnell but open to a compromise, if one could be found which commended itself to the Chief. It was this very reasonableness of temperament which left Redmond open to the accusation by his critics of wavering and even duplicity at the time of protracted Boulogne negotiations in January 1891 when attempts by moderates on both sides to negotiate the terms on which Parnell might step aside foundered.[35] Accused later of being willing to throw over his Chief, Redmond insisted that what was involved was never more than a 'sham retirement'.[36]

In a letter to his wife, Lord Randolph Churchill described Parnell's manifesto as 'a masterpiece. He lifts the issue between himself and Mr Gladstone from the small ground of the divorce up to the large ground of a great political question. He may hold his own; but it must mean a complete smash-up of the Home Rule alliance.'[37] If Parnell's intention was to move the debate away from the divorce issue and on to the high ground of Irish autonomy and British interference, he was only temporarily successful. The condemnation of the Catholic bishops brought the moral issue back to the fore where it remained for the duration of the increasingly acrimonious conflict waged across Irish constituencies in a series of by-elections, in Kilkenny in December 1890, north Sligo in April 1891 and Carlow in July. The Parnellite candidate was defeated decisively in each case. As the tide moved increasingly against Parnell, Redmond became more uneasy, particularly after Parnell's marriage in June 1891 which even some of his close supporters considered politically ill advised.

Shortly after the Committee Room 15 split, Redmond responded to criticism of his support for the morally reprehensible Parnell from his long-term friend and confidant in Wexford, Fr Patrick Furlong, admitting his unease but insisting that he was guided solely by his 'clear and strong conception of what is best for the country'.[38] That remained his position as the temperature boiled over in the following months. He repeatedly condemned what he regarded as improper interference by the clergy in by-elections between pro and anti-Parnellite candidates. As a conservative Catholic, Redmond was never comfortable with the moral dimension of the Parnell Split. In a speech in February 1890, he asserted the right of freedom of conscience on political questions when the bishops advocated a course of action which he considered the wrong one, reminding his audience of the regularity in Irish history with which the prelates took actions which proved to be short-sighted and unpatriotic.[39]

The frankest exposition of Redmond's thinking was provided at a public meeting in Wexford in May 1891 on his first visit to the county since the crisis began. When a local newspaper suggested that he dared not make an appearance in Wexford, he travelled by train from his home in Dublin. The trip was not without controversy, but the reception was warmer than he might have feared, albeit with the clergy conspicuous by their absence. In an impromptu speech on the platform in Gorey in his North Wexford constituency, he spoke emotionally about 'the trying and heart-breaking months' he had experienced but insisted that his actions were actuated by pure and disinterested motives. In Wexford, he was met by a band and addressed a large crowd at the Bull Ring. He promised to speak his mind with perfect candour and did not disappoint. He deprecated the bitterness which had attended the struggle between Parnellites and anti-Parnellites and expressed his absolute loathing 'for the personalities, the insults, the scurrilities' which had brought disgrace on the country. Coming to the heart of the matter, he insisted that 'Parnell's leadership was a purely political as distinguished from a moral question'. He accused those who said he condoned adultery of libel but went on to implicitly accept that Parnell was guilty of such a sin: 'While they detested the sin laid at Mr Parnell's door, they denied that his political leadership depends in any degree on his private life.'[40]

Redmond assured his audience in Wexford that he was satisfied that the course of action he had taken was the honourable and political course, but he grew increasingly uncomfortable as divisions intensified and the bitterness deepened. He was conspicuous by his absence from the National Convention of Parnellites held in Dublin in late July and did not join Parnell at meetings in Westport on 6 September, Listowel on 13 September and Creggs on 27 September. This was cited at the time and since as an indication of a wavering commitment on his part, or even, as John Dillon alleged, of a plan to desert. However, the evidence to support the latter charge is unconvincing. Redmond spoke at Parnellite gatherings elsewhere at or around the time of the meetings in Listowel and Creggs, and he shared a platform with Parnell at Cabinteely on 20 September 1891. At the latter meeting, he condemned the scurrility and intimidation of their opponents and spoke forcefully about the future of the national cause. Looking towards the general election due the following year, and beyond to the prospect of a new Home Rule bill being introduced, he echoed comments by Parnell that they had no reason for anxiety. No measure of Home Rule had any chance of being a final settlement of the Irish question which did not have the sanction of Parnell speaking on behalf of those he represented in Ireland.[41]

Parnell's death at Brighton on 6 October was unexpected. While it was known to his close colleagues that he had been unwell, news of his passing came as a thunderbolt. Redmond was deeply shocked by the news and hurried to Brighton with colleagues to assist in making the funeral arrangements. It was they who chose Glasnevin for the burial rather than the family plot at Mount Jerome on the basis that 'his body belonged to Ireland' and Glasnevin was the national necropolis. It was also they who conveyed to the press that the Chief's dying words were 'Give my love to my colleagues and to the Irish people'. The message was emblazoned on the walls of City Hall in Dublin the following Sunday at Parnell's lying-in-state and, in subsequent years, on pewter medals distributed as part of the Ivy Day ceremonies. It detracts only somewhat from the sentimental power of the message that Parnell almost certainly said no such thing, as his wife who was with him in his last hours later confirmed.[42]

The death of Parnell removed the central figure in the drama and, in other circumstances, might have paved the way for reconciliation. Had Redmond actually been on the brink of deserting his Chief, he might have taken that view, but he did not. The bitterness had gone too deep and the emotion of Parnell's funeral, which was an extraordinary political demonstration, only helped to entrench the divisions. On the morning of the funeral, Redmond was elected chairman of the Parnellite wing of the Irish Party. Ironically, the vitriolic Tim Healy helped elevate Redmond's claims. A fortnight earlier, Healy had singled Redmond out for opprobrium. Describing him as callous and calculating, he said that 'the main share, the capital responsibility for the split in the Irish Party will always be found, next to Mr Parnell, on the head and shoulders of Mr John Redmond'.[43]

Virtually Redmond's first act as leader was to resign his seat in Wexford to contest Parnell's vacant seat in Cork City. It was an uncharacteristically bold move, worthy of Parnell himself. In the event it almost proved disastrous as Redmond, faced with the combined forces of anti-Parnellites and clergy, was roundly defeated. This might have presaged the end of the Parnellite cause, but a vacancy arose in Waterford a short time later and Redmond was duly elected to a seat he held until his death in 1918. His opponent in the Waterford election was none other than Michael Davitt so the contest pitted against each other two of the leading protagonists in the Split. Redmond's victory in a bad-tempered contest arrested the decline in the fortunes of the Parnellites and helped establish Redmond's leadership. That process was assisted by the inability of the anti-Parnellite majority to unite under a credible alternative leader and the disappointing outcome of the Second Home Rule Bill, the long-promised carrot offered in return for jettisoning Parnell. The Bill passed the House of Commons by 307 votes to 276, but unsurprisingly, it was decisively rejected by the House of Lords, 419 votes to 41.

The position adopted by Redmond is instructive as to the changing context and the development of his thinking since 1886. In a major speech on 'the national demand' on St Patrick's Day in 1892, Redmond, quoting Parnell, had defined the essential element of Home Rule as being the supremacy of an Irish parliament in the management of Irish affairs.[44] In his critique of the 1893 Home Rule Bill, he left no doubt that he considered that the measure fell well short of meeting that test, highlighting among other deficiencies the withholding of control customs and excise, the limitations on the power of taxation and the temporary withholding of power over police, judiciary and land. Nevertheless, he voted for the measure, safe in the knowledge that it was likely to be rejected by the Lords. In contrast to 1886, he insisted that the proposed bill could be not considered as 'a full, a final or a satisfactory settlement', and he invoked Parnell's famous warning about not setting boundaries to the march of a nation.[45] In addressing Ulster opposition to the bill, Redmond was less conciliatory and more dismissive than he had been in 1886 but that did not betoken a hardening of his position. On the contrary, over the next decade he cultivated relationships with moderate unionists and worked constructively to support reform. The democratisation of Irish local government in 1898, the creation of the Department of Agriculture in 1900, and the continuing process of land reform which culminated in the 1903 Wyndham Act all owed something to his cooperation and support.

This conciliatory policy was not always met with approval from his own supporters, many of whom favoured a return to a more radical agrarian campaign. Redmond, like Parnell, had resisted a move in this direction earlier, and he remained consistent in that regard. When William O'Brien sought to reinvigorate the broad nationalist movement from the bottom up through the establishment in 1898 of the United Irish League, with the motto 'the land for the people', the socially conservative Redmond was alarmed. However, the rapid growth of the UIL which hastened the re-unification of the Irish Party eventually forced Redmond to change his position and to take nominal control of the League when it merged with existing Irish National League and the Irish National Federation and became, in effect, the local constituency organisation of the Irish Party. It was a development which foreshadowed Redmond's take-over of the Irish Volunteers more than a decade later. In both cases an initial under-estimation by Redmond was followed by a belated assertion of control with the intention of neutralising a potentially troublesome rival.

A central feature of Parnellism before 1891 was the drawing together of various streams of Irish nationalism in a single movement. After the Split, the elements of that movement gradually reverted to their separate courses amid a contest for the Parnell legacy.[46] Although the leader of a minority faction in the 1890s, Redmond was in pole position to claim that legacy and shape it for his own purposes. As Mathew Kelly has demonstrated, by inheriting the Parnell mantle Redmond inherited the same coalition of interests that Parnell had assembled.[47] Largely under his direction, between 1891 and 1911, Ivy Day, the annual commemoration of Parnell's death, became a symbolic national rallying point. On the first anniversary of Parnell's death, the *Irish Daily Independent* carried an advertisement calling on Parnellites to wear the ivy leaf in token of their fidelity to their lost leader's independent principles.[48] Until 1901, the annual Ivy Day parade and ceremony was a significant social and political event. While he took a background role on Ivy Day itself, Redmond used the event and the Party meeting which was invariably held the following day to promote his version of Parnellism. He invoked the ghost of Parnell in his political rhetoric to promote unity, contrasting the cohesiveness of the movement at its height under Parnell with the division and recrimination which attended his fall. In his speech at the laying of the foundation stone of the Parnell monument on 8 October 1899, Redmond spoke of the national determination to fittingly honour Parnell and the related desire to blot out memory of past dissensions. He believed that the Parnell monument 'might be the means of bringing Irishmen together' and expressed the hope that before it was unveiled 'Ireland might be once more united, as she was when Parnell made her power felt'.[49]

The moves which culminated in the reunification of the Party had already begun at this point and within a matter of months, Redmond was chairman of the re-united Irish Party. Redmond was never regarded as an inspired or dynamic leader in the mould of Parnell but 'more prosaically, and correctly, as its Chairman'.[50] His selection was a testament to his diplomatic skills and temperament, and he can claim some credit for reunification. Old animosities remained though, and the unity and central control which was such a feature of the Party under Parnell was never fully regained. The independence of powerful maverick figures, such as Healy and O'Brien, was never curtailed, and John Dillon, Joe Devlin and others continued to work through the UIL and the AOH to pursue agrarian and other agendas. Even if he wanted to, Redmond never quite moved from being chairman to being chief. Arthur Lynch, who was an Irish Party MP between 1901 and 1902 and again between 1909 and 1918, was no admirer of Redmond but he recalled him as an impressive chairman, 'dignified and yet sufficiently concessive in manner, with the aspect of a Roman Senator.'[51]

The disturbances which attended the ceremony to unveil the foundation stone of the Parnell monument point to another area of vulnerability for Redmond. During the Split, Parnell had commanded the loyalty of the majority of the Fenian element and during the 1890s the Parnellite group under Redmond retained much of the support. The 'symbiotic relationship' between advanced nationalists and Redmondites persisted for most of the decade.[52] As the successor of Parnell, Redmond inherited a residue of sympathy and support from advanced nationalists. For a time at least, he cultivated that support, backing amnesty campaigns and paying lip service to radical nationalism. By the end of the decade, that alliance was fracturing, a development which was highlighted by the conflict between those organising the Parnell memorial and the supporters of the existing Wolfe Tone memorial group who complained that their hero was being side-lined in favour of Parnell.[53] As the division between Parnellites healed, an *Irish Times* reporter discerned a 'new split' – between those who preferred Parnell to Wolfe Tone and those who preferred Wolfe Tone to Parnell.[54] In the years which followed, with Redmond focusing his efforts on incremental reform at Westminster, that division became more rather than less entrenched. When he asked rhetorically at the unveiling of the Parnell statue where were the enemies of Parnell now, it was Sinn Féin who responded caustically that some of them were behind him on the platform.[55] The failure to keep the leaders of the Fenian tradition inside his broad nationalist movement was to have considerable implications later for Redmond and for Ireland. In this, historians have fairly detected a notable contrast with Parnell. According to Oliver MacDonagh, whereas Parnell first outmanoeuvred, then tamed and deployed the 'hillside men', Redmond first under-estimated them and then allowed them to seize the initiative.[56]

The appointment of Liberal leader Henry Campbell-Bannerman as Prime Minister in December 1905 and the subsequent 'Liberal landslide' in the January 1906 Election presaged a new phase in Redmond's leadership. The virtues of the Liberal alliance which had been much disputed in the Split re-emerged in Redmondite rhetoric alongside the well-worn mantra about the absolute necessity for an independent Irish Party. It was a productive trade-off which resulted in a series of measures beneficial to Ireland including further land reform, a Town Tenants Act (1906) and the long-awaited settlement of the Irish University Question (1908). The apogee of the alliance was the passing of Home Rule in the shape of the Government of Ireland Act which received royal assent on 18 September 1914 following a prolonged period of constitutional crisis. Although the measure was suspended for the duration of the war and until some provision was made for Ulster, it was a significant achievement for Redmond who, it appeared, had done what Parnell had failed to do, win Home Rule for Ireland.

Redmond had predicted in 1893 that any future Home Rule bill would be a compromise and that was certainly true of the measure as passed. For 40 years, the ambiguous slogan 'Home Rule' had been the demand of constitutional nationalists: translating that slogan into practice in a volatile political climate was always going to be difficult. For some, Home Rule meant a large measure of devolution; for others, it was a code-word for full independence. Inevitably there would be disappointment. The 1914 Act fell short of the full legislative and fiscal autonomy which Redmond and most constitutional nationalists had sought and, of course, it left the Ulster question dangerously un-resolved. The prospect of temporary or permanent exclusion of Ulster continued to hang over Ireland. However, while Redmond's leadership has been criticised, the Act undoubtedly represented a considerable advance on the earlier Home Rule proposals.

When Parnell was accused by English critics of never defining precisely what he meant by Home Rule, he responded in his memorable speech at the Cork Opera House in January 1885 when he said that 'no man has the right to fix the boundary to the march of a nation'. The words were intended to reconcile what was currently achievable with possible future developments. Redmond's choice of these words for inscription on the Parnell monument in 1911 clearly indicates his approval of the sentiment but it would be misleading to interpret their use on the monument as a comment by Redmond on the interim nature of the anticipated settlement. The inscription was chosen five years earlier, when there was no prospect of Home Rule and all that was on the horizon was a modest measure of devolution. In any case, Redmond did see the Home Rule Act as an acceptable compromise settlement. While it can be argued plausibly that the Home Rule movements led by both Parnell and Redmond were separatist, in effect, neither leader was separatist in his instincts or aspirations. Redmond, who was much influenced by his travels in Australia, envisaged legislative autonomy for Ireland within the British Empire: in his own words, the goal was 'national freedom, imperial unity and strength'.[57]

The events of the Great War and the story of how Redmond's generous response to the war effort redounded on constitutional nationalism lie beyond the scope of this chapter. Redmond was certainly unfortunate in the turn of events, but he compounded matters by being slow to appreciate how the context had been transformed. With conventional politics in cold storage for the duration of war, the Irish Party lost its leverage, and the Liberal alliance became irrelevant. In Ireland, other forces emerged to fill the vacuum and constitutional nationalism foundered.

In the light of his achievements, it may seem unfair that Redmond's reputation as a leader has been discounted by historians. However, that judgement is based not simply on an unfavourable comparison with Parnell but also on the events of the period 1914–18 when, as Nicholas Mansergh reflected, Redmond preferred compromise at a time compromise had gone out of Irish politics.[58] The qualities which made him a good choice of leader of the Irish Party in 1900 when the warring factions were re-united were precisely the qualities which were a liability after 1914. Redmond himself identified a key contrast between himself and Parnell. In November 1896, during a visit to the United States, he told an audience in New York that the English people first hated and then respected Parnell but that they always feared him.[59] The same could never have been said about Redmond whose reasonableness, dignity and moderation were both endearing and ultimately damaging. J. J. Horgan who was an admirer of both concluded perceptively that Redmond 'lacked the daemonic spirit which frightens as well as inspires, and which made Parnell a great leader'.[60]

CHAPTER 4

John Redmond & Edward Carson: Bloodshed, Borders, and the Union State[1]

Alvin Jackson

John Redmond and Edward Carson together dominated the politics of Irish Home Rule and unionism between 1910 and 1918 and were major influences on Irish and British politics for an even longer period than this. Yet though contemporaries routinely viewed them together, and though they had a strong political and personal relationship, the hermeneutics of much modern Irish historical scholarship have precluded any systematic comparison. In fact, comparing Redmond and Carson provides important new illumination on the central themes of their careers, as well as on the political cultures of the multi-national union state within which they each operated.

Comparing John Redmond and Edward Carson

These men were the two greatest Irish parliamentarians of their generation: they were perhaps the best-known Irishmen of the time. And their achievements – and their mistakes – lastingly shaped the political landscape of modern Ireland and indeed of the United Kingdom. Their careers say much about the working of the multi-national union state wherein they found themselves. Their careers, and in particular their role in the Irish and British Home Rule crisis of 1910–14, speak to other concerns which have a real contemporary resonance.

They were of course, on the face of it, political opposites: John Redmond was the leader of the nationalist Irish Parliamentary Party from February 1900 through to his death in March 1918; Edward Carson was the leader of the Irish unionists from 1910 through to 1921, when he became a law lord. And yet the parallels between the two are clear. They were of the same (mid-1850s) Irish generation. They were educated at the same university, Trinity College Dublin. They pursued the same profession (the law) at King's Inns, Dublin, and mixed in the same legal circuits. They sat together for over 25 years in the one parliament. They were tireless political opponents, but they also professed a friendship and mutual respect. One was a Home Rule nationalist, the other an Irish unionist; yet they shared some monarchical, imperial, federalist, and indeed anti-suffragist sympathies.[2]

Contemporaries of all kinds – from the king to cartoonists – routinely linked them. Even their own families – Harry Carson (Edward's son) and Louis Redmond-Howard (John's nephew) – came together in presenting a number of bitter patricidal critiques of their elders (including a co-written one act melodrama in 1914).[3] And yet the two protagonists of the Home Rule struggle have rarely been brought together analytically.

WHY, THEN, HAS THERE BEEN NO COMPARISON OF THIS KIND?

It is notable that where comparative biography of great political rivals is a common place elsewhere (there are, for example, the several joint lives of Disraeli and Gladstone, Wellington and Napoleon, Hitler and Stalin), comparative political biography and comparative political history are relatively underdeveloped genres within modern Irish historiography. This is perhaps because the kinds of connection which might be made (say) between constitutional nationalist and physical force separatist or – as in this case – between nationalist and unionist cut across still acute political sensitivities. It is also the case that the two 'lives' have been separated out by the division of the island into two popular and opposing political narratives. 'Partitionist history' within an Irish context can be defined partly as dealing with nationalists and unionists exclusively in their separate silos, and ignoring common political environments, the cross-fertilisation of ideas and cross-communication (however fractious).

WHY DOES ALL THIS PARTICULARLY MATTER JUST NOW?

The year 2018 brought the centenary of the death of John Redmond, with a surge of commemorative activity on or around the day of the anniversary, 6 March, including the conference from which the contributions in this collection are drawn. But the era of the Third Home Rule Bill, and the careers of Redmond and Carson, and the contexts to their activity, have a much wider contemporary resonance for both Ireland and Britain. This period of Home Rule, so dominated by Redmond and Carson, was one of unusually intense and concentrated political passion not just for Ireland but for Britain too, and it serves as a reminder that while the stability of the United Kingdom is often taken for granted, there has been a history of threatened conflagration and near melt-down. The tone and content of political discourse over Home Rule in 1910–14 – the anger, division, and brinkmanship – bear some resemblance to those which have prevailed in Britain over Brexit.[4] The period was one of intense and bitter passion, especially for Carson's Conservative allies – who were split over Britain's trading relationship with the wider world – and in particular over the issue of free trade. In seeking to 'make [Edwardian] Britain great again' the conservatives in 1912–14 turned to Irish unionists like Carson with a dangerous passion.

But the era not only defined issues and problems of lasting importance; it also threw up projected solutions which remain in play. There were different, hard, and soft, versions of what constituted partition; for example, the partition envisioned in 1914 or 1916 was very different from that enacted in 1920–22. Many, including both Carson and Redmond, believed that a federal reform of the British constitution – still very much relevant as a possibility – might reconcile Irish nationalism to a reformed union or imperial state.[5]

More generally, for some influential twenty-first-century Scots (such as the former First Minister, Alex Salmond) the struggle of Irish nationalists for Home Rule and independence has been a frequently cited inspiration. But it was Charles Stewart Parnell – aggressive and charismatic – whose portrait Alex Salmond chose to display in his parliamentary office at

Westminster, and not that of the more emollient and genteel John Redmond.[6] In a sense, therefore, understanding Mr Salmond's choice of interior decor provides a pointer to some of the central themes of this chapter.

How did their personal formation impact upon Redmond and Carson's political roles?

Redmond's parents were estranged. Carson was the favoured sibling in a relatively stable family environment. And, while this is not the place to unravel the intricacies of attachment theory, it is still likely that these circumstances were linked to Redmond's conspicuous lack of wide networks of friends and allies – as well as to Carson's indomitable self-confidence and theatrical braggadocio.[7]

Redmond was from the Catholic professional and landed classes and there was money in his family networks. Carson's family was *arriviste*: there are hints of a somewhat louche quality. Though Carson was a southern Irish Protestant, he was not a landed Protestant; and there is evidence to suggest that after his father's death the family were left (as one of his sisters later affirmed) in 'straitened [financial] circumstances'.[8] In other words, Redmond was materially secure, but personally insecure in terms of background; Carson (on the other hand) was well anchored in his family affections, but he felt materially threatened until the day he died, leaving in his will the modern real price equivalent of over €10 million.

Redmond and Carson were both lawyers, but here the similarity ended. Carson can be defined by his social and professional role as a lawyer in ways which do not apply to Redmond. Carson's success in the law courts generated leverage within a British parliament increasingly professional in its makeup and values – even with political opponents like H. H. Asquith or T. M. Healy (who were by no means easy to impress). Indeed, Carson's legal career was reaching its peak at precisely the moment that Home Rule was returning to centre stage (in 1910): he defended George Archer-Shee, the 'Winslow boy' of Terence Rattigan's later (1946) drama, in early 1910.[9]

Recent history weighed heavily with each in terms of their outlook and strategies. Part of the problem with Redmond was the extent to which the legacy both of Charles Stewart Parnell and of the profound 'split' within constitutional nationalism (1891–1900) after the latter's death weighed down upon him. This partly illuminates his own relentless concern for unity. However, in some ways Redmond was loyal to the letter but not necessarily to the spirit of Parnellism. Carson (who was occasionally compared to Parnell by contemporaries) was clearly influenced by a particular historical reading of successive British governments' willingness to respond to Irish political mobilisation.

Finally, each of them was a compromise leader, and each was circumscribed by this. Each of them was in some ways marginal to the central concerns of the parties that they ended up leading – Redmond as a Parnellite in a largely anti-Parnellite united party – Carson as a southern unionist in a largely northern unionist movement. The resulting limits on Redmond's freedom of manoeuvre are well-known; but there was also a considerable distance between Carson's public certainties over the union and his much more circumspect private behaviour in 1910–14.

WHAT, THEN, DO THE TWO CAREERS SAY ABOUT THE CULTURES OF THE UNION STATE OF THE NINETEENTH AND EARLY TWENTIETH CENTURIES?

Each of the men worked with a particular set of personal legacies; however, each also worked within, and was defined by, a particular type of political environment. One way of thinking about Redmond and Carson, and the social and political roles that they occupied, is to look at the structure of the state in which they operated.

Those multi-national union states, like the UK, which emerged in the late eighteenth and early nineteenth centuries were created often in similar circumstances, against the backdrop of European warfare, and they shared some common characteristics. This is not the place to reflect at length about the conceptualisation of union, but a couple of fundamental points are worth highlighting.[10] The UK (like other united kingdoms) was of course an asymmetrical union – one overwhelmingly 'predominant partner' (to use the language of Lord Rosebery) and several (like Ireland, Scotland, and Wales) which were much smaller.[11] It was also an imperfect or an incomplete union – in so far as distinctively Scottish or Irish institutions remained after 1707 and 1801.

Empire was conceptually relevant to these union states, which were not only often connected to overseas colonisation, but were sometimes founded upon forms of internal colonialism.[12] The types of governance which they sustained and the kinds of political culture also overlapped with empire: in the Irish case there was a viceroy, favoured social and political classes through whom government was largely sustained, and complex or hybrid political cultures which were often pulled between the metropolitan power as well as local traditions. Partition (as in Bengal in 1905) was also an imperial stratagem which was ultimately applied to Ireland.

As K. T. Hoppen has recently reminded us all, the politics of the Westminster elite through much of the period of union were characterised often by a relative ignorance of Ireland and of the union and by a relative lack of any lastingly coherent vision of union. This expressed itself in cyclical shifts between integrationist approaches to the government of Ireland and exceptionalist or even devolutionist approaches.[13] Moreover, Irish politicians, whether nationalist or unionist, fought for attention, and then fought to educate or inform British ministers and party leaders. The corollary of this was the deepening of political division within Ireland itself, since the competing parties tended to look for external support and validation rather than internal reconciliation. But there was little of this pathology that was unique to Britain and Ireland: for example, Austrian politics in the later decades of the Dual Monarchy have been described (by Steven Beller) as an ever more 'vertical hierarchical system – where the parties bargained with the government ... rather than with each other ... the aim of the game was to put one over on the opponent rather than to come to a compromise with him'.[14] This – in essence – was the 'system' in place in Ireland.

How does all of this relate to Redmond and Carson? Redmond and Carson had a low-key but persistent friendship from about 1890. But there was a striking absence in their political relationship: there is little to suggest that – despite all of the ties mentioned earlier – they had much direct negotiation with each other particularly when their British allies were not present. Each of them looked primarily to the British parties to represent their cause. For each this carried an ongoing risk of dependency or clientelism – which in the past was only off-set by highly combative constitutional nationalist leaders such as Daniel

O'Connell and Parnell or through the studied defiance of the militant separatists enrolled within the Irish Republican Brotherhood (or Fenians). There were also (as we shall see) clear distinctions between the ways in which Carson navigated the politics of the union parliament and government, and Redmond's ways.

Carson had a critical advantage: British Conservatism relied upon the union as a unifying mechanism since the Party was otherwise still wrangling over tariff reform and free trade, and over its leadership in 1910–11. In addition, the Conservatives' embroilment in Ulster obscures the fact that Carson had partly liberated himself from Westminster politics through the popular political mobilisation which had occurred in the north after 1911–12. The central irony of the period was of course that the strength of Redmondite nationalism hinged largely upon its position in the British parliament, while that of unionism now lay in Ireland itself.

Redmond's essential difficulty was that he was coping with a still fragile constitutional nationalist tradition (nominally – but only nominally – united after the internal conflagrations of the 1890s) and seeking to collaborate with a broadly united Liberalism which was sympathetic towards, but not passionate about, Home Rule. Moreover, it was a Liberalism which believed that (as Asquith said in 1913) 'the Nationalists without the support of the Liberal Party were powerless'.[15] Redmond's relative weakness was expressed in terms either of lack of communication from Liberal ministers, debilitating partial affirmation, or broken promises (this was particularly clear in the negotiations of February/March 1914 and of June/July 1916). This relative weakness was also directly expressed in terms of discourse. His vocabulary and pitch (in dealing with ministers) were often, seemingly, those of a supplicant. He frequently invoked the language of 'fair play'.[16] A characteristic motif of his correspondence was anxious petitioning: a characteristic tone, on the other hand, was offended gentility. Even Redmond himself recorded on occasion that he felt 'really humiliated in having to run after them [British ministers] in the way I have done'.[17] All this was not a feature of Parnell's communication – nor, for that matter, of Carson's. A striking contrast between how the two men navigated the British establishment came with their respective meetings with Lord Kitchener on 6/7 August 1914: Carson responded to Kitchener's various threatening suggestions with a sarcastic 'you're a damned fine fellow' and 'I'd like to see you try'; while Redmond gently recorded that he had been 'rather disquieted' by his parallel conversation with Kitchener.[18] 'Rather disquieted' and 'I'd like to see you try' are an eloquent conjunction or introduction to their two styles.

Turning finally to wider contexts – most analysis of the survival or demise of union states or multinational empires of the nineteenth century stresses the role of monarchy and loyalty and its associated institutions (like the army) as critical binding agents and as engines of a supranational state identity. Oszkár Jászi, the Hungarian-born sociologist of the Austro-Hungarian Empire, stressed the role of the Habsburgs as a key 'centripetal' force, and more recent work by Pieter Judson and others has done likewise.[19] Work on the Bernadotte monarchy in the United Kingdoms of Sweden-Norway points to a similar set of unifying functions.[20] Both Redmond and Carson were primarily Irish in terms of their identity (indeed Carson was sometimes accused of stage-Irishness); but each acknowledged a supranational set of imperial and monarchical loyalties. Redmond's monarchism, imperialism, and commitment to the British war effort are generally seen unflatteringly or uncomprehendingly in the context of either unionism or (by contrast) a purist republican separatism. But there is a case for understanding him partly by looking back to the O'Connellite tradition of nationalist 'loyalty'; and also, partly by looking sideways to a wider European phenomenon of nationality and state loyalty, brokered through the agency of the crown and its institutions.

Redmond's and Carson's fundamental characteristic was that they reflected the hybridity of Irish political culture under the union – the janus-faced looking to union or imperial as well as national themes. This again is only surprising if judged by the standards of an essentialist Britishness or Irishness, or judged from the standpoint of an uncompromisingly partitioned Ireland. And, indeed work on identity in other multi-national union states conventionally emphasises the contingency and negotiability of identity, as well as its linkages and layers.[21]

Bloodshed

Violence, whether real or threatened, was also a common feature of Europe's united kingdoms of the nineteenth century. This should scarcely surprise since these supranational unions were being constructed at precisely the moment of mounting national sentiment across the continent. And each of the two careers poses questions about how essentially constitutional politicians operate in a society where there are strong cultures either celebrating or practising violent political resistance. A number of points may be highlighted in illuminating this theme. To start with, a water-tight distinction between 'constitutionalist' and 'militant' in modern Irish history is generally hard to sustain. There is in fact some analytical value behind Seán Lemass's notion (applied to the newly founded Fianna Fáil Party in 1926) of being 'slightly constitutional'.[22]

Why did Redmond, as a great parliamentarian, shift to a greater militancy in 1913–14, as the political crisis over Irish Home Rule developed? He did so firstly, of course, as a response to unionist mobilisation in the north of Ireland. But the question has also to be grasped in terms of his own long-standing relationship with physical force nationalism, and in particular, with the Irish Republican Brotherhood (or Fenian movement). He had a strong sense of the history of national insurgency and was at the forefront of the centenary commemoration of the 1798 Rising. He built links with Fenians and Fenianism in the 1890s. The issue was not therefore that his relationship with the militants was ever absent. But Redmond's closest links with Fenianism had come in the 1890s – and by 1914 he had a conception of Fenianism which was both outmoded and incomplete. Moreover, Redmond did not absolutely oppose political violence in principle; he saw instead conditions in which the Irish might legitimately resort to arms. There are overlaps here with Catholic – Thomist and other – teaching on the notion of the just war. One aspect of his reasoning certainly related to the overwhelming strength of British firepower, the impracticality of any Irish assault, and the inevitability of bloody Irish defeat.[23]

Why was Redmond evidently so unimpressed by unionist militancy in 1912–14? This was essentially because he believed that he understood and shared their strategic calculations. In 1908 he wrote that 'there are friends of ours who say that any violent action in Ireland will alienate support here [in Britain]. But the sounder view ... is that you have got, in some way or another, once more to impress the English mind that the Irish question is a real, urgent, one'.[24] In Redmond's view Carson's militants were bluffing in 1912–14 because like him they understood that tackling the military might of the British Empire would produce a bloodbath; but he also 'knew' that they were bluffing because he saw that they, like Irish nationalists, were primarily seeking to 'impress the English mind' through their militant postures.

Why, then, did Carson shift to militancy in 1910–14? The answer to this rests partly again with 'impressing the English mind'. But unionist militancy also came at the end of a long period of northern reorientation towards local organisation and initiative.[25] Did Carson introduce the gun into Irish politics? He unquestionably helped to illegally introduce large numbers of guns into Ireland and its politics. There is certainly a case for saying that he introduced the gun into Redmondite politics – or perhaps that he *reintroduced* the gun into Irish politics more generally. But, of course, he was not the first militant Irish politician, or the first to threaten the British government with armed insurgency. In the end the key point about Carson and militancy was not primarily that he was the first to introduce guns into Irish politics. It was rather that he was the first who deliberately wanted to be seen introducing guns into Irish politics.[26]

Were Carson and Redmond the effective architects of the partition of the Ireland?

Neither Carson nor of course Redmond invented partition as a concept, or even as a concept with an Irish application. It was in fact privately mooted with the First Home Rule Bill in 1886, and had been given imperial applications before 1912. As is very well known, Carson was a driver of partition, while Redmond reluctantly acquiesced in an increasingly difficult range of partitionist proposals forced upon him by his Liberal allies. As is relatively well known, they were ultimately divided not by the principle of partition, which Redmond loathed, and Carson disliked, but by its practicalities and potential application: Carson sought ultimately the indefinite exclusion from Home Rule of the six counties which became Northern Ireland, while by 1916 Redmond was prepared to countenance a term-limited or otherwise clearly 'temporary' exclusion.

But a number of under-explored issues are worth highlighting, especially perhaps given contemporary concerns. Part of the problem in dealing with partition in Irish history is that it is such a heavily freighted and teleological term; but the Brexit debates arising from the 'backstop' over the Irish border have served to underline that there is – and has been – no single definition of either partition or its associated frontiers. Home Rule, as defined in the summer of 1914, did not give an Irish parliament any untrammelled right to disrupt free trade. Therefore, opting out of Home Rule did not create an economic or necessarily a 'hard' political border any more than such existed between Northern Ireland and Britain in the years of devolution. It was not eastern Ulster opting out of Home Rule which created the form of partition which we have been living with in Ireland for a century; it was rather eastern Ulster opting out of the revolution.

In some ways partition was an example of the law of unintended consequences in politics. For Carson partition was a tactic which became a compromise which was reimagined as a fundamental goal: the unity of Ireland was pragmatically replaced in 1914–16 by the idea of a soft border and then almost accidentally in 1920–1 by a hard border. Carson began as an all-Ireland unionist who long knew that the concentrated industrial wealth and unionism of the north-east posed a problem for Liberal Home Rulers. Only from about the autumn of 1913 onwards did he look seriously at partition as a meaningful compromise position.[27] And only from 1920 did he publicly and retrospectively define partition as the immutable objective of northern unionism.

For Redmond partition was an anathema and remained an anathema. He and his senior lieutenant, John Dillon, had a particularly well-organised northern support base through the charismatic Belfast nationalist, Joseph Devlin; and Party and national unity were fundamental to his vision of politics in the wake of the Parnell Split. One of the central planks in the posthumous defence case for Redmond (mounted by Dillon) was that he had fought partition tooth and nail – and had left Ireland united at the time of his death in 1918.[28]

Indeed, while Redmond and Carson were famously opposed on the national question; they both tentatively explored (as many do within the UK today) federalism (or explicitly shared sovereignty) as a means of bridging their political positions. For Carson federalism was a means of creating an Irish parliament within the overall context of a reformed union government of the United Kingdom. For Redmond, federalism was a means of redefining the government of the whole empire. But federalism also worked for Redmond within an Irish environment, allowing the possibility of the north enjoying a distinctive status but within an all-Ireland rather than a British context. Here again Redmond was simultaneously looking forward to later (often republican) thought on the shape of an all-Ireland state; but he may also have been looking back to the precedent of other European composite monarchies like Austria-Hungary, and to the Home Rule relationships (such as those experienced by Croatia) within the two halves of that state. In short, federalism – whether in 1914 or now – offered a common vocabulary and a hope of bipartisanship, which perhaps masked conceptually very different approaches and goals.

Linked with this, Redmond and Carson each looked beyond national borders to wider supranational and (in the case of Redmond) diasporic concerns. Redmond sought to counterbalance the power of London using the devices of the empire and the Irish diaspora. Strikingly, Carson did not have the same vision of empire as did Redmond – nor did he have the same active and constructive engagement with colonial ministerial networks and communities. Ultimately, Carson talked the talk about empire; but it was Redmond who envisioned and practised it.

We know of course that Redmond's vision of Irish self-government was superseded by that of Sinn Féin, and that he died over a century ago, a disappointed man. We know, too, that Carson shifted gradually from an all-Ireland unionism to a six-county exclusionist or partitionist stance. But Carson's public acceptance of the role of patriarch of Northern Ireland (which flourished in the 1930s) concealed a profound bitterness about the condition of all of Ireland in the 1920s. This was repeated in private communications: in 1918, Carson wrote privately that he had 'already agreed to the exclusion of six counties, although I think that arrangement unstatesmanlike and a poor solution'.[29] Despite his standing as patriarch of Northern Ireland he wrote in 1922 that 'I feel I am a citizen without nationality or anything to be loyal to'.[30] In 1928, he confided that he thought 'there'd be more decency in a Republic than in this [Free State] humbug. In fact, I'd rather see a republic'.[31] He claimed in private at this time that 'looking back at politics, I think we made a great mistake in not accepting Mr Gladstone's first Home Rule bill'.[32]

The difference between Carson and Redmond on partition was in the end essentially the difference between explicitly arguing and implicitly thinking in partitionist terms – or (alternatively) the difference between disliking and loathing partition.

Overview

After a century it is surely worth reuniting Redmond and Carson analytically. In reality, neither could ever wholly be understood without recourse to the other. Nor can each be fully understood without some recourse to the shape and functioning of the multi-national union state. Redmond's approach to a succession of fundamental issues – such as militancy and partition and the endorsement of the war effort – was at least in part influenced by Carson's actions and strategies. Carson's own actions in key areas were partly conditioned by a particular view of Irish nationalism and the ways in which successive union governments operated. Redmond had vision, but lacked passion; Carson lacked vision, but could provide the theatrical passion in spade-loads. Each, however, was in part confined by the contours and precedents of the union state.

Redmond on the whole played by the parliamentary and political rule book, including the opaque Parnellite rule book; indeed, he became the key executor of the great man's highly fraught and ambiguous legacies. He sought for consistency and honour in his private and public dealings. Carson bent and broke rules and revelled in contradictions while all the while proclaiming his directness, simplicity, and consistency. Yet he was at times the lawless lawyer; the disloyal loyalist; the all-Ireland partitionist. He bequeathed complex legacies to his compatriots in the north, including legacies of dangerous brinkmanship.[33] He simultaneously embraced and owned his standing as a state-builder in Northern Ireland, while privately complaining at length about the new dispensations of the 1920s.

Ireland for long has been a land of secret histories, of hybridity and liminality, where the reality of political experience has sometimes been buried, and often kept far apart from the ideal. The ideal has been a treasured vision of pristine political struggle: the reality has often involved day-to-day compromises with power, ambiguous family heritages, and quotidian and understandable (if not very glamorous) struggles for survival and betterment. Edward Carson lived long enough to rewrite his own history, and thereby to mask the shifts and failures in his political life: he lived long enough to impose a form of consistency on a long and inconsistent career whose central themes were simultaneously the law and the breaking of the law. It was John Redmond's tragedy that he all too clearly embodied compromise, ambiguity, and struggle. But at the same time these complexities also reflected the reality of much individual and collective Irish historical experience. And herein lie both Redmond's authenticity and his importance for us all today.

CHAPTER 5

THE IRISH PARTY: RECRUITMENT AND THE GREAT WAR, C.1914–1915

Michael Wheatley

The Redmond symposium held in March 2018 marked not only the centenary of the death of John Redmond, but also of the death of 'Redmondism', of Redmond's hopes for all-Ireland Home Rule, peacefully achieved, embracing all creeds and classes and within the British Empire. Redmond's own nationalism was suffused with small 'c' conservatism, but for 18 years he had to preside over a movement that was mostly radical, sometimes democratic, and often belligerent – if distinctly male and middle-aged. As that archetypal Scottish Liberal fixer and chief whip, the Master of Elibank, put it after Redmond's death, 'I found him a thorough gentleman and absolutely reliable. Apart from the Home Rule principle…he would have been known as a rigid Conservative and Constitutionalist.'[1] The verdict of historians on Redmond's leadership during the war has not necessarily been unkind, but virtually all have acknowledged the totality of his failure. Home Rule was lost. Ireland was irretrievably divided. The use of violence to achieve political ends was vindicated.

Recent histories have greatly enhanced our understanding of Ireland's participation in the Great War, and also of Redmond's role, both in promoting wartime recruiting and in getting a limited measure of Home Rule legislation passed into law after the outbreak of war.[2] However, significantly less has been added to our knowledge of the Irish Party during the war. By the Irish Party, I mean that broader movement in Ireland that at the outbreak of war encompassed a range of nationalist organisations and retained the loyalty of much of nationalist Ireland.

It was not just Redmond who failed so completely in the Great War. His party, the Irish Party, was comprehensively discredited and largely destroyed, though its demolition was hardly unique. Right across Europe, the war brutalised and sometimes crushed political cultures, parties, and leaders. For many years to come, however, the Irish Party in particular would be portrayed as an elderly, corrupt movement that was already in terminal decline, just waiting to be blown away by the first hurricane that came along.[3] That hurricane might have been the pre-war Home Rule crisis, had that crisis not been cut short by the outbreak of war. As it was, the destruction and transformation wrought by the war was judged to have been more than adequate for the task.

I find this interpretation, of the inevitability of the Irish Party's decline and fall, hard to accept. At the outbreak of war, it was still a credible, self-renewing, broad alliance, embracing the large majority of Irish nationalists. Elements within it were, certainly, decaying, but others were in rude good health and the party was more than capable of disciplined, decisive action. Its goals, rhetoric and support base continued to evolve. The vigorous, growing, openly-sectarian Hibernians and what the party now hailed in its rhetoric – but barely, if at all, controlled – as 'Ireland's army', the Irish Volunteers, were both in full flow before the war. Perhaps both of these movements were more indicative of the future evolution and militancy of the Irish Party than they were of its inevitable obliteration.

However, these movements and their associated rhetoric represented anything but 'Redmondism'. Rather they reinforced the impression that Redmond and his party had never been synonymous. When Redmond had tried to set a more moderate course – over conciliation and devolution in 1903–04, over the Irish Council Bill in 1907, over federalism in 1910 and even over volunteering in the winter of 1913–14, he was pulled back towards his more militant, belligerent movement. Nevertheless, when it came to the greatest crisis of all, in August 1914, Redmond, off his own bat and hardly consulting the rest of his party, immediately committed Ireland to friendship with and support for England in the emerging European war, despite the fact that Home Rule was still unattained. The Irish Volunteers, he declared in the House of Commons on 3 August 1914, would lock arms with their brethren in the north [i.e. the unionist Ulster Volunteers] to defend Ireland's shores, freeing the British Army to be withdrawn from Ireland.[4] As T. P. O'Connor would state in October 1914,

> ...no nation was ever asked by its leaders and by new conditions to take such a sharp curve in its point of view.[5]

This time, however, Redmond carried the overwhelming majority of his party with him and, once this commitment was made, there was no going back. The Irish Party set out on a course that it could not abandon without losing Home Rule, but which, before the war ended, would lead to its own destruction.

As with the other nations of the United Kingdom, the outbreak of war came as a surprise and shock to almost all Irish opinion formers. It was seen at once as a massive upheaval and dislocation. Few, if any, saw it as a jaunty adventure that would be over by Christmas. Whatever its expected duration, whether short or long, the war was considered to be a tragedy; a terrible slaughter. According to the ever-moderate *Wicklow People*:

> With all the progress that has been made it is sad to think that our great powers are still just as barbarous as they were generations ago, but have invented much more effective methods for the slaughter and destruction of soldiers.[6]

For the *Dundalk Democrat:* 'this terrible struggle, in which all the great Powers of Europe are now involved, will be the greatest struggle in the history of the world'. All countries would emerge financially exhausted, if not crippled. 'Countless lives will be lost'.[7] For the party's leading national mouthpiece, the *Freeman's Journal*, the outbreak of war on such a gigantic scale was a catastrophe for humanity and civilisation. 'We are confronted by Armageddon as the climax to all our boasted modern progress...No nation that is free, or hopes to be free or to maintain its freedom, can escape the fortunes of this conflict.'[8]

In common with every other belligerent country, Irish public opinion rapidly identified a clear, external threat and aggressor.[9] Germany was immediately seen as a brutal, militarist aggressor against England's allies (in particular France and small, independent, Catholic Belgium). The cause of the Allies was clearly seen, in nationalist Ireland, to be just. As the Royal Irish Constabulary County Inspector for Roscommon put it at the beginning of September:

> The War is the absorbing topic of interest now. Nothing else is discussed and there is a fine spirit of loyalty in evidence. Germany is hated and France beloved.[10]

The drama and damage caused by the war immediately became apparent, manifesting itself in panic buying, price hikes, spy scares, a financial credit crunch, industrial layoffs and short-time working – and also booming farm incomes. More patriotically, the outbreak of war also saw a surge of recruiting, enthusiastic crowds cheering departing soldiers (from both Irish and British regiments) the launch of relief funds, and the establishment of welfare committees.[11] Across provincial Ireland, nationalists backed Redmond's offer of the Irish Volunteers for home defence. In making this offer, Redmond was in no way going against the grain of popular nationalist opinion as the huge shock of the outbreak of war sank home. Indeed, for the Irish Party to have adopted a more neutralist stance at that time, in that context, seems inconceivable. In this, they were hardly alone. As Conor Mulvagh observed, 'the actions of the Irish Party in 1914 conformed closely to the actions of politicians across Europe.'[12]

Redmond's personal commitment to the justness of England's cause in the war would never be in doubt. He would even come to join in singing 'God Save the King', drink the Loyal Toast and fly the Union Jack beside the Green Flag at his country retreat.[13] However, his party's motives in backing his initial offer were decidedly more mixed. High-minded idealism was diffused with low parliamentary manoeuvring, as Redmond and his colleagues sought to secure the passage of the Home Rule Act through the British Parliament and to match any offer to Britain that might be made by Carson and the Ulster unionists. Nobly appealing to Ulster unionists to unite in a joint purpose with Irish nationalists coexisted with the far harsher objective, as James McConnel has shown, of obtaining training and arms for the Irish Volunteers for their use after the war, very probably against the Ulster Volunteers.[14] There was, certainly, a belief that Ireland now had a duty to ally with 'England' in a just cause, but there was also a pervasive fear – that to betray England in a terrible war would kill any chance of Ireland obtaining Home Rule for years to come. Ireland's rights and interests were still paramount. The *Wicklow People*, though lamenting the barbarism of the great powers, trusted Redmond and the Irish Party to play Ireland's game. For the *Dundalk Democrat*, 'Mr. Redmond has shown the world a new Ireland – calm, self-reliant, prepared to defend her shores and her rights, seeking to injure or offend none, but resolved to have and keep that which is hers.'[15] It is a truism that motivations for political decisions are rarely, if ever, simple. The fact that virtually all contemporary considerations, whether noble or selfish, supported alliance with 'England' in the war made the Irish Party's policy axiomatic. More neutralist nationalists inside and outside the party were relegated, if only temporarily, to the fringe.

From the start of the war, the party's support for England was, therefore, joined at the hip to the eventual achievement of Home Rule. Indeed, for the first six weeks of the war, the party refused publicly to promote army recruiting – until, that is, the Home Rule Act finally became law at Westminster. Recruiting meetings were simply not held. Advertisements for Kitchener's New Armies were largely absent from the party press. Welfare committees were formed by the score but recruiting committees remained conspicuous by their absence. Such was the party's discipline that possibly only one MP, Arthur Lynch, broke ranks publicly to promote recruiting.[16] The energies of the party's great and good were concentrated instead on parliamentary manoeuvres at Westminster, on war relief and on building the Irish Volunteers. The public, civic, civilian mobilisation that exploded into life to support army recruiting in Britain (and, from the beginning of September, in unionist Ulster), by-passed the Irish Party and was largely absent in nationalist Ireland. Even in Cork, the fervently pro-war, pro-recruiting rhetoric of the dissident nationalist William O'Brien proved ineffective in the face of the blatant inactivity of Redmond's party. In March 1915, O'Brien and his followers were still fuming at the damage done to recruiting by Redmond's failure to endorse it early in the war:

> He [Redmond], who now professes a fanatical zeal for Lord Kitchener's Army, has allowed his organisers and fuglemen in Cork to institute a merciless boycott of those nationalists who decided Ireland's attitude towards the war while he and his were three months still shivering in terror of pledging themselves to anything less lackadaisical than 'the defense of the shores of Ireland!'[17]

Already by the end of August 1914, the War Office put out a public statement, widely reported across Ireland, that Lord Kitchener was disappointed with poor level of enlistment into the first of Ireland's New Army divisions, the 10th (Irish) Division. If things did not improve, Kitchener believed, the new division would have to be completed with non-Irish recruits. Moreover, nationalist discontent was building over further parliamentary delays to Home Rule. At the beginning of September, John Dillon reported to T. P. O'Connor on the souring mood. Government 'shilly-shallying' meant that 'the country is seething with suspicion and disappointment...Our friends are disheartened and bewildered.'[18]

The Home Rule Act did finally gain the royal assent in mid-September and the party's pro-war commitment duly evolved. Redmond, in particular, now made a series of calls for men to serve 'in the firing line' in an 'Irish Brigade', which in practice became focused on the army's new 16th (Irish) Division. This new policy was proclaimed from mid-September in parliament, in a public manifesto and then in Redmond's supposedly spontaneous speech to an Irish Volunteer parade at Woodenbridge, Co Wicklow on 20 September. Here he proclaimed that it would be a disgrace for young Ireland if it remained 'confined at home' to defend Ireland against 'an unlikely invasion'. To the assembled Volunteers on parade Redmond went on: 'Go on drilling and make yourselves men, not only in Ireland itself, but wherever the firing line extends, in defence of right, of freedom and religion in this war'.[19]

In making this shift, the party leadership undoubtedly anticipated an open, public split with neutralist, advanced-nationalist opponents, particularly within the Irish Volunteers, whom it swiftly came to ridicule as 'Sinn Féiners'. The party moved rapidly to undertake a well-organised campaign to take over the Volunteers once and for all. During a two-month programme of Volunteer parades and rallies – 'packed' in both senses of the word – over

90 per cent of Volunteer companies were put firmly under party leadership. However, even those few MPs who went the extra mile at these meetings, to advocate joining the British army, stressed that no man would be coerced – the decision to join the army was a matter for free, individual choice. Though the police described the meetings and parades, wrongly, as 'recruiting' meetings, their purpose was to confirm the party's control over Irish nationalism and head off any threat to the party's wartime policy – to support Britain in the war and thus secure the implementation of Irish Home Rule.[20]

Though the success of this campaign was a confirmation of the party's strength, it was also, with hindsight, its last hurrah. First, it won victory at the cost of defections into outright opposition, or at least semi-detachment, of a number of formerly loyal politicians and, particularly, newspapers. Possibly the most significant publication to defect was the *Irish World* newspaper in New York and this period saw the beginning of the end for the United Irish League in North America.[21] Secondly, the prize won by the campaign – the renamed National Volunteers – proceeded to crumble in the party's hands. Far from the Volunteers now being trained for any wartime or post-war role, they withered away. The numbers attending activities slumped, funds ceased to be raised, drills and route marches did not take place, reorganised companies ceased even to meet. Their leadership had been decapitated twice – first by the call-up of army reservists and then by the party's purge of its opponents. More important, perhaps, was the fear of many that organised, public Volunteer activity made them liable to be called up and even conscripted into the British army en masse. The first serious conscription scare in Ireland, triggering hundreds to emigrate to the United States, occurred as early as October 1914. Party speakers, perfectly aware of this fear, went out of their way to stress that they were not 'recruiting sergeants' for John Bull and that recruiting was solely a matter for individual conscience – such niceties of language proved useless. Thirdly, public, civic support for army recruiting in the south and west remained minimal. Monthly recruiting nearly halved in the south and west between September and October 1914, and then languished over the winter.[22] Though Joe Devlin would lead an effective, mass enlistment into the 16th (Irish) Division by more than 1,300 National Volunteers in Belfast, this campaign had to wait until November even to begin. The perceived slowness of nationalist recruiting triggered fresh public attacks by unionists on Redmond, on his party and on nationalists in general. In November the *Irish Times* was moved to mockery:

> Long live our National Volunteers!
> May none their reputation mar;
> Invincible in times of peace,
> Invisible in times of war.[23]

The foremost nationalist advocate of recruiting remained Redmond himself, but already, he had to make the case that the Ireland's recruiting numbers were not as bad as they appeared. The explanations that he offered rightly included the importance of Ireland's agriculture, her small industrial base, and her rural depopulation and emigration, which had left behind the 'old and infirm'.[24] Though Redmond bulled up the numbers enlisting (by adding in those serving pre-war, reservists who were called up, and Irishmen enlisting in Britain and overseas) and proclaimed the justness of Ireland's participation 'in the sacred cause of justice and liberty', he also had to address what he called 'the infamous falsehood' or 'the slanders that constantly appear in unionist newspapers', that Irishmen were shirking in the war.[25]

By the end of 1914, the Irish Party was committed to a policy of support for Britain and the Allies that, given the terrible circumstances and sacrifices of wartime, it simply could not row back from. One striking aspect of the party's succeeding trudge to obliteration is that so little appeared to change prior to the Easter Rising. Superficially, and certainly in public, party discipline appeared to hold in 1915.[26] The party still won parliamentary by-elections. It put some effort into restoring the registration of local United Irish League branches and even supported two temporarily successful recruiting campaigns, in the spring and November 1915, though both were initiated and run by the authorities. In the first, from February to May 1915, recruiting advertisements did, for the first time, appear across the party-supporting press, and party MPs and dignitaries were organised to speak at local recruiting meetings. The 16th (Irish) Division did still attract recruits but, dogged by persistent War Office resistance to 'political' soldiering (at least if by nationalists), the division remained firmly anchored as a unit of the British army rather than as the 'Irish Brigade'. In the second recruiting campaign, in November 1915, despite a blitz of advertising across almost all of the Irish press and a direct, postal appeal to all men still deemed eligible to enlist, local party involvement was minimal. Redmond was, however, involved in planning this latter campaign and spoke publicly in support of it. Indeed, throughout 1915, Redmond remained the most prominent advocate of recruiting and his rhetoric became more emphatic as the year progressed. Ireland's future liberty and happiness now rested upon her loyalty to her pledged word in this war. The whole civilised world was in a death struggle with despotism and barbarism.[27] Redmond's use of the language of blood sacrifice was also evident after his own, much-publicised trip to the Front in November and his declaration on returning that:

> Let Irishmen come together in the trenches and spill their blood together and I say that there is no power on earth that when they come home can induce them to turn as enemies one upon another.[28]

A significant gap did open, however, between Redmond and the bulk of his party during 1915. His repeated, ardent, public recruiting was actively supported by fewer than 20 of his MPs – with only a handful of them in uniform. The pressures of a colossal war – mass casualties, military defeats, swingeing tax rises, rapid price inflation, suspended land purchase and the indefinite postponement of actual Home Rule – instead combined to create a climate of gloom and grievance. A repeated mantra became that of the unfair treatment of Ireland relative to England. In June, the Athlone-based *Westmeath Independent*, whose proprietor's sons had both enlisted and which had carried the headline 'Bravo England!' at the outbreak of war, now wrote as follows:

> Nationalists of the most self-sacrificing description – and there have been many such – do not always like to feel they are mere puppets in a continuously losing game...We look for light and guidance in the darkness and wilderness in which we feel we are entangled.[29]

After the spring of 1915, the party's local promotion of recruiting declined. Political campaigning slumped even more, with Home Rule becalmed, hardly any elections to organise and next to no land purchase after wartime public spending cuts. Of the party's organisations, only the Hibernians appeared remotely robust. Worst was the state of the National Volunteers. Though thousands did turn out for their last significant, Dublin parade before Redmond and Dillon, on Easter Sunday 1915, the overall condition of the movement was dire. In September, their Inspector General, Colonel Maurice Moore, wrote to disillusion Redmond, who was even then mulling over whether to revive the idea of a 'defence army' with the War Office;

> ...nothing can be done with the Volunteers or anything like them
> ...the enthusiasm has gone and they cannot be kept going.

In Moore's judgement, the National Volunteers had exhausted their usefulness.[30] Some of the party's wartime campaigns worked directly against Redmond's hopes for post-war Irish unity and British goodwill. One particular effort, promoted for months through the 'Hibernian Notes' that were syndicated to much of the nationalist press, consisted of repeated attacks on the 36th (Ulster) Division. Why, it was asked, were the Ulster unionists not at the Front when thousands of Catholic Irishmen had already died? This unfairness, it was claimed, held back nationalist recruiting. Were the Ulstermen so incompetent that they were unfit for service? Were they 'funkers' or were they being 'favoured' by the War Office, held back intact for more sinister purposes after the war?[31] The other consistent party refrain throughout 1915 was that conscription, if imposed on Ireland, would, in the words of John Dillon, create 'conditions no responsible man could contemplate.'[32] Again and again, party speakers declared that conscription would be resisted by every means in their power. The Mayo MP William Doris exemplified party policy when speaking in December:

> The elected representatives of Ireland are heart and soul with the Allies and against the brutal, barbarous Germans...For this reason they have asked their young countrymen to do their duty as Irishmen to take their part in what is the defence of their own land.

But he went on, they have also declared that they will not have conscription 'under any circumstances' and would oppose it 'tooth and nail...to the last'.[33]

The formation of the wartime coalition government, in May 1915, was particularly disheartening and also triggered another conscription scare. As what he called 'the greatest enemies of Ireland' took office, J. P. Farrell MP – the epitome of the loyal, local party boss – was horrified. For him, the coalition was 'the greatest and grossest betrayal of this country that had occurred since the flight of the Earls'. Farrell, the MP for North Longford, publicly described himself as having been 'like a chained dog'.[34] However, for him, and for his party, there was no alternative. As Farrell asked rhetorically, in a public letter to an American writer who had denounced the Irish Party as traitors, did the writer really want 'the defenceless Irish again to be driven from their homes as a result of a vain rebellion?'[35] Farrell would remain loyal to the party's policy to the end, declaiming even some months after the Easter Rising: 'We can always revert to the policy which will revive the rule of Cromwell in Ireland! Any fool can do that'.[36]

As 1915 progressed, the Irish Party came to be seen by much of its leadership and press, by its opponents and by Dublin Castle, as being in trouble. The chances of winning unionist goodwill after the war for Home Rule, let alone for all-Ireland Home Rule, looked increasingly remote. The party faced declining morale, falling membership, a decaying – in the case of the Volunteers, disintegrating – organisation and no way out of its policy impasse. Conversely, the party's anti-war opponents were experiencing exactly the reverse. As Dillon put it to T. P. O'Connor in July 1915:

> It is VERY bad, worse than I have known it since 1900. The Clan men are exceedingly active, and have eight organisers traversing the country with plenty of money. Our men are disheartened and puzzled, an increasing number of the clergy are very hostile.[37]

In December 1915, at the height of yet another conscription scare, the government's Chief Secretary for Ireland, Augustine Birrell, wrote privately to Redmond of the rising numbers of the anti-war Irish Volunteers and of the 'increasing exaltation of spirit' of their press. 'I feel the Irish situation is one of actual menace'.[38]

The greater part of this chapter has, inevitably, focused on the years 1914–15, describing why the Irish Party formed its wartime policy and became stuck in a cul-de-sac from which it could not escape. Subsequent events – above all the Easter Rising and the British government's reaction to it – overwhelmed a party that, in wartime, was incapable of a response that could ensure its preservation as the leader of Irish nationalism. The destruction of the party after the Easter Rising was sudden and rapid:

- The panic, callousness, and confusion of the government's wildly varied responses to the Easter Rising were themselves completely inexplicable outside the context of war. They formed a perfect storm for the Irish Party. Redmond and his party became seen as complicit with English brutality and tyranny – as selling out Irish unity by then acceding to permanent partition and then as a dupe of yet another English betrayal when the negotiations of June and July 1916 collapsed.
- The executions and mass arrests that followed the Rising divided Redmond from the bulk of his party. In the Rising's aftermath, a substantial majority were far more sympathetic to the common depiction of the rebels as brave, honourable fools than they were to Redmond's view of them as enemies of Home Rule. By far the most overused word in this period was not 'traitor', but rather 'misguided'.[39]
- The government's rapid swing, from executions and mass arrests to opening new negotiations, validated the Rising. The view became commonplace that that one week of bloody fighting had achieved more than decades of parliamentary agitation. With the negotiations came the immediate fear that the exclusion of Ulster from Home Rule would be anything but temporary. The unravelling of the party, across Ireland, was under way well 'before' the negotiations collapsed acrimoniously in July. Local party bosses, councillors, UIL branches, Hibernian divisions, even constituency committees, and, of course, newspapers, broke with the party's leadership on a scale far greater than seen in the autumn of 1914. The humiliating collapse of talks at the end of July only advanced this process. The demoralisation of the party was nearly complete by the beginning of 1917. Though local pockets of organisation lingered on, particularly

in Ulster, co-ordinated, national activity was now *de minimis*. The vacuum left by the party was rapidly filled, in provincial Ireland from the spring of 1917 onwards, by a resurgent and soon-to-be reconstituted Sinn Féin. The Irish Party's by-election successes in early 1918 were in no way a harbinger of national revival, owing more to residual local influence, in Ulster and pockets such as Waterford, and to tactical voting by local unionists.[40]

- The party was already way beyond redemption when, in April 1918, the final conscription crisis erupted. Again, the actions of the government were inexplicable outside of the context of the war. The government acted against local, official advice because of the far greater crisis of the war in general, irrespective of the damage that it knew would be caused in Ireland.[41] Short though it was; the conscription crisis confirmed Sinn Féin as the undisputed leader of Irish nationalism and read the last rites for the Irish Party.

Some years ago, I wrote that the Irish Party broke under the strain of following the wartime policies of its leader, and that Redmond's wartime goals went against the historic grain of nationalist public opinion.[42] I still stand by both statements, but I also believe that to blame Redmond alone for the party's destruction is little better than simplistic. For the party, as well as its leader, there was no alternative policy in 1914, 1915 or 1916. The party at the outbreak of war was, for all manner of reasons, as closely aligned with its leader as at any stage of his long leadership. It was the war – the awful shock of its outbreak, its indefinite, terrible duration – that gravely weakened the party. Moreover, the events that supplied the coup de grâce – the Rising and the government's panicky, cruel stupidity in its immediate aftermath – were inconceivable outside the context of the war. I still believe that Redmond's vision of Home Rule could not be realised peacefully, war or no war, but it was the war alone that finished off his part.[43]

CHAPTER 6

WOMEN'S SUFFRAGE, JOHN REDMOND, AND THE IRISH PARLIAMENTARY PARTY

Margaret Ward

In the decade prior to the First World War the campaign by British and Irish women for the vote, which was met by the repeated failure of suffrage bills introduced into the House of Commons, has commonly been portrayed as a battle between British suffrage militants and the Liberal government of H. H. Asquith. Much less attention has been given to the voting record of the Irish Parliamentary Party (IPP) and to the impact upon the suffrage campaign of the party's determination to win home rule for Ireland. The grand narratives of Irish history and monographs covering aspects of these years disregard the gendered implications of a Home Rule settlement that omitted the female half of the population. In so doing they ignore the misogyny that existed within the Irish Party. The opposition of Ulster unionists to Home Rule and the efforts to mollify their concerns dominate the historical discourse. One has to turn to histories of the suffrage movement and to the suffrage newspapers in Ireland and Britain to construct a narrative that does justice to the feminist campaign, putting into context the anomaly of men doing their best to assure other men that Home Rule posed no threat to their political and cultural identity, while continuing to deny Irish women of any political persuasion the right to citizenship in the forthcoming constitutional arrangement.

IRISH PARLIAMENTARIANS AND WOMEN

The reality was that the IPP was a party resolutely opposed to the participation of women within its ranks. In this it differed substantially from every other political party in Ireland or Britain. From the late 1880s the Conservatives had the Primrose League; Liberals had the Women's Liberal Federation, and women were full members of the Labour Party. In 1911, the Ulster Unionists formed the Ulster Women's Unionist Council in order to enlist women's services in the cause of combatting Home Rule. Attitudes towards women's suffrage in these organisations were varied. Within Ulster unionism Edward Carson was anti-suffrage while James Craig was a supporter, but the significant factor is that they recognised women's importance in mobilising support for the unionist cause, albeit under male direction. There was no woman's organisation attached to the IPP, although from 1910 women were able to join a Ladies' Auxiliary of the Ancient Order of Hibernians, a religious society aligned to the parliamentarians.[1] In 1914, speaking to women in Belfast, Redmond admitted he had never before addressed an audience of ladies. It was, concludes Pašeta, 'an extraordinary admission, which suggested once again that the Party, at the highest level at least, had done very little in the way of recruiting women to its ranks.'[2] Hostility to women in political life did not, however, begin with John Redmond. Irish parliamentarians in the Parnell period had driven women out of the Land League through starving funds to the Ladies' Land League in order to wrest back control of the land movement. After the women dissolved their organisation rather than remain in a subordinate position to men, the parliamentarians formed a new organisation, the National League, described as an 'open organisation in which the ladies will not take part.'[3] The exclusion of women continued into the following decade, as the young Maud Gonne, searching for an entry point into nationalist political life, found herself 'working as a freelance' as she was refused entry into any organisation.[4] It was not until 1900 that she met others who 'resented being excluded, as women, from National Organisations'.[5] Inghinidhe na hÉireann was then formed, as a determinedly feminist and nationalist organisation. As a result, nationalist women developed the necessary contacts and confidence which enabled them to become involved with Sinn Féin, the Gaelic League and other nationalist groups.

The IPP had another organisation, the United Irish League, which was to act as a support organisation to the parliamentarians after John Redmond assumed leadership of the parliamentary party following many years of discord caused by the split over Parnell's divorce. The party, aware that it was losing touch with young nationalists, welcomed the formation of a Young Ireland Branch of the League (known as the YIBs), which was formed in Dublin in 1906. Most of the young men were graduates of University College Dublin (UCD) and regarded as rising stars within the movement.[6] However, the YIBs were notable for another reason: they had female members. The women, most notably the Sheehy sisters, three of whom were married or about to be married to YIB members, were there partly because of the support they received from the men. The testimony of Hanna Sheehy Skeffington revealed little enthusiasm from the party. The branch was originally to be called the 'Young Men's Branch' she said sarcastically, as young men were invited to join. On the occasion of its second meeting, however, 'several of us students determined to put the matter to the test, and invaded the League offices, plonked down our entrance fees to an amazed official, who though visibly reluctant and embarrassed, did not openly refuse us, murmuring something of course about a 'Ladies' Branch', which we ignored.'[7]

This account was written in 1909, long before the advent of suffrage militancy in Ireland and the controversies over the lack of women's enfranchisement in the Home Rule bill, nevertheless, even at that date, Sheehy Skeffington declared that 'the growing estrangement between Irishwomen and the parliamentary party is now acute, almost to alienation.' Why was this? There was a gender-based gulf between parliamentarians and women: 'Members returned to a male parliament by males, shut in by the male-club atmosphere which pervades the House of Commons'. As a result, parliamentarians were 'naturally predisposed to discount the influence of women in public life.' In the three years of membership of the YIBs she had experienced women being denied a place, even as visitors, to the National Conventions organised by the party. She believed the reason was that women were voteless and could therefore be ignored.[8] There was little pressure within the IPP to support suffrage measures coming before the Commons – what pressure there was, came from individuals within the YIBs. While the party contained defenders of women's suffrage, notably Willie Redmond, Tom Kettle, Stephen Gwynn and Joe Devlin, their support was contingent on not alienating Asquith and the Liberal government and it disappeared when matters became critical. Sheehy Skeffington, in calling for women to be enfranchised, 'even by an alien and grudging parliament', asked the question: 'Will the Irish Party be bold enough to make this act of faith and help the citizenship of women?'[9] It would not be long before the party's reluctance to give any support became clear.

When the chronology of events in the period 1909–1912 is examined, it becomes clear that Redmond and many of his colleagues were opponents of women's suffrage long before they raised the pretext that Home Rule would be jeopardised if a women's suffrage measure was passed.

The Irish Women's Franchise League and the Irish Party

The Irish Women's Franchise League (IWFL) was formed in November 1908 as Irish women grew tired of the fruitless years of attempts at persuasion. Taking their inspiration from the 'Deeds not Words' motto of the Women's Social and Political Union in Britain, they declared themselves to be a militant organisation calling for the right of Irish women to have the vote on the same terms as men. One of their priorities was to persuade every Irish member of parliament to vote for all woman suffrage bills coming before the House of Commons. They also wanted to ensure that votes for women would be included in any bill for Irish self-government that might be introduced into parliament. Margaret Cousins, co-founder with Hanna Sheehy Skeffington, explained that they were 'as keen as men on the freedom of Ireland'. The problem was that the men showed 'no recognition of the existence of women as fellow citizens.'[10]

The men of the YIBs continued to support the women's cause. In February 1909 Frank Sheehy Skeffington, responding to a request by the IWFL, introduced a motion at a Convention of the United Irish League calling for women's suffrage to be given support by the Irish Party. At the last moment Tom Kettle reneged on his promise to second the motion. Skeffington described this as 'Mr Kettle's first breach of faith with the women's suffrage party'.[11]

A delegation of IWFL members finally manged to meet Redmond in December 1909. The women were told that Redmond would not commit the IPP into supporting suffrage bills as it was a matter for each individual MP, and his own personal views, the delegation reported, were 'somewhat vague' on the question. Most damningly, Redmond would not use the political influence of the IPP to have suffrage prisoners in English jails treated as political.[12] Redmond's most recent biographer provides a different account of the meeting, stating that Redmond agreed to have imprisoned suffragettes treated as political rather than as ordinary prisoners, although he added, 'I regard some of them extremely foolish in what they have done.' He congratulated the Irish women on not having resorted to militancy, 'you are much more likely to advance your cause by taking the course you are now, and in reasoning and arguing and putting your case with the ability and moderation that you have done this afternoon'. In referring to his voting record he told them that he had begun as a supporter, then voted against women's franchise, but he was not 'a confirmed or bitter enemy' although he remained to be convinced that Irish women wanted the franchise.[13] While this is a more sympathetic portrayal of Redmond, there is no evidence that he ever campaigned on behalf of suffrage prisoners, and in his description of his views on suffrage, 'somewhat vague' is a fair description as Redmond adroitly avoided any commitment to support the women's cause. Privately, he told Hanna Sheehy Skeffington that he feared clerical domination if women had the chance to vote but asked her not to quote him on this.[14] Sheehy Skeffington also remembered an occasion when a member of a delegation to Redmond used the word 'feminism'. In response he 'interrupted sneeringly': "I do not know what the word means." He did not wait for an explanation.[15]

Redmond's lieutenant, John Dillon, was more direct on his opposition to female suffrage, telling a delegation, 'Women's Suffrage will, I believe, be the ruin of our Western civilisation. It will destroy the home, challenging the headship of man, laid down by God. It may come in your time – I hope not in mine!'[16]

Westminster, Suffrage, and the Irish Party

By 1910 the issue of women's suffrage was top of the agenda in Westminster. That January the Liberals had lost their overall majority in the House of Commons and an all-party Conciliation Committee was formed to sponsor a women's suffrage bill. Prime Minister Asquith, as historian Constance Rover has said, 'made his dislike of any measure of women's suffrage perfectly clear during the whole of the pre-war campaign'. Even the non-militant feminist Millicent Fawcett saw him as 'our chief antagonist.'[17] Asquith's contempt of women, whom he described as 'dim, impenetrable...for the most part hopelessly ignorant of politics, credulous to the last degree...'[18] was different from John Dillon's fear of the radical challenge to the established order that enfranchisement might herald, but mirrors what suffragettes felt were Redmond's views, even if he preferred not to make those views public.

The 70 members of the IPP now held the balance of power in the Commons, keeping the minority Liberal Party in power. Their price was Home Rule. The 1910 Conciliation Bill on women's suffrage was revised to meet Liberal objections and reintroduced to parliament in May 1911. Irish suffragists from all organisations embarked on a concerted lobbying campaign of nationalist MPs in the months before the bill was introduced. A number of members of the IWFL waited upon Redmond at the Gresham Hotel the week before the party's annual general meeting, presenting him with 'an excellent, and moderately worded statement asking for the Irish Party's help in securing facilities for the Conciliation Bill and pointing out that if these were refused the Irish Party would be jointly responsible with English members for any adoption of militancy.' On this occasion Redmond promised to put the matter before the party.[19] Shortly before the debate Marguerite Palmer and Mary Sheehy Kettle of the IWFL went to London to canvass Irish MPs, who found themselves 'snowed up' with correspondence on the subject.[20] This Conciliation Bill passed by 255 votes to 88 with 31 nationalists voting in favour and 9 against. The only Irish MP to speak in its favour was Hugh Law, who talked about his wish for a society based upon 'broad principles of equality, comradeship, justice and equity.' Willie Redmond voted in its favour, but John Redmond did not.[21] It failed to gain government time and did not progress.

Another bill came before the House in March 1912 and there was what Rover has described as a 'whispering campaign against the bill' to the effect that Asquith would resign if it were passed. It was considered that this fear 'occasioned the defection of Irish nationalist supporters of the cause.'[22] The bill was narrowly defeated by 208 votes to 222. On this occasion not one member of the IPP voted in favour of women's suffrage. Only William O'Brien, Tim Healy, and James Gilhooley of the O'Brienite faction of nationalists continued their support. This defection was decisive in terms of defeat. Redmond refused to take responsibility for the voting, insisting that the action was 'the action of individuals – as a Party we took no action'.[23] There was condemnation of this betrayal of women from all quarters, in Ireland and in Britain. Irish suffrage militants gave voice to their anger by joining protests in London. Altogether, 18 Irish women were to serve time in Holloway jail. In Britain, the Women's Social and Political Union (WSPU) declared war on the Irish Party and Christabel Pankhurst announced: 'No votes for women, no Home Rule.'[24] This was not the case in Ireland. The objective of the Irish militants was 'Home Rule for Irishwomen as well as Irish men', in addition to urging support for all suffrage bills in Westminster.

Criticism of the IPP came from several quarters. Within Ireland there was considerable support for the suffrage cause. UCD Professor Charles Oldham[25] wrote an open letter to Redmond, 'from Daniel O'Connell all the way down to the Boer War and English labour movements – how clean was the record of Irish Nationalists! That is our moral strength. You are the first Irish leader to smirch our record – when you threw the party vote to kill the Women's Bill.'[26] The justification of the IPP was that if the Conciliation Bill had passed it would have eaten into the time available for discussion on the Home Rule bill. The *Irish Times* commented, 'Redmond gained a week of parliamentary time and alienated the sympathies of every woman suffragist in Ireland.'[27] Frank Sheehy Skeffington made the obvious point that if the Irish Party had simply abstained, the bill would have passed. The Home Rule bill was about to be passed and the parliamentarians regarded the women 'not only (as) enemies of Home Rule, but rebels as women.'[28] The stage was now set for outright hostilities between feminists and parliamentarians.

Home Rule and Women

On 31 March, two days after the defeat of the Conciliation Bill, the IPP organised a celebratory 'Home Rule Day' in Dublin, as a pointed reminder to the Liberal government that Ireland was impatient for self-government. A small group of 20 women draped with sandwich boards marched through the crowds to remind the party that the demand for votes for women had not gone away. As they approached the Mansion House they were attacked by members of the Ancient Order of Hibernians, acting as stewards for the IPP. One participant, the artist Maud Lloyd, who had served a prison sentence in Holloway Prison in November 1911, wrote an account of her experience, positive that 'the treatment of the poster paraders by the official National stewards was in itself proof positive that the Irish Party had taken the field against our cause'. She believed men like Tom Kettle (who had assured a meeting addressed by Christabel Pankhurst that he intended being an MP in a Home Rule parliament, and that he was quite certain he would be elected by women as well as men) were dangerous allies who had 'lulled' Party women into the belief that women's suffrage would be included in Home Rule.[29]

The following day four members of the IWFL met Redmond. This time he said he was 'entirely and absolutely opposed' to the insertion of a clause in the Home Rule bill that would give votes to women. It was 'essentially a local question', to be decided by the Irish Parliament when it came into being. He would give no undertaking to introduce such a bill in the Irish Parliament either – if and when established. In addition, Redmond declared he was not prepared to allow the proceedings to be published in the press. Deborah Webb, head of the delegation, rose from her seat, 'stated that under such conditions the deputation would be a farce and serve no useful purpose, and left the room, followed by the rest of us.'[30] The women were left in a dilemma on how to proceed. They sent a confidential statement to members, explaining the situation and this was published, without their consent, in the *Freeman's Journal*.[31] Frank Sheehy Skeffington accused Tom Kettle of knowing how this had happened. Kettle was still an associate member of the IWFL and would therefore have received the circular from the delegation. This was a turning point in relations between feminists and the IPP. The Skeffingtons resigned from the YIBs (Young Ireland branch), and Hanna urged women to leave every organisation connected with the party, threatening that the women of Ireland would 'break the power of the party';[32] a view not accepted by all suffragists, many of whom were uneasy at the choice between suffrage and nation.

The Home Rule bill was introduced into the House of Commons on 11 April and a National Convention to discuss its contents was scheduled to be held at the Mansion House on 23 April. The IWFL, in their confidential circular to their members, had stated that they would ask the National Convention to receive a deputation, which they hoped would be 'representative of women from every part of Ireland' in order to lay before the convention their demand for inclusion within the Home Rule bill. They expected opposition to their presence and if they were refused admission warned 'a demonstration may be made'. Volunteers on the delegation were instructed to 'be prepared, should occasion arise, for resolute action.'[33]

Considerable opposition to this escalation in tactics was voiced by some who had formerly been supporters of the suffragists. The Limerick branch of the IWFL declined to take part as members considered it 'unreasonable, ill-timed and likely to do harm to the cause of women's suffrage in Ireland in the present circumstances'.[34] The historian Mary Hayden, Professor of Modern Irish History at UCD and Senator in the new National University of Ireland, was a strong suffragist, but not an advocate of militancy. She urged women not to confront the Irish Party, 'women's franchise if it comes in a few years, as come it surely will, will be as good as if it came tomorrow, not for Home Rule, for want of which our country is now bleeding to death.' Similarly, Agnes O'Farrelly, Professor of Irish at UCD, argued that, with a cabinet divided on the issue of women's suffrage, it would be 'extremely dangerous' to insist on its inclusion within the bill for Home Rule.[35]

As expected, militant women were barred from the convention proceedings, although the artist Sarah Cecilia Harrison, the first woman to be elected to Dublin City Council, was admitted. The big front door of the Mansion House closed quickly on Hanna Sheehy Skeffington and Margaret Cousins as they tried to enter the building. Police cordoned the area to prevent protestors from getting too close. In the afternoon, after Redmond had left the building, an attempt at a public meeting was held, with the help of a chair from the Mansion House smuggled past the police cordon. Hanna Sheehy Skeffington was lifted down by the police after uttering no more than a few words while her husband was 'turned practically upside down by a couple of policemen'. After a scuffle the crowd was escorted towards Grafton Street.[36]

Tom Kettle had promised to move a motion on suffrage, as he made plain in a note left at the Skeffington household before the event: 'Dear Hanna, I called to let you abuse me. I am of course going to move a motion but also to make it clear even if no amendment whatever to any clause can be carried, I think the Bill should be accepted.'[37] Kettle, who had resigned his parliamentary seat in 1910, once again failed at the last moment to speak on suffrage. Patrick Maume, a noted authority on constitutional nationalism, reckoned he 'lost his nerve'.[38] Party loyalty came first, and Redmond had made the party position unambiguously clear.

On 1 June 1912 a last attempt was made to appeal to the Liberal government to introduce a women's suffrage clause to the Home Rule bill. The Irish suffrage movement now had its own newspaper, the *Irish Citizen*, which first appeared on 25 May, giving the movement an opportunity to shape its message. A mass meeting of women, presided over by Mary Hayden, was held in the Antient Concert Rooms. Hayden stressed that they were asking in 'a perfectly constitutional manner', and she called on all political parties in the British Parliament to help obtain this measure of justice for women.[39] Nineteen organisations were represented, and a petition was sent to the government and to the leaders of the political parties. It was emphasised that this included women from all different societies and political persuasions – nationalist and unionist, militant and non-militant. Women put wider political differences aside in order to unite around the principle of their right to citizenship. As the speaker from Leinster, Hanna Sheehy Skeffington warned that this was the last constitutional chance women had to achieve their goal:

> If the Liberal govt refuses to respond to our resolutions, there is no further chance for constitutional agitation. The franchise is deliberately tied up for three years after the establishment of Home Rule. We demand now the safeguard of the vote, not for a minority but for a majority...We have helped to build up the house out of which we are now to be shut.[40]

The joint appeal by women was ignored. The limits of constitutionalism had been reached. On 13 June eight members of the IWFL went out to smash the windows of government buildings, including Dublin Castle, the GPO, and the Custom House. They received sentences of two and six months, according to the number of windowpanes smashed. Over the next two years there would be 35 suffrage arrests in Ireland.

Suffragists were only too aware that a private member's bill without government backing had no chance of success. Philip Snowden, Labour MP, on 5 November 1912 nevertheless attempted to introduce an amendment to include women's suffrage within the Home Rule bill. His measure was based on the local government register which would have enfranchised 1000,000 women. Before the debate Christabel Pankhurst, referring to women's campaign for inclusion in a Home Rule settlement, had written 'never did so great an issue – that of the enfranchisement or disfranchisement of half a population under a new constitution – receive more cavalier treatment...the government ought to have made woman suffrage an integral part of the Home Rule bill. Their refusal to do so is in itself a provocation to militancy.'[41]

In opening the debate Snowden paid tribute to the strength of the women's movement in Ireland by reading out a list of women's suffrage organisations. It was, he maintained, proof of the demand for the measure. In countering Snowden, Hugh Law, no longer a supporter of the women, was scathing about the extent of support for suffrage within Ireland, 'Is there an effective demand among Irish women for the franchise? I am bound to say that I think there is not.' As far as he was concerned, Irish MPs 'were not elected on the question of woman suffrage, we were elected to advance Home Rule'. Willie Redmond, another former supporter, also argued that adoption of Snowden's amendment 'would prejudice the success of Home Rule' and should be left to the Irish Parliament. John Redmond, while saying he was reluctant to speak on the issue, echoed his brother in arguing that the amendment was being used 'simply as a political weapon for the purpose of inflicting injury upon the Home Rule bill.' He also assured members that the IPP would be as free as the Liberals to vote as they wished on a Franchise Bill that would come before parliament in due course. MPs objected to this line of reasoning with several expressing scepticism over his promise of a free vote. Much of the debate revolved around a constitutional issue: was the granting of the vote to Irish women one for the British Parliament to decide or should it be left to the Irish Parliament? Their arguments were dishonest and disingenuous. Lord Robert Cecil, a strong suffrage supporter, could not understand why giving the vote to women in Ireland should imperil home rule. He believed that the time to deal with woman's suffrage in the Irish Parliament was with the Home Rule bill, and not under a Franchise Bill for the United Kingdom. Some MPs put forward the argument that as Westminster would continue to deal with the army, navy and other imperial affairs, the Home Rule legislature, subordinate to the British, would be eminently suitable for Irishwomen to engage with, as the issues to be dealt with would be purely domestic and not concerned with the 'physical force' issues women were unsuited to or incapable of considering. The government refused to accept Snowden's amendment, putting the Whips on MPs and the measure was lost by 173 votes. Eleven Irish MPs did vote for Snowden, but 72 voted against.[42]

The first acts of suffrage militancy in Ulster were committed following this vote, when windows were broken in the GPO in Donegall Square, telegraph wires were cut, and letter boxes attacked. No arrests were made.[43] In Dublin two members of the IWFL smashed windows in the Custom House. In court Kathleen Emerson declared the vote on the Snowden amendment was a 'deliberate insult' to the women of Ireland, while Meg Connery explained to the judge that she did not break the law 'because she liked it, but because she had been driven to adopt these methods to draw public attention to the intolerable grievances under which women had to live. She was an outlaw; she was not a person'.[44]

While sympathetic to the Irish cause, the response of the WSPU to the vote centred around Redmond's influence in preventing the vote being granted to women in Britain:

> Short of saying in so many words that he refuses to allow women to have the vote, Mr Redmond could not have expressed his hostility more clearly than he did. It is obvious to the least intelligent that Mr Redmond, when he claims that the Irish Parliament shall decide whether Irish women shall have the vote, necessarily means that he is determined, if he can, to prevent the passage of any Woman Suffrage Amendment to the coming Franchise Bill.[45]

Following the vote Redmond had announced grandly, 'What we want is that the Irish Parliament should be representative of every element in the country. We want every class represented. We want equality. We will not have, and we will not tolerate an ascendancy of any class or any creed.'[46] The omission of any mention of women, despite extensive lobbying by women in Ireland and Britain and prison and hunger strike on the part of a large number of militants, was significant. Christabel Pankhurst retorted, 'Sex ascendancy is the only ascendancy which Mr Redmond dare defend, and upon that sex ascendancy he absolutely insists, the reason being that, as women are neither voters nor sufficiently violent, he can afford to trample upon their interests.'[47]

This refusal to acknowledge women's existence was extraordinarily gendered myopia. Redmond's stubborn refusal to acknowledge the existence of female campaigners and women prisoners was evident in an emotional address to members of the Irish community in Birmingham. When he spoke of the impact of British rule over Ireland, 'the years that had passed had been marked by famine, by continued depopulation, by coercion, by suffering in the prison cells of thousands of Irishmen, himself amongst the number,' he was heckled from the audience, 'And you ought to be there now for supporting a government that tortures and coerces women.'[48]

ULSTER UNIONISTS, HOME RULE AND THE IRISH PARTY

Feminists were quick to point out the dishonesty of the IPP view on suffrage and Home Rule and their excuse that this was an issue that had to be settled by Irish men and an Irish Parliament. They pointed out that this reasoning would apply equally to every other question settled by the London Parliament regarding Home Rule. Most pertinently, if Westminster was not entitled to give the political safeguard of the vote to Irish women, how could it be entitled to give safeguards to Ulster men? The conclusion of Christabel Pankhurst was that, 'The Government and Mr Redmond are afraid of the armed and drilled men of Ulster and therefore they are offering to these men all sorts of concessions and safeguards.'[49] It was an incitement to further militancy. Using the tactics of heckling and shadowing cabinet ministers, women attempted to demonstrate the double standards of politicians. When Cabinet Minister Runciman, addressing constituents, stated, 'I would not underrate for one moment the seriousness of feeling in some parts of Ulster about the passage of the Home Rule bill,' a woman called out, 'You underrate the seriousness of women's feelings, sir.'[50] After the formation of the UVF and running in of guns to Larne, the government failed to prosecute. John Dillon, speaking in June 1914, stated openly that the nationalists had been strongly opposed to any prosecution of Ulstermen, 'You do not put down Irishmen by coercion. You simply embitter them and stiffen their backs.'[51] The same line of reasoning did not extend to militant women. The WSPU issued a poster, 'Men & Women Note These Facts!' outlining significant differences in government treatment of suffragettes and the UVF:

> The government arrests women's deputations
> The government allows gun running in Ulster
> The government raids Suffragettes' houses
> The government permits explosives in Ulster [52]

In June 1914 a delegation of women representing all Irish suffrage interests in Ireland travelled to Westminster in a final attempt to persuade Asquith and Redmond to include women within the Home Rule Act. Although the women waited for several hours the men failed to meet them. As they held a protest meeting in Westminster Hall Margaret McCoubrey from Belfast shouted out, 'They only mind the militants with guns' and another woman said, 'had we had been men they would have heard us'.[53] That charge of failing to take women seriously continued to permeate the narrative of the Home Rule crisis as the focus remained with the militants with guns – the unionist men of Ulster.

Cat and Mouse Act

Women's suffrage was again a dominant issue in parliament in April 1913, when the government brought in a measure to deal with hunger strikes. For many in Ireland, the voting by the IPP on the 'Cat and Mouse Act' was the ultimate betrayal of the principles of Irish nationalism. Tim Healy was the only Irish nationalist to vote against. None of the Irish MPs spoke in the debate. John and Willie Redmond were both in parliament and both voted in its favour. The Act's formal title was *The Prisoners (Temporary Discharge of Ill Health) Act*, and it was intended as an alternative to forcible feeding. Women were released from prison when their health was compromised and then were supposed to return to prison to serve the remainder of their sentence. They were only released 'on licence'. The Lord Mayor of Dublin granted the use of the Mansion House for a public meeting of protest against the application of the Act to Ireland. While Tom Kettle moved the resolution for repeal of the act as 'a dangerous instrument of political oppression in the hands of any Government', he added he was, 'prepared, not to sacrifice, but to postpone, any social or franchise reform for the sake of seeing Ireland mistress in her own household.' This was greeted with angry retorts 'that's not the woman's view' and 'you're not a woman'.[54] While Irish women arrested in Dublin under the terms of the Act were not re-arrested, the Act was put into practice in Belfast after the WSPU began militancy in Ulster.

There was one further attempt to pass a woman's suffrage measure in May 1913, when Liberal MP Willoughby Dickinson put forward a Representation of the People Bill to grant the vote to women over the age of 25, women householders, and the wives of householders. It would have enfranchised six million women. This measure was lost by 47 votes, with 54 nationalists voting against. While Willie Redmond voted in favour, John Redmond and his son, William Archer (who had taken over the East Tyrone seat in the December 1910 election, following Tom Kettle's decision to leave parliament) were again in the 'no' lobby. So too was David Sheehy, father of Hanna Sheehy Skeffington, who remained an anti-suffrage voter, despite his daughter's leading role in the suffrage campaign.[55] Georgina Manning was fined 25 shillings for daubing green paint across a bust of John Redmond on display in the Royal Hibernian Academy, also leaving the message, 'Why didn't you get us votes for women Mr Redmond? A traitor's face is no adornment to our picture gallery'.[56]

Nationalist women and the Irish Party

What was the response of nationalist women to the actions of the Irish Party? Many nationalist women were also members of suffrage organisations, and as the Home Rule issue intensified, felt they had to make a decision regarding their primary loyalty. Jennie Wyse-Power, who had been a member of the Ladies' Land League when a young woman and was vice-president of Sinn Féin and a former member of the Irish Women's Suffrage and Local Government Association, referred to her past experiences when she argued that votes for women should be included in a Home Rule bill because if not, women would be excluded from an Irish Parliament for at least three years. While she would not press for suffrage if it 'imperilled' the bill, she gave the example of the Ladies' Land League, when women 'stepped with one stride into the place vacated by the men and by their tenacity and purpose saved the organisation that otherwise would have vanished.' Wyse Power tried to appeal to parliamentarians with this example, claiming the women's contribution had enabled the parliamentary party 'to remain a party of power and influence'.[57] This reminder of women's past activism would not have found favour with many members of the parliamentary party, who appeared to remain wary of militant women.

Two years later Mary MacSwiney, who had been a member of the Munster Women's Franchise League, wrote in support of Redmond, thereby setting off a debate within the pages of the *Irish Citizen*. While she admitted that many nationalist women believed Redmond had made 'a big tactical blunder in opposing the Conciliation Bill', she argued that he had been helpless, because he could not risk the Home Rule bill by opposing Asquith on his pet prejudice. 'Mr Redmond's one and only business in Westminster is to secure Home Rule. He received no mandate for Woman Suffrage and thoughtful and fair-minded Irishwomen of every political belief recognise that.' She added, 'The women of Ireland want the vote, but they do not want it, nor would they take it at the expense of Home Rule – even if we have to wait three years! What are three years in the life of a nation?', she asked.[58] In this she echoed the words of Mary Hayden two years previously.

An editorial in the same issue of the *Irish Citizen* dissected MacSwiney's argument. Referring to the assertion that Redmond 'could not even if he had wished' given support to the Conciliation Bill because that would have been to oppose Asquith, the question was asked, 'Why did Mr Redmond not say so?...had he said frankly that his action in deliberately killing the Conciliation Bill was due to the exigencies of the English political situation, and had he accompanied that plea by a promise to take up Votes for Women in a Home Rule Parliament – Miss MacSwiney's position would be a logical and tenable one.' The *Citizen*, however, identified in Redmond's personality 'the most virulent anti-feminism'. He had denied in the face of all the evidence that he had anything to do with the killing of the Conciliation Bill. He stated categorically that he would always oppose Votes for Women, in a Home Rule Parliament as well as at Westminster.' This 'double treachery and hostility' was what had promoted opposition to him and to the Party, which was described as 'the weak instrument of his will.'[59]

Conclusion

It has been argued that John Redmond's opposition to female suffrage was merely strategic, an outcome of his determination to win Home Rule. However, as one biographer admits, he 'always disliked the intervention of women in politics, and he had particularly avoided the social functions which were conducted with such energy and ability by Mrs Asquith.'[60] There is no evidence to show that he ever contemplated a time when women in Ireland would possess a vote – either for the Westminster Parliament or for a Home Rule legislature. His limited interventions on the issue in parliament were not supportive of women. The only time political women occupied his consciousness was when they succeeded in meeting him in delegation — or when he found himself confronted with a militant suffragette through heckling or, more than once, having objects thrown at him. His response like many prominent politicians, was to construct a *cordon sanitaire* between himself and suffrage campaigners, eventually refusing interviews and barring them from public meetings. Even in the war years suffragists continued, without success, to try to change his mind. In early 1918, as the Representation of the People Bill was being debated, the non-militant suffragist Lucy Kingston said of him that 'antagonism to woman suffrage seems to have been inextricably melted into Mr John Redmond's system by some malign fairy.'[61]

Redmond's triumph was the passing of the Third Home Rule Bill. But with that achievement he ignored half of the Irish population. Would the inclusion of women's suffrage have seriously damaged the prospects of Irish Home Rule? Could women have had faith in a party which had, on so many occasions, reneged on its promise to vote in favour of women's suffrage? What one can say is that John Redmond was an extraordinarily single-minded individual and party leader; a politician not afraid of using the whip to ensure strict compliance to party policy. Cliona Murphy in her study of Irish suffrage and society, weighing up the evidence, concluded that 'certain inconsistencies in their arguments would lead one to the conclusion that all but a very few cared not a whit for women's suffrage. For them nationalism did not only win over suffragism, it was the only issue.'[62] While a significant number of Irish women devoted years to the campaign for suffrage and did everything they could to win over politicians to their cause, it is obvious that John Redmond's vision of a 'new' Ireland never included the citizenship of women.

CHAPTER 7

THE IRISH PARLIAMENTARY PARTY AND ITS SUCCESSORS

Martin O'Donoghue

Interviewed by the *Irish Times* as part of a special feature on the Irish Parliamentary Party in 1940, ex-MP John Lalor-Fitzpatrick declared that after the 1918 electoral defeat, 'its members certainly proved their belief in democratic methods of government; for they stepped quietly back into private life, and since then not one of them has raised a voice in opposition to the elected governments or to any verdict of the people'.[1] In so doing, he implied that 1918, as much as 1932, needs to be recognised for its importance as a peaceful transition in the history of Irish democracy. Certainly, it is the 1932 transfer of power from Cumann na nGaedheal to Fianna Fáil that is often held as evidence of the stability of democracy in the Irish Free State in an era of instability globally.[2] However, the 1918 ballot which took place across the entire island, was described by Peter Mair as Ireland's 'mobilising election', and occurred at a moment of enormous geopolitical significance as the First World War ended and old orders across Europe lay in ruins.[3] As one nationalist party largely ceded its claims to leadership, it can be argued that the Irish Party/Sinn Féin transition is therefore more significant than any other – providing both an apparent rupture with the past and a foundation stone for party politics in the years that followed. If Cumann na nGaedheal peacefully stepping aside for Fianna Fáil is important due to the Civil War split between both sides of the old Sinn Féin, it is surely worth reflecting again on the influences of the older Irish Party on Sinn Féin itself and nationalist politics generally.[4]

Lalor-Fitzpatrick's experience of the transition was, however, hardly a typical one: he had only been elected in 1916, he was still alive in 1940, and willing to contribute to the *Times*'s endeavour when many of his colleagues were not. Most problematically, for his own argument, many of his colleagues had not stepped back into private life and it was certainly not the case that 'not one of them... raised a voice in opposition to the elected governments'. While the fact that many criticised and even opposed governments in elections and in parliament may actually have been a sign of a healthy democracy, examination of this point helps to shed light on the influence of the older party on those that followed it and on the evolution of thinking among those from Home Rule backgrounds. As dramatic as the 1918 election was, transfers of Irish Party support occurred at specific pressure points before and after that poll which must be seen in context while exploring the relationship between each new party and the one first established after the success of Butt's Home Rule League in the 1874 Westminster election.

In assessing the transition from the Irish Party, some observations are necessary. The 1918 transformation was not the transition that Irish Party MPs would have foreseen before the First World War. In 1905, Michael Davitt had imagined the end of the Irish Party, but in a scenario whereby Home Rule was granted and an Irish House of Commons broke into conservative and liberal parties with Sir John Waterford (read Redmond) a conservative prime minister despite perhaps 'the new forces which universal suffrage was destined to bring into the arena of Irish public life'.[5] Even as the Ulster crisis threatened Irish unity in the early months of 1914, IPP MPs and supporters expressed little doubt of their place in history given their view that the Irish Party had worked its part in the chain of Irish nationalism that would be handed over to the next generation.[6] Few home rulers would have seen themselves as having broken from the highest traditions of Irish nationalism whether constitutional or otherwise. However, Irish political leaders and parties have not always rushed to claim themselves as successors of the Irish Parliamentary Party. As this chapter shows, the history of the IPP and its successors was one of interaction, with elements of overlap and lessons learned by later leaders as pertinent as examples of any 'clean break'. Transitions in nationalist politics played out in necessarily different ways in the Free State and Northern Ireland. The two polities were conceived and constructed in different ways; Sinn Féin provided a revolutionary touchstone for the major parties in the south but had a more mixed political legacy in the north where Redmondism, or perhaps more accurately, Devlinism persisted. Yet, despite the centrality of the styled 'Civil War politics' in independent Ireland, a discernible legacy of the Irish Parliamentary Party survived both north and south – in terms of individual politicians, parties, and the persistence of particular forms of political activism.

THE IRISH PARTY AND SUCCESSION, 1918–22

In his pioneering study of county Clare, David Fitzpatrick highlighted how the coalition of political, cultural, and social groups that gathered around post-Rising Sinn Féin mirrored the phalanx of support bodies that the Irish Party had previously attracted.[7] The IPP's coalition was of course a 'broad church', and it was part of its enduring success that, prior to the First World War, this coalition had remained largely intact. It lost supporters along the way certainly – it often struggled to present itself as the defender of both larger and smaller farmers as well as labourers – and it faced internal dissension at regular intervals, most notably during the Parnell split which led to a decade of division.[8] The Parnellite and anti-Parnellite parties reunited in 1900 and, apart from the Unionist Party, no sustained electoral challenge appeared until the First World War. Sinn Féin had first emerged as competitor to the Irish Party in 1907 only to falter and retreat – its presence in representative politics largely confined to local government in Dublin.[9] Movements such as the agrarian United Irish League and the Catholic fraternal Ancient Order of Hibernians were auxiliaries to the party while the All-for-Ireland League, set up by former IPP MP William O'Brien, was strongest in its leader's Cork fiefdom and is best seen as a splinter party, or perhaps simply *sui generis*.[10]

It was only after the Easter Rising that Sinn Féin emerged as a party to displace the IPP and become the new voice of nationalist aspirations. It is worth remembering though that Sinn Féin presented itself clearly as a rejection of the 1918 IPP and its methods rather than a successor per se. The rhetoric of the Parnell era was noted in advanced nationalist propaganda, but the post-Parnellite party was openly derided. It was in this way that Sinn Féin could claim to represent untarnished elements of previous nationalist movements while discarding the IPP's policy of attending Westminster as articles in the party's paper, *Nationality*, engaged in constructive ambiguity about what measure of sovereignty would satisfy Sinn Féin's demand for self-determination.[11] It remains difficult to compare how Sinn Féin operated as a political party – either before or after the election – with the IPP given the fact that so many members were either in jail or on the run (Irish Party MPs had not faced such a level of suppression since the Land War).[12] However, the party's focus on international recognition and creation of a counter-state from 1919 provided for a radically different agenda to the more incremental parliamentary approach of the home rulers. Yet, it remains inescapable that Sinn Féin became a national movement as the Home Rule movement had been, though it espoused certain tactical and philosophical differences. After all, from 1917, Sinn Féin, revitalised by new activists and the change in public opinion after the Rising, had fought and defeated the Irish Party at its own game – electoral politics.[13]

In terms of membership, Sinn Féin also acquired much support from former political movements – including the Irish Nation League, formed in 1916, which briefly threatened to capture attention in the political flux of post-Rising Ireland, and the All-for-Ireland League which stood aside in its Munster powerbase.[14] The Irish Party's tendency to encompass both radicals and conservatives allowed local activists and politicians to shift allegiance over the course of the war. Many had drifted from the party after the failure of Home Rule negotiations in 1916; the 1918 conscription crisis wounded the IPP further still. As Wheatley has shown, there was regional variation, and in some areas, many party activists simply retained old allegiances or disappeared.[15] John Redmond's son, Capt. William Archer Redmond, held the party's seat in Waterford city while with the benefit of the electoral pact with Sinn Féin in Ulster brokered by Cardinal Logue, the IPP retained five seats in the northern province.[16] The level of transfer at national level among politicians from the Irish Party was a longer and more sensitive process than is often appreciated.

While Fitzpatrick showed crossover at activist level in Clare, Fergus Campbell has suggested a greater tendency for Sinn Féin members in Galway to be more distinct on both class and generational lines; it was certainly the case that Sinn Féin was more hospitable to younger activists and women – an important factor as the franchise nearly tripled in 1918.[17] However, as Tom Garvin has observed, the level of transfer between Sinn Féin and the Irish Party was 'rather weak' at elite level.[18] The reasons for this are partly structural given the age profile of IPP MPs by the end of the First World War. Of the TDs returned for Sinn Féin for the First and Second Dáil, only two had experience as Irish Party MPs at Westminster: James O'Mara who had renounced his IPP affiliation in the first Sinn Féin flowering of 1907, and Laurence Ginnell who as the 'MP for Ireland' was an independent from 1910.

Its last leader, John Dillon, was unwell in the early months of 1919 and thereafter remained a largely passive observer, offering advice to activists but urging caution and avoidance of any action that might appear to favour the British government by undermining Sinn Féin.[19] The futility of the seven remaining Nationalist MPs' existence in the Commons was heightened by the evolution of violence in Ireland as Belfast MP Joe

Devlin in particular struggled to adapt to the changed dynamic at Westminster. Dillon was rarely impressed by the behaviour of IPP MPs who did not act in consort with Devlin and Liverpool MP T. P. O'Connor in the Commons – a marked contrast with the proud discipline shown by the fabled party bloc of previous decades.[20] Former MP Stephen Gwynn formed the short-lived Centre Party a month after the 1918 general election and welcomed former colleague Thomas Grattan Esmonde into the fold. The party advocated for federal self-government with assemblies for each province in Ireland (unlike the Buttite impulse towards federalism on a UK basis), but it bore little relation to the old party organisation and enjoyed little support from Dillon or other former colleagues.[21] The same could be said of Sir Horace Plunkett's Irish Dominion League which later merged with Gwynn's movement.[22] Although the Irish Party had attracted 224,000 voters nationally in 1918, circumstances and decisions made by its remaining leaders ensured that the Irish Party organisation in its pre-1918 form quietly departed the Irish political scene – outside of Ulster at least.

Joe Devlin and northern nationalism

Many nationalists of the Irish Party tradition remained distinct at local level and did well in urban areas in local elections held in 1920 under Proportional Representation by Single-Transferable Vote [PR-STV] on a more restrictive franchise though the old party structures were decaying by that point.[23] Support in in Belfast increased, and nationalists won 15 per cent of the seats in Ulster compared to nine per cent for Sinn Féin – an illustration of the popularity of Joe Devlin and the enduring significance of the AOH. Often viewed as a 'green Orange Order' and a political machine for the advancement of Catholics, the fraternal body – exclusive to Catholics born in Ireland or of Irish descent – was a bogeyman for unionists as well as Sinn Féin activists who resented a religious test on nationalism. While the Order declined in many areas with the IPP, it retained support in its northern powerbase where it had built on the legacy of the Ribbon tradition and provided an organisational ballast which many of Devlin's colleagues further south lacked as the UIL atrophied. Nationalists from the Home Rule tradition therefore remained an important thread in northern nationalism after partition, but nationalist politics in Northern Ireland bore little resemblance to the IPP in terms of strength, cohesion, or tactics.

Even in Ulster, the AOH declined; Eamon Phoenix has argued that only in Belfast where love of Devlin was strong did 'old nationalism' retain its former prominence as branches lost members to Sinn Féin in the early 1920s.[24] Devlin used his time in Westminster to seek to defend his constituents and draw attention to the worsening violence in the north-east during the summer of 1920, with the Belfast MP implicating James Craig in expulsions of Catholic workers in the city.[25] As the Government of Ireland Act provided for partition and separate parliaments north and south, John Dillon and Captain Redmond announced that they would not contest the 1921 election for the southern parliament.[26] More isolated than ever, Devlin and northern nationalists entered into a pact with Sinn Féin for elections in the new six-county territory on basis of opposition to partition though it was nationalists who were copying from Sinn Féin as they agreed to their former opponents' policy of abstaining from parliament.[27] Nationalists would contest and win six seats in the northern parliament in May 1921; Devlin was victorious in two constituencies while John Dillon

Nugent and Patrick O'Neill were also returned alongside Thomas Harbison and George Leeke.

As Alvin Jackson has noted, the implementation of a 'Home Rule' settlement in Northern Ireland remains one of the ironies of partition.[28] From the beginning, however, Devlin and his colleagues doubted the credentials of what they viewed as a unionist state – a stance which governed much of their policy. Devlin in common with others from old nationalist backgrounds were also largely marginalised as the Treaty was debated by the Dáil.[29] While Devlin managed to preserve some of the structures of the old Home Rule movement in Northern Ireland, cooperation with Sinn Féin remained difficult and fault lines among nationalists in the north were visible not just between former Irish Party and Sinn Féin followers, but also among nationalists along the border who hoped for relief from the findings of the Boundary Commission (set up under the Treaty) and those further north-east. Amidst serious violence in 1922, some 'old Nationalists' were keen to abandon abstention, but even in Belfast, supporters opposed the move.[30] As the Unionist Party dominated parliament and government, Devlin's AOH retained an organisational structure. In March 1924, it recorded 5,372 members in the six counties and held meetings as it awaited the outcome of the Boundary Commission.[31] The Order faced many challenges though as the border divided its insurance interests and it no longer had an effective, unified political party to support.[32]

After the 1925 elections to the Belfast parliament, Devlin finally took his seat along with T. S. McAllister; fellow Hibernian George Leeke followed in 1926 and Harbison took his seat in 1927.[33] However, abstention remained a recurrent theme for decades and it is therefore difficult to compare the IPP in its heyday to the struggles of northern nationalism – despite the number of Hibernians and others with Home Rule heritage. In 1928, an alliance was formed between Devlin and Cahir Healy of the Sinn Féin tradition, a movement which the AOH backed – in the view of National Secretary and former MP John Dillon Nugent, 'Catholics are all in the one party fighting for the maintenance of Catholic rights and the unity of Ireland'.[34] Although the first-past-post system was introduced in the 1929 parliamentary election, it was Labour which was worst affected and Nationalists won eleven seats – an increase of one. From 1933, however, Nationalists struggled to reach double figures. Devlin returned to Westminster in 1929, representing Fermanagh and Tyrone alongside Harbison and Cahir Healy as the only Nationalist MPs in the London Parliament until his death in 1934.

The organisation of the late Home Rule movement in Ulster had been Devlin's greatest success, earning him a loyal following in Belfast and entry into the Irish Party leadership's inner circle.[35] The 1920s were a difficult time for him; his role in securing the support of northern nationalists for the exclusion proposals in the 1916 Home Rule negotiations were raised in newspapers and public debates, and he never contributed to parliament in Belfast in the way he had done in London.[36] Unsuccessful as an independent Labour candidate in Liverpool Exchange in 1922, Devlin turned down opportunities to run for Dáil as former home rulers sought to reorganise in the Free State. Like colleagues south of the border, Devlin encountered the difficulties of encompassing the IPP's catch-all tendencies in changed circumstances. His working-class appeal often saw him to the fore among defences of the IPP as 'Ireland's Labour party'.[37] Nationalist politics clashed with the Northern Ireland Labour Party, however, and Devlin endorsed colleagues like Belfast Falls MP Richard Byrne who he had once described as a 'Tory'.[38]

Although always a minority party at Westminster, the IPP achieved prominence and, at times, was able to exercise a leverage which Nationalists never did (or could) in Northern Ireland. Devlin led Nationalists out of parliament in 1932; after his death, Byrne and T. J. Campbell showed the greatest loyalty to a parliamentary heritage and opposition to abstention. However, the biggest legislative achievement was arguably Campbell's Wild Birds Protection Act (1931).[39] The AOH remained a force but one in 'relentless decline' in the decades which followed, and though an Irish Party tradition was visible in Northern Ireland, the difficulties of nationalist politicians at Stormont made for a stark contrast with the Irish Party's pre-war dominance across Ireland and its ability to command attention at Westminster.[40]

Home rulers and 'Civil War politics'

Despite the achievement of the Free State, nationalist parties also remained in the south though the Irish Party was moribund. Instead, Sinn Féin was the stem for what came to be characterised as 'Civil War' politics in the decades which followed. To what extent can Civil War parties be seen, perhaps conversely, as successors to the IPP? To assess this, it is necessary to consider their tendency (or not) to absorb old Home Rule support and politicians (and the implications of this) – but also to compare how nominally nationalist parties functioned in the changed politics of independent Ireland.

As the country split over the Anglo-Irish Treaty, former home rulers resistant to Sinn Féin charms were at first largely uncultivated. The great majority of unreconciled home rulers supported the Treaty (it offered self-government as well as welcome peace and stability), but they were not always prepared to endorse the new pro-Treaty Cumann na nGaedheal party. Ex-Home Rule politicians in the Free State were often representatives without a party. Capt. William Redmond refused an invitation to stand for Cumann na nGaedheal in 1923 and was comfortably elected in Waterford as an independent. Such local fidelity was visible too in the success of James Cosgrave in Galway, and, especially, Alfie Byrne in Dublin.[41] In addition to prominent figures like ex-MPs, a number of those active in nationalist politics at local level prior to 1918 began to drift gradually towards the backbenches of Dáil Éireann.

In a new multi-party system, which contrasted sharply with the political culture of Home Rule pre-eminence before the First World War, other groups absorbed some elements of the Irish Party's old movement without being a successor in any meaningful sense. Former activists from the O'Brienite Irish Land and Labour Association joined the Labour party.[42] The relationship between land and politics remained important, and as Tony Varley has observed, 'a party-centred clientelist politics organised around the Treaty/Civil War split and the class appeals of the main pro- and anti-Treaty nationalist parties' helped to fill the vacuum left by the collapse of the UIL.[43] In the early 20s, local representatives from the Home Rule era remained members of the Irish Farmers Union and some found their way into its political wing, the Farmers' Party.[44] Although the IFU had unionist and Sinn Féin members, some ex-Irish Party activists were therefore in a party which mostly represented larger farmers: some of the very people who had gained from the IPP's work.[45] Three of the seven Farmers' deputies returned in 1922 were ex-Nationalist councillors or poor law guardians. In the August 1923 election, its 15 elected TDs included one ex-Westminster candidate and six ex-Nationalist councillors.

Conversion was more notable (and perhaps difficult) for more prominent ex-home rulers such as MPs than local politicians, but it was also the case that embracing either Cumann na nGaedheal or anti-Treaty Sinn Féin represented a break with the Irish Party in a way which standing as a Farmers' Party, independent or Labour candidate did not. British MP Andrew MacCullum Scott likened his switch from the Liberal party to Labour in 1924 to 'changing one's religion.'[46] Yet, notwithstanding the long-standing closeness between the Irish Party and the Liberals at Westminster, both parties (and Sinn Féin and British Labour) were different in character – as was the nature of the respective transitions in both countries.

While the work of Catherine Ann Cline and John Shepherd have shown that the Liberal-Labour transference also occurred in stages, the Liberal party did not disappear suddenly like the IPP.[47] The party, split over David Lloyd George's advocacy of coalition with the Conservatives, lost support in 1918 but did not disappear (though Asquith's anti-coalition ticket was decimated). Despite a surge in support in 1918, the vagaries of the first-past-the-post system meant Labour's seat gains were not comparable to Sinn Féin's victory either. Labour's rise also incorporated former Conservatives to broaden its appeal to middle-class opinion; pre-war Ireland only had one big political beast as the Unionist Party had little electoral success outside of Ulster and south Dublin. Ultimately, Labour succeeded the Liberals as the progressive competitor to the Conservative party; Sinn Féin replaced the IPP as the central plank of Irish political nationalism. In the 1920s, the Liberals remained as a third force even if divided, and some members found roles in the national governments of the 1930s.[48] In the Free State, former IPP supporters were part of an even more fragmented party system. Liberal voters and members abandoned their party as it went into steep decline; it was the Irish Parliamentary Party which abandoned its surviving members and followers as it retreated from politics outside Ulster. It is therefore testament to IPP loyalty that conversion to new parties could still prove so difficult.

It has, after all, been argued that constitutional nationalism had found a successor in the party of government in the Free State: Cumann na nGaedheal.[49] Some 'old Nationalists' would undoubtedly have argued that Treatyites had only come to realise that a republic might be desirable, but not possible and the value of peace over an unwinnable war, much later than the IPP had done. Yet, while the Treaty may not have delivered unity, it offered greater sovereignty than any Home Rule measure which had previously been proposed. Sinn Féin abstained, and Cumann na nGaedheal and other parties helped to establish the Dáil as a national parliament as the IPP had once hoped to do – even if it met in Leinster House rather than College Green and the old site of Grattan's Parliament which had loomed large in the Redmondite political imagination.[50] For many former home rulers, however, the violence of 1916 onwards, partition, and the lack of official respect for the party and John Redmond, left political scars that would take a long time to heal.

Cumann na nGaedheal, for its part, saw itself as a successor of Sinn Féin and not the IPP. It was led by a 1916 veteran in W. T. Cosgrave and venerated Arthur Griffith and Michael Collins, signatories of the Treaty, as the state's founding fathers.[51] As recent research has shown, the Treatyite accommodation with Commonwealth should not be conflated with Redmondite attachment to empire – nor should Treatyite articulation of republican ideals from the revolution through to the Free State period be overlooked.[52] In personnel, the Treatyites did not garner huge number of converts initially. The appointment of Governor-General was a break with convention as the Free State appointed someone from the dominion: ex-MP Tim Healy. Healy, however, had been outside the IPP fold for some time and while it was a nod to the old constitutional tradition, it was a move only likely to further antagonise John Dillon.

Healy was proposed by his nephew-in-law Kevin O'Higgins – a central figure in John M. Regan's analysis which, stressing the increasingly conservative middle-class character of Cumann na nGaedheal by the mid-20s, examines the absorption of a number of former Irish Party and Unionist Party figures into the Treatyite fold.[53] O'Higgins's colleague, Patrick Hogan, sprung from a similar class background while Patrick McGilligan was the son of former Irish Party MP for Fermanagh. However, while Regan's analysis is stimulating in terms of assessing the class character and policies of the Treatyite party, seeing Cumann na nGaedheal as simply the IPP redux would simplify the variegated nature of what Conor Mulvagh has termed the Irish Party's 'green umbrella' and the differences between grassroots and elite home rulers shown by Wheatley.[54] It would certainly not satisfy TDs with purely Sinn Féin lineage – or John Dillon, Tom O'Donnell and members of the AOH in the Free State who criticised the government and refused to renounce older loyalties.[55] Yet, for O'Higgins and Cumann na nGaedheal, home rulers were more obvious targets for support than republicans. While there were few Home Rule links in pro-Treaty Sinn Féin, from 1923 onwards, several Cumann na nGaedheal TDs had Irish Party links – the same was not true of anti-Treaty Sinn Féin.[56]

The 'new' Irish National League

Other former Irish Party devotees found expression in a party that can unquestionably be ascribed the role of direct successor to the IPP: the Irish National League led by Captain Redmond and fellow ex-MP Thomas O'Donnell from 1926 to 1931. Both men capitalised on the persistence of Home Rule loyalty, but also an uncertain political situation where the collapse of the Boundary Commission had left the government more vulnerable than ever. Former MPs, however, were unused to facing to such a crowded field as multiple new parties appeared, including Fianna Fáil – founded by Éamon de Valera four months before the League's launch. Redmond and O'Donnell's party sought to navigate a path where it cast itself as a 'new' party despite drawing explicitly on the old IPP. Made up chiefly of former IPP politicians, activists, and support networks, it criticised Cumann na nGaedheal on partition and government expenditure – a significant trope in O'Donnell's public speeches since 1918. In so doing, it would face several challenges – not least building a nominally 'catch-all' nationalist party from the ashes of another which had prospered in an era of restricted franchise and few competitors.

The League's claims to be a new party were unconvincing from the outset. Its launch in Waterford had clear echoes of the John Redmond anniversaries of previous years while the symbolism involved was also that of a pre-1918 world. The flags at the launch were the old green flag with golden harp rather than the tricolour; the name chosen for the party was the same one used by Parnell in the 1880s while even the membership cards were the same as the old UIL cards and handbills often concluded with the Manchester Martyrs' invocation, 'God Save Ireland', printed on the bottom.[57] Arguably, it echoed the old IPP's attitudes to gender too; it alienated Mary Sheehy Kettle at an early stage through its neglect of women.[58] While it outlined policy documents (in consultation with John Dillon who did not take a public role), it failed to convert former backers in the Farmers' Party, and its attempts to appeal to workers were too shallow to challenge the Labour party. The only sectors of society with which it had real success were vintners and town tenants – two groups associated with support for the IPP.

The League's very existence saw historical debates about the Irish Party regularly raised during the June 1927 general election campaign, and 23 of its 30 candidates had some IPP link as did six of its eight successful candidates.[59] It polled best where the old party had retained support in 1918, but it certainly did not live up to the IPP's famed parliamentary discipline. In the aftermath of Kevin O'Higgins's assassination in July 1927 and with Fianna Fáil effectively forced into the Dáil by W. T. Cosgrave's subsequent legislation, the National League attempted a risky coalition deal with Labour and the tacit support of de Valera's party. This venture ended in farce as one TD opposed the deal and another, John Jinks, failed to vote on a motion of no confidence in Cosgrave, leading to rapid decline for the League and it folded in 1931. While defenders of the League subsequently argued that it helped to smooth Fianna Fáil's entry into the democratic process, the party did play an important, if brief, role in Free State politics.[60] It highlighted the extent and strength of Home Rule loyalty (as well as dissatisfaction with the government), and ultimately, it almost succeeded in putting a Redmond in cabinet in a self-governed Irish state. The League's collapse also, however, demonstrated that the Sinn Féin tradition was then the foundation for party politics. Former home rulers would have to join with those from advanced nationalist backgrounds if they were to achieve real political success.

THE LEGACY OF THE LAND LEAGUE?

Even in 1927, the National League had not succeeded in winning over all former home rulers as Cumann na nGaedheal continued to attract those with Irish Party heritage. In the aftermath of the League's collapse, assimilation was accelerated, and the majority began to embrace a Treatyite identity. The shifting forces of electoral politics as de Valera's Fianna Fáil grew in popularity meant that former home rulers were increasingly forced to choose a side or risk being left on the margins. The most significant recruit to Cumann na nGaedheal was unquestionably Capt. Redmond in 1931. It was ironic, however, that he sold his decision on the importance of supporting the Treaty and opposing de Valera – the exact reason so many National League supporters deserted Redmond in 1927. Patrick Maume has rightly pointed out that memoirs by former MPs such as Stephen Gwynn and William O'Malley, along with the Home Rule links of figures like O'Higgins, have helped to obscure a radical wing of IPP support which was absorbed into Fianna Fáil in later years.[61] Tom O'Donnell was highly critical of the government, in particular its absorption of former unionists, and was a high-profile Fianna Fáil candidate in 1932. James Cosgrave canvassed enthusiastically in Galway in the same year while the longer-term arc of nationalist and feminist activism includes Ladies' Land League veteran Jennie

Wyse-Power and Honor Crowley, daughter of former MP John P. Boland, who was elected Fianna Fáil TD in 1945.

Despite these and other examples, the National League's policies had been broadly conservative and the threat of Fianna Fáil saw many more side with Cumann na nGaedheal. Just under a third of Treatyite TDs returned in 1932 had traceable Home Rule roots.[62] As Mel Farrell has shown, from the late 1920s onwards, Cumann na nGaedheal and Fianna Fáil, began to occupy recognisably centre-right and centre-left positions; Sinn Féin divided into opposing forces as Michael Davitt had once imagined that the Irish Parliamentary Party would after Home Rule.[63] The shadow of Davitt, however, would prove a long one and it certainly stretched over the Free State in the 1930s as both parties competed for a Land League, if not quite an Irish Party inheritance.[64]

The names of Land League leaders were invoked by both parties to defend their respective positions on the issue of land annuities owed to the British government under the land reform legislation won by the Irish Party. For Treatyite speakers, the Free State had to honour the bond of Parnell, Davitt, and Dillon while Fianna Fáil, appealing to its support base of smaller farmers, summoned the Land League message to represent its defence of rural Ireland against British mistreatment.[65] While Cumann na nGaedheal recruited Davitt's son, Robert Emmet Davitt, such rhetoric was not the preserve of any one party or movement. Some from Home Rule backgrounds, for example, remained resistant to both Treatyite and anti-Treatyite charms. James Dillon, son of the last IPP leader, and Frank MacDermot, a former Irish Party activist, remained independent of the major parties and were more forward-looking politicians than those in the National League in the 20s. Both were vocal on the constitutional status of the state, but it was the annuities issue and the 'economic war' with Britain which animated supporters of their Centre Party, founded in 1933, absorbing along the way the remnants of the Farmers' Party and other former home rulers.

The Centre Party's moniker and MacDermot's declaration that it was a 'frail boat on a stormy seat' echoed appeals of centrist parties in Germany and the Netherlands to resist parties of the right and left in the polarised politics of the interwar period.[66] In an Irish context, its Home Rule-tinged leaders could also be seen as taking up a tradition of using rural mobilisation to promote a national movement. Yet, the Centre Party's nominal neutrality belied the fact that the party was far closer to Cumann na nGaedheal than Fianna Fáil.[67] Although it claimed to appeal to all farmers, its support base was almost exclusively larger cattle farmers threatened by the government's dispute with Britain. In truth, despite the tensions and division within the original Land League, no party in the 1930s could claim anything as broad-based as the movement of the 1880s.

The mass movement of the 1930s – the Blueshirts led by Eoin O'Duffy – capitalised on rural unrest but provided divisiveness rather than any sense of national coalition. Its merger with Cumann na nGaedheal and the Centre Party reflected fear and distrust of the de Valera government and Treatyite malaise as well as the influence of continental Fascism.[68] Conversely, the new party formed in 1933, the United Ireland Party/Fine Gael, at first seemed to reflect a victory of sorts for Dillon and MacDermot who secured equal representation on the party's committee, commitment to Commonwealth membership, and a name which reflected their preoccupations with unification and ending 'Civil War' politics.[69] However, O'Duffy's leadership would force both men to stand by speeches and policies clearly inimical to a parliamentary tradition. By the time O'Duffy departed in September 1934, the damage done to the new venture was clear, and, contrary to Dillon and MacDermot's initial intentions, Fine Gael subsequently became very much seen as a successor to Cumann na nGaedheal.[70]

Between 30 and 40 per cent of Fine Gael's TDs in the 1930s and 40s had Home Rule backgrounds but were thus confined to opposition.[71] Any frustration experienced, however, hardly compared with the issues of northern nationalism which remained a mixture of various legacies and organisations as the shadow of the IPP became more distant.[72] Richard Byrne passed away in 1942 and was succeeded by Fianna Fáil's Eamon Donnelly who refused to take his seat. After Byrne's death, Campbell remained the sole representative at Stormont until Glasgow-born James McSparran became Nationalist leader in 1945.[73] Politicians from Irish Party backgrounds south of the border rarely drew explicitly on Home Rule heritage after the foundation of Fine Gael. James Dillon's opposition to wartime neutrality stressed the importance of American and British allies and the need to defeat Nazi Germany rather than allusion to the First World War.[74] Politicians with Home Rule heritage from both sides of the border were active in the Anti-Partition League, but the post-war optimism that partition could be ended did not last.[75] By 1946, de Valera was happy to declare that Sinn Féin and the Volunteers had taken up the work from the Land League generation.[76] The inter-party government formed in 1948, however, contained almost all remaining representatives with Home Rule heritage in the Dáil and a Taoiseach, John A. Costello, who had been a home ruler in his youth.[77] However, despite 'the accommodation with the crown' that neo-Redmondism might have been seen to imply, individuals such as Dillon, Bridget Redmond, and ex-MP John Lymbrick Esmonde largely accepted the declaration of the republic and leaving the Commonwealth – a move which bore little continuity with the rhetoric of John Redmond in 1914.[78]

A Genius for Organisation? Successor parties and political activism

Assessing the implications of partition during the third Home Rule crisis in 1913, Arthur Balfour speculated that the north would retain the island's industrial strength, and that any southern polity would be left only with 'the Irish genius for parliamentary debate and political organisation'.[79] Despite the pejorative undertones of such sentiments, Balfour's view was perhaps a strange tribute to the Irish Party's discipline and organisation, prized by Parnell and maintained thereafter by Dillon and Redmond. It was certainly a valuable inheritance for any successor with designs on winning and retaining power in a parliamentary democracy. Yet, as already noted, early Sinn Féin and other opponents ridiculed the late Irish Party's organisation at local level as a closed shop associated with jobbery. By the time of the Irish revolution, any genius for organisation or discipline which the Irish Party displayed was viewed in very different terms by those who felt a new vision for Ireland was possible. For Eoin MacNeill, writing to Maurice Moore in September 1916, Irish Party MPs were 'hopeless... because no able, honest man could sell his soul to his leaders in the way in which the Irish Party rank and filer is expected to do'.[80] The primacy of the whip system in Dáil Éireann, however, and the persistence of 'parish pump' appeals highlight threads of continuity far beyond the early decades of independence.[81]

The 'hybrid' nature of Ireland's position within the United Kingdom and the wider empire from the Act of Union, and the Irish Party's success and discipline under Parnell from the 1880s had helped to create a political culture which for nationalists centred on a single party elected to Westminster 'with the aim of leaving it'.[82] Other large nationalist movements sometimes dominated electoral competition in emerging systems throughout the British Empire it is true, but examples like the Indian National Congress did not get to make their case from within the United Kingdom by sitting at Westminster.[83] In the first instance, the modus operandi of the IPP was not therefore a model that could be easily applied to a self-governed state or a conventional multi-party system. Analysing the Home Rule movement alongside the parliamentary party, however, Mulvagh adopted the typologies of Moisei Ostrogorski, arguing that the Irish Party 'at least at grassroots level functioned more like a municipal political model' in an almost one-party system.[84] While Irish politicians had demonstrated a flair for organisation in municipal politics in many US cities (including formidable machines in Chicago, Albany, New York city and San Francisco), pre-independence Ireland itself had distinctive characteristics – not least the fact that the party had no rivals in many nationalist areas. The Irish-American examples were, by contrast, organs of the Democratic Party and fought elections against regular competitors. They were also built on the distribution of patronage (though more limited than is often assumed) and the advancement of ethnic groups in the metropolis.[85] Elements of such an approach may be detected in the activism or rhetoric of Home Rule organisations in the early twentieth century.[86] However, as McConnel's work on backbench politicians has illustrated, Irish Party MPs at least, operated as brokers rather than actual distributors of patronage – interceding on behalf of constituents as representatives of the Irish nation in the British parliament in London.[87]

Partition and the arrival of self-government might have been expected to change this political culture profoundly. In Northern Ireland, politics was largely focused on a nationalist-unionist divide and a unionist majority; the Nationalist Party's organisation resembled more a collection of fiefdoms run by prominent politicians than the kind of unified structure associated with the IPP.[88] But in the south, many aspects were not altered. Proportional Representation by Single Transferable Vote and party fragmentation were features of the Free State, but a culture of expectation persisted from the Home Rule era too as supporters expected reward from the Treatyite regime as part of the spoils of victory.[89] The tradition of appealing to the local politician as a conduit between the state and the citizen also remained and the TD often took on the role of broker once held by the MP despite any sense that a parliament in Dublin might be less remote than one in London. Cumann na nGaedheal, home to many with Irish Party roots from the mid-1920s, often sent inclusive invitations to selection conventions in the vein of the IPP and pre-Treaty Sinn Féin.[90] Ironically, however, it was Fianna Fáil, dominated by former Sinn Féin and IRA veterans, which excelled at organisation boasting more membership branches in 1932 than its rival or the UIL at its peak.[91]

As Richard Dunphy has pointed out, de Valera's party took up the tradition of identifying party with nation – building a party with mass appeal attracting a number of different interest groups.[92] In its appeal to smaller farmers, Fianna Fáil echoed the party of Parnell while even its parliamentary behaviour in opposition in the late 1920s, focused on constituency matters and obstructing Dáil business, followed Irish Party traditions – a contrast with the increasingly lackadaisical attendance of Cumann na nGaedheal TDs and the abstention of Nationalist MPs in Northern Ireland.[93] In government, its long period in power saw it face accusations of jobbery – in this way at least the evolution of nationalist parties came full circle.[94]

Conclusion: the IPP and Sinn Féin

The example of the IPP therefore ensured legacies on both sides of the border – but with noticeable ironies. In Northern Ireland, the Nationalist Party, was led by former Redmondites and Hibernians, but in some ways, resembled pre-Rising Sinn Féin – it abstained from parliament, was successful only in its strongholds, and ultimately could do little to disrupt the political status quo. In the south, Sinn Féin parties dominated but absorbed individuals from Home Rule backgrounds and embraced constitutionalism – working through parliament, representing constituents, and largely continuing pre-independence norms and tactics with all their attendant virtues and flaws. The 'two Irelands' were of course very different entities; 'Civil War' politics had its origins in Sinn Féin which had learned to overcome the IPP at electoral politics while Northern politics was defined from the beginning by the reality of permanent unionist government. Yet, both polities highlight important issues in assessing the IPP and its successors.

In independent Ireland, the importance of revolutionary inheritance ensured there was electoral value in claiming Sinn Féin roots, and with the exception of the short-lived National League, no grouping self-consciously looked back to the Irish Party. Nonetheless, while former home rulers ultimately had to join with those from Sinn Féin backgrounds to enter government, those who did so often exercised significant influence. A Redmondite legacy may have seemed obscure as the republic was declared, but James Dillon was minister for agriculture. He later led Fine Gael from 1959 to 1965, remained President of the AOH while leader of the opposition, and defended the role of the Irish Party on the fiftieth anniversary of the Rising in 1966.[95] In 2016, another former Fine Gael leader whose family joined via the Centre Party, made similar interventions as iar-Thaoiseach, as John Bruton argued for Redmond's place in history and that the Easter Rising was ultimately unwise.[96]

In Northern Ireland, the Nationalist Party ensured the survival of Devlinite nationalism buttressed by the weakened but persistent AOH. Devlin, Campbell, and Joseph Stewart, leader at Stormont from 1958–64, all had IPP backgrounds.[97] Others such as Hugh McAleer and Gerry Lennon remained prominent Hibernians – the latter serving as vice-president from 1951 and President from 1975. The party remained the voice of nationalism in the north up until the 1960s with members such as Lennon participating in the early civil rights movement. Nevertheless, the party was viewed as lacklustre and ineffective by that period; the Social Democratic and Labour Party, founded in 1970, provided a better level of constituency organisation and even an initial willingness to engage at Stormont as well as a centre-left policy platform.[98]

Undoubtedly, IPP leaders would have been forgiven a rueful thought that their work helped to forge a culture of party activism which was used against them in 1918. Yet, it might be argued given the merits and defects often associated with Irish politics that the party bequeathed a parliamentary culture as much as a democratic culture; as

McConnel has noted, former MPs recognised the priorities and constraints of a TD's work as similar to their own.[99] Local issues and party discipline were prized as much as ideology. While Irish Party loyalty persisted for decades after 1918, individual home rulers and their descendants found themselves in new circumstances. Captain Redmond opposed compulsory Irish language policy in 1927 while Dillon and MacDermot defended Commonwealth membership, but neither position found favour in independent Ireland despite the Treatyite absorption of home rulers; Joe Devlin exercised less influence in a Belfast parliament than he did at Westminster. It was the political circumstances of the 1920s and 30s which eventually forced recalcitrant home rulers to join Sinn Féin parties in the south while the Nationalist Party in the north eventually collapsed in the face of more dynamic alternatives in the 1960s. The Irish Party provided a model of organisation and a range of tactics for achieving political aims, but its successors which utilised them had to do so in very different contexts. Therein lies the IPP's enduring relevance: the party's successes, failures, and even its ultimate collapse still provide lessons for any party negotiating periods of political, social, or economic change.

CHAPTER 8

THE PARLIAMENTARY CAREER OF BRIDGET REDMOND TD, 1933–52: A GENDERED ANALYSIS

Claire McGing

For nearly two decades, Bridget Redmond served as an elected representative for the constituency of Waterford in Dáil Éireann. Her journey into elected office was intertwined with personal tragedy, a common narrative for many women TDs in the early decades of the twentieth century who inherited seats left vacant after the passing of male relatives.[1] In an unexpected turn of events in 1932, at the age of 28, Bridget Redmond was unanimously selected as a parliamentary candidate for Cumann na nGaedheal – a role she likely never envisaged herself to hold. This decision arose following the untimely death of her husband, Captain William Archer Redmond, who served as a sitting TD in Waterford. Captain Redmond, son of John Redmond, the leader of the Irish Parliamentary Party (IPP), had won a seat at Westminster in the Waterford city constituency in 1918 and held it until 1922. In 1923 he gained a place in the Dáil for the new multi-seat constituency for Waterford city and county.[2] Since the early 1890s, the Redmond family had enjoyed an almost mythic status in Waterford, particularly in the city, where they were held as local heroes among supporters spanning a diverse range of backgrounds, including groups unable to vote until 1918. After her first general election in 1933, Bridget Redmond assumed the role of the 'keeper of the Redmondite flame', a responsibility she held until she died in 1952.[3] Her diligent commitment to serving the constituents of Waterford, coupled with her active participation as a party member of Cumann na nGaedheal and later Fine Gael, secured her consistent re-election through seven general election contests.

This chapter examines Bridget Redmond's political role and historical significance as a candidate and TD for Waterford. Importantly, it contextualises her story within the broader framework of women's participation in politics following the establishment of the Irish Free State. In 1933, the political landscape was increasingly conservative, authoritarian and had a patriarchal ethos. This was evident in the minimal representation of women in the lower and upper houses of parliament.[4] Although, she did not identify as a feminist figure at a time when women's citizenship rights were being eroded by legislative means, which was a source of disappointment for her contemporaries engaged in the women's movement, Bridget Redmond's mere presence subtly challenged male dominance in the Dáil. As a woman TD who represented one of the most prominent surnames associated with the Irish parliamentary tradition, she was both an insider and an outsider to institutional politics in the formative decades of the new state.

Drawing from archival records and secondary sources, this chapter weaves together various strands of Bridget Redmond's parliamentary career. The analysis encompasses the circumstances leading to her selection as a Cumann na nGaedheal candidate in 1932, marked by the tragic death of her husband. It explores her active role in shaping a political alternative to Fianna Fáil during the tumultuous years of 1933 and 1934, including her membership of the 'Blue Blouses'. The chapter examines her legislative and constituency priorities as a backbench TD, providing insights into her ideological positions, along with her electoral performances in Waterford. Employing a gendered analytical framework,[5] the research offers a nuanced portrayal of Bridget Redmond's public life, set against the backdrop of her navigating an emerging political system designed for and predominantly operated by men.

CONTEXT: WOMEN AND POLITICS IN POST-REVOLUTIONARY IRELAND

Early political milestones achieved by women in the general elections of 1918 and 1921 were rolled back in the decades following Irish independence. Opportunities for women to enter politics became progressively limited during this period. Six women TDs, all members of Sinn Féin, secured seats in the 1921 general election (four were related to dead republican heroes); by 1933, when Bridget Redmond first won a seat, this figure had dropped to three women TDs. In the subsequent four decades, no Dáil would have more than five women TDs. In contrast to the revolutionary period of the early twentieth century where women were actively involved in the struggle for Irish independence, albeit typically in gendered auxiliary roles, the post-revolutionary era imposed significant restrictions on women's participation in the public sphere.[6]

Affirming a commitment previously articulated by the Provisional Government in March 1922, the Irish Free State Constitution, enacted in December of the same year, granted suffrage rights to women citizens on par with men (Article 14). This provision faced no opposition in either the parliament or the mainstream press.[7] While the passage of the Representation of the People Act 1918 had marked a significant triumph for suffrage campaigners in Britain and Ireland, it imposed gendered restrictions by granting voting rights only to women over 30 who met certain property or education criteria (essentially a class barrier), while enfranchising all men over 21. In 1922, women in the Irish Free State attained full suffrage six years before their counterparts in Britain and many other European democracies, which was widely celebrated.[8] The debate on Article 3, however, was more contentious. The draft equality provision was watered down several times before a final wording was agreed upon. According to Thomas Mohr, 'there can be little doubt that the 1922 Constitution, and Article 3 in particular, proved weak and ineffectual in protecting the vision of equal rights reflected in the drafts produced by the Constitution Committee'.[9] Despite Article 3 referencing the privileges and obligations of citizenship 'without distinction of sex', feminist activists had concerns that the new constitution aimed to confine women's rights to 'mere political equality'; in other words, limiting their participation in the broader economic and social spheres of the Irish Free State.[10]

Despite feminist resistance, which included vocal opposition from women senators (but not the small number of women TDs), a series of legislative reforms were implemented by Cumann na nGaedheal governments throughout the 1920s, severely restricting women's participation in public and political affairs. Notable among these gender-based statutory changes were the confinement of senior civil service posts for men only in 1925, the exemption of women from jury service in 1927 and the censorship of birth control in 1929. Although feminists lobbied against the curtailment of women's citizenship rights, they constituted a vocal minority.[11] The government, aligned with the Roman Catholic Church and likely a majority of women citizens, regarded women's primary role in independent Ireland as domestic, as had been the case before independence.[12] Surveying Cumann na nGaedheal's ten years in office, Maryann Gialanella Valiulis writes:

> The [Cumann na nGaedheal] government and its supporters authoritatively asserted that the primary role of women was marriage and motherhood, that women's place was in the home, tending to the needs of their husbands, raising their children. From this stereotypical role flowed the belief that women, therefore did not belong outside the home, be it in the civil service or the jury box.[13]

The reversal of women's rights continued when Fianna Fáil assumed government in the 1930s, which was unsurprising given the party's alignment with Cumann na nGaedheal's gender ideology. Legislative changes during this period included the introduction of the 'marriage bar' in 1932, a prohibition on the sale or importation of contraceptives in 1934 and the authorisation given to the Minister for Industry and Commerce to control and restrict the number of women working in any given industry in 1936. Additionally, several articles in the 1937 Constitution of Ireland further restricted women's participation in the public domain. The document solidified women's domestic and maternal roles, additionally recognising the family as the natural primary and fundamental unit group in society. Alpha Connelly highlights the patriarchal ethos of the 1937 Constitution, revealing Fianna Fáil's willingness to integrate Catholic values into the constitutional framework of the state:

> The use of such language and the ascription of particular historical and social roles to women and men is that power and status in Irish public life are the preserve of the male. Women's power and status are of a different order. They pertain to private life and derive women's essential role as nurturers of the next generation.[14]

As for electoral politics in this period, although women had the right to vote and formally stand for office, the opportunities for women to secure political representation at the national or local level were increasingly restricted due to these legislative and socio-cultural shifts. Gendered structural barriers were exacerbated by a political culture that became more localised as the 'revolutionary generation' of politicians exited the political arena. In their place, men with strong local connections to the constituency, established mainly through their profession or prior involvement in local councils, gained advantages in party selection processes.[15] Another factor in the stagnation of women's representation was the opposition of the six female TDs of the Second Dáil to the terms of the Anglo-Irish Treaty in 1921 and 1922.[16] Their strong rejection of the Treaty constructed a narrative among political and religious leaders and within wider society, suggesting that women were too inflexible and emotional for institutional politics.[17] This belief provided the state with justification to suppress and control republican women. Ultimately, this gender-based discourse had a detrimental and lingering impact on political opportunities for all women, even those on the pro-Treaty side and the party organisations that arose from this faction.[18]

Thus, for various reasons, a limited number of names, including Bridget Redmond, dominated the small cohort of female TDs in the early decades of the Irish state. The majority of these women were close family members of deceased male TDs, primarily widows and daughters. Similar to the first generation of women TDs elected in the 1920s, the entry of women candidates from the 1930s until the early 1970s often resulted from a vacancy due to a death. In these cases, political parties sought to leverage the 'sympathy vote' following a TD's passing. However, in a highly gendered culture, even women representing political dynasties were not guaranteed a straightforward path to candidacy or election, and they were not always the obvious choice for the local party organisation.[19] Despite these challenges, many women TDs sustained prolonged careers in Dáil Éireann during this era and achieved notable electoral successes, due to their diligent record of constituency service. Nevertheless, as will be further explored later in this chapter in the context of Bridget Redmond's story, historical research has tended to downplay the roles these women played in public life in the twentieth century.

Bridget Redmond's Selection as a Candidate, 1932–3

Despite a large collection of academic works on women's political representation in Ireland in the post-suffrage years, Bridget Redmond was a largely overlooked figure by scholars until the detailed biographical works of McDermott[20] and, subsequently, Pat McCarthy.[21] Born on October 30, 1904, at the Curragh in county Kildare, she was the second of four children to John and Bridget Mallick (née Sex). In contrast to the material circumstances of most women at this time, her class background was marked by privilege. Her father was a landowner, racehorse owner and hotelier and 'the Mallick colours' were known at racing meetings in England and Ireland.[22] Educated at the Ursuline Convent in Waterford City from 1916 to 1922, Bridget Redmond likely never anticipated that she would return to the constituency as a TD only a decade later. During her time at the Ursuline Convent, she acquired the nickname 'Tiny' due to her petite stature, a moniker affectionately used by family and friends throughout her life. Although she had a talent for singing, her shyness curtailed her musical ambitions.[23] Upon completing her formal education, Bridget returned to county Kildare to live with her parents, engaging in activities befitting a young woman of her social standing, such as horseracing, hunting and motoring.[24]

In 1930, mutual friends introduced Bridget Redmond to Captain William Archer Redmond, a serving National League TD and barrister. During the First World War, Redmond served in the British Army as Captain in the Irish Guards, being one of seven nationalist MPs to serve during the conflict.[25] The couple were married in Monkstown, county Dublin, when she was 26 and he was 44.[26] They had no children.

Captain Redmond represented one of Ireland's most important political dynasties. After serving the constituency in the House of Commons for 27 years, the future of Redmondism in Waterford City had seemed 'apparently neither possible or probable' when his father, John Redmond, died on 6 March 1918.[27] 'Redmondism' as a political phenomenon in Waterford[28] emerged upon his first election to the constituency in 1891, and even though John Redmond had no connections to Waterford City before his election, it 'subsequently fostered and developed as a distinct dogma in the district'.[29] McDermott argues that nobody outside the core faction of the MP's supporters 'could have anticipated that Redmondism was by 1918, vital, necessary, and strong enough to survive the death of the man who had inspired it in the first instance'.[30] However, supporters asked John Redmond's only son, Captain Redmond, Home Rule MP for East Tyrone at the time, to contest the by-election to fill the vacancy. Captain Redmond resigned his seat in Tyrone and won the Waterford City by-election just three weeks after his father's passing. Reported to be the 'mirror image' of his father, physically and politically[31], Captain Redmond achieved 62 per cent of the vote in a two-candidate race against the Sinn Féin challenger, Dr Vincent White. The result was notable in the context of rising electoral support for Sinn Féin in the aftermath of the 1916 Easter Rising and escalating levels of public disenchantment with the repercussions of the world war.

A general election was called for December 1918, the first parliamentary election in eight years. Franchise reforms increased the Irish electorate from around 700,000 to approximately 2 million eligible voters. Nationally, Sinn Féin won 73 seats, leading to the establishment of the illegal First Dáil in 1919. Unionist candidates secured 26 seats. The IPP's vote collapsed, with the party returning only six MPs on the island of Ireland (down from 71 seats in 1910): five in Ulster counties, helped in part by the electoral pact brokered by Cardinal Logue, and Captain Redmond in Waterford City, who attained 53 per cent of the vote against Dr Vincent White (with a majority of 484 votes).[32] Although Captain Redmond's vote had decreased significantly since the by-election earlier that year, partly a consequence of a larger, more diverse electorate, his success highlighted the enduring resilience of Redmondism as a political force. While most constituencies apart from Ulster had turned towards the 'green tide' of radical nationalism articulated by Sinn Féin, in Waterford City, support for the moderate nationalist vision of Home Rule endured amongst the local Redmondites. Even after Ireland was granted dominion status pursuant to the Anglo-Irish Treaty in 1922, Redmondism retained its prominence within Waterford City. As opposed to being a staunchly ideological movement, it gradually shifted towards 'maintaining a shrine to John Redmond while, simultaneously, welcoming the two later Redmonds as members of his hallowed family and caretakers of his legacy'.[33]

The Ballybricken Pig Buyers' Association was among Captain Redmond's core supporters. His father fostered their loyalty after successfully negotiating a settlement in the pig buyers' dispute of 1892–97, which had almost destroyed their livelihoods. Ten association members were pallbearers at the funerals for both father and son, and they would later remain faithful to Bridget Redmond during her tenure as TD. Working class women in the city also played a central role in the dynasty's support base. This trend commenced with John Redmond's election in 1891, before the extension of voting rights to women. The Waterford Women's Nationalist Association, a local Redmondite organisation, regularly paid tribute to the family throughout their years in office, including holding an event in honour of Captain Redmond's marriage to Bridget Redmond in 1930. The deputy told those gathered that while his new wife was not from Waterford, she was 'no stranger to the city', having been educated there.[34]

Captain Redmond declined to contest the 1921 and 1922 general elections for 'Southern Ireland' and the Free State respectively, but entered the Dáil chamber in 1923 as an independent TD. In that election, he polled in second place after anti-Treaty candidate

Caitlín Brugha, who succeeded her husband, Cathal Brugha, following his death at the hands of Free State Forces; she was the first 'Dáil widow' to directly inherit a seat. Captain Redmond was re-elected in every general election until his death. In 1926, he co-founded the short-lived new Irish National League Party, which 'filled a niche, appealing to former constitutionalists, conservatives and ex-servicemen.'[35] Following the dissolution of the National League in 1931, Captain Redmond joined Cumann na nGaedheal – in many ways, it was the natural successor of the IPP and its former supporters[36] – and was elected as a party candidate in the 1932 election contest.

Bridget Redmond often accompanied her husband on formal visits to Waterford. As with the years she had spent in Waterford as a schoolgirl, the important connection she cultivated with his followers in the city 'was to become significant a lot sooner than she, her husband, and their supporters would have wished'.[37] The bonds she forged with her spouse's supporters would ultimately benefit her path to candidacy. As Eleanor Lowe observes in relation to women MPs who inherited seats in post-suffrage Britain: 'Their relationships with their husbands provided them with attributes that were necessary to forge a parliamentary career when many were still so resistant to lady members'.[38]

After only 18 months of marriage, in April 1932, Captain Redmond died suddenly at the funeral of his long-time friend and loyal supporter, Patrick F. Hogan. Bridget was at home in Dublin when she heard that her husband had collapsed, but she was not aware of his death until she arrived in Waterford.[39] He had previously been complaining of ill health. Newspapers reported the extent of shock and grief felt throughout the city. The *Irish Press* described 'poignant scenes' witnessed by spectators when the 27-year-old widow went to the cathedral mortuary to see her husband's body.[40] According to the *Munster Express*: 'To those outside Waterford it would be difficult to realise the depth of the people's grief when the sad news spread. Women wept in the streets, and many shops closed at once'.[41]

Bridget Redmond received many messages of sympathy, such as the following from the Waterford Pig Dealers' Association:

> For a period of 41 years, the Redmonds – father and son – have given not only to our calling but to Waterford generally, a service and a friendship unique probably in the history of any municipality. Not soon will their name be forgotten by their faithful and grief-stricken followers in the ranks of our Association.[42]

The Waterford Women's Nationalist Association wrote that:

> The members of the Waterford Women's Nationalist Association assure you and Captain Redmond's relatives of their deep and heartfelt sympathy in the tragic loss of our beloved leader. His personality, name and life-work can never be forgotten by his devoted followers in his old constituency.[43]

Captain Redmond's passing seemed to mark the end of the Redmond [political] dynasty. John Kiersey, the other Cumann na nGaedheal TD in Waterford, expressed his condolences to Bridget Redmond, remarking that 'it was an unfortunate thing to have the last of the family taken from them [the people of Waterford and Ireland]'.[44] No immediate by-election was scheduled to fill the vacancy, and local party activists initiated a search to find a suitable candidate to succeed Captain Redmond. His widow was not the obvious choice of candidate at this point. In the local newspapers, only the *Waterford Standard*, a few days after Captain Redmond's funeral, raised the possibility of her inheriting the vacant seat:

> The heartfelt sympathy of everyone in the city and county of Waterford goes out in this time of sorrow to the grief-stricken widow… we are sure when the time comes, she will not hesitate to carry on the tradition as a representative of the people.[45]

Two days later, a report in the *Kerry News* newspaper stated that any discussions about her potential candidacy 'may be taken with some reserve'.[46] Deeply affected by her husband's unexpected death, the young widow had not engaged in discussions regarding her nomination in the by-election, according to her brother, who informed reporters that he was unaware of any decision made by her in this regard.[47] No other mainstream newspaper suggested Bridget Redmond as a potential candidate for several months, and it was assumed that she would grieve for her husband and father, who had died a year previously, in private.[48] She only visited Waterford on rare occasions, for example, to attend a meeting of the Nationalist Women's Association in July 1932.[49] A month after the funeral, a meeting of the county and city executive of Cumann na nGaedheal discussed the constituency's seat vacancy. Still, they could not agree on a suitable candidate, and a decision was deferred.[50] The delayed invitation to Bridget Redmond may be explained by considering how few women held parliamentary office in the years after suffrage.[51] Nevertheless, a year earlier, Cumann na nGaedheal had selected another widow, Mary Reynolds, to contest for her late husband's seat in Sligo-Leitrim after he was shot during the 1932 election campaign – the party had already set a precedent around the symbolism of 'widow's weeds' in constituency politics.[52]

McCarthy provides a detailed account of Bridget Redmond's journey to ultimately being selected as a Dáil candidate in 1932.[53] Dr Vincent White, whom Captain Redmond had defeated in the 1918 general election, maintained a visible presence in the constituency, particularly through his active involvement in establishing a local branch of the newly formed Army Comrades Association (ACA). Traditionally, the party that had lost the Dáil deputy initiated the writ for the by-election, but 'Cumann na nGaedheal seemed to shy away from an electoral contest, a situation that suited the minority Fianna Fáil government'.[54] The party's standing committee was aware of local discussions but opted not to intervene. Fianna Fáil, the Labour Party and the National Centre Party selected their candidates in November, with active campaigning underway by December. Cumann na nGaedheal finally scheduled a selection convention for Sunday, 18 December, with General Sean Mac Eoin as chair. Dr Vincent White was the only nominee, but after he was proposed and seconded, the chair announced that Bridget Redmond had agreed for her name to go forward – a development already highlighted in multiple newspapers in the days leading up to the convention.[55] Amidst resounding applause and a standing ovation from about 200 party members, the widow entered the town hall in Dungarvan.[56] After Dr Vincent White withdrew his nomination, Bridget Redmond was unanimously chosen as the party's candidate to uphold her husband's legacy in securing his seat. McCarthy concludes: 'It was a perfectly stage-managed event. Cumann na nGaedheal had got their ideal candidate for Waterford'.[57] Given her family association, local supporters were reported to be 'fairly certain of a victory'.[58]

Her acceptance speech clearly shows that she proudly saw herself as carrying on the Redmondite tradition in Waterford:

> Nobody can realise more than I do what an honour it is to represent Waterford. I have been hearing about Waterford since my marriage and for a long time before it. Waterford always came first. I fully realise the decision you had to make was a very hard one. When you think of the man who is gone and the one who went before him, the late John Redmond, I am sure you will make allowance for my shortcomings. I hope however I can do one thing and that is at all times to have the interests of the people at heart and the country in general which the late Captain Redmond served so loyally and so well. I hope to be able to deserve and retain the affection of the people of Waterford...[59]

Éamon de Valera dissolved the Dáil in January 1933 before a by-election could occur, and a 'snap' general election was called for 24 January. The Cumann na nGaedheal organisation in Waterford nominated three candidates to contest the four-seat constituency: incumbent TD John Kiersey, Bridget Redmond and Dr Vincent White. As customary, her nomination papers were signed by the Chairman and Secretary of the Ballybricken Pig Buyers' Association. There were 30 additional papers for her, compared to 20 additional forms for her two running mates. Notably, one set of papers was signed exclusively by women voters from Jail Street and Ballybricken, the heartland of Redmondism in the city. After submitting her documents, Bridget Redmond's departure from the courthouse was met with enthusiastic cheers.[60]

Tumultuous Years, 1933–4

The campaign for the 1933 general election was bitter, and many Cumann na nGaedheal meetings were marred by incidents of violence.[61] Bridget Redmond campaigned extensively in Waterford, mainly in the city and surrounding areas.[62] Her position as the torchbearer of the Redmond dynasty was highlighted throughout the election campaign. For instance, at a rally in the city, party leader W. T. Cosgrave introduced her to the crowd as 'the widow of their late distinguished representative, Captain Redmond'.[63] In a political climate marked by escalating hostility, Bridget Redmond forged a link between the principles of her late father-in-law and Cumann na nGaedheal's election manifesto, employing this association to advocate for constitutionalism and law and order.[64] She stated at a public rally disrupted by republican activists that, unlike Fianna Fáil, Cumann na nGaedheal stood for 'construction, not destruction'.[65] The economy was also central to her platform and that of her party, particularly the detrimental impact of the economic war on Irish agriculture, as was the need to observe the terms of the Anglo-Irish Treaty.[66]

The general election was disastrous for Cumann na nGaedheal. The party lost nine Dáil seats, in many cases at the expense of the new National Centre Party, marking their second electoral setback within a year. Fianna Fáil won 77 of the 153 Dáil seats and re-entered government with a comfortable working majority, supported by the Labour Party. The Cumann na nGaedheal vote in Waterford fell by 12 per cent compared to 1932. Bridget Redmond, who won the first seat, was the party's only successful candidate in the constituency. The incumbent TD, John Kiersey, saw his vote fall by nearly 50 per cent, and he decided to retire from electoral politics, as did Dr Vincent White. Both of

Cumann na nGaedheal's incumbent women candidates, Margaret Collins-O'Driscoll and Mary Reynolds, were defeated. Bridget Redmond found herself in a parliamentary party where she was the sole female member among 47 TDs. Fianna Fáil secured the election of two new women candidates: Helena Concannon (National University) and Margaret Mary Pearse (Dublin County).

During the initial two years of the Eighth Dáil, the flurry of political activity happened outside of Leinster House: the rise of the Blueshirt movement; the impact of the economic war; the move to withhold the county rates; and the formation of a new party, all meant that the political focus was on the constituencies and on the streets.[67]

In Waterford, Bridget Redmond was an active participant on all these fronts. This is reflected in the Dáil record, to which she did not contribute in the second half of 1933 or at all in 1934. She was heavily involved in the re-organisation of Cumann na nGaedheal at constituency level following the party's abysmal showing in the 1933 election contest. As a newly-elected deputy, she visited the constituency most weekends over the summer of 1933. She addressed multiple public meetings, criticising government policies and emphasising the need for her party to be returned to power at the next general election.[68] Speaking at a public meeting under the auspices of a local branch meeting in June 1933, she declared (to loud cheers):

> It was high time the economic war was ended. What was wanted was a sane, equitable, sensible settlement between the two countries [Ireland and Britain]... It was, therefore, time for all to waken up and realise that they must organise. Waterford would then be able to take its place in the march to sound and sane government... They must stand for law and order, which was now being flouted and refuse to be carried away by the chimerical shadow of a Republic which they had heard so much about.[69]

Cattle prices were badly affected by the impact of the economic war, especially for larger farmers, and this provoked many farmers across the country to withhold their rates as a form of protest. In response, the Gardaí seized livestock and other assets from farms, and the state auctioned off the goods to pay the monies owed. Bridget Redmond gave visible support to farmers withholding their rates, particularly in the high-profile case of the 'Gaultier Nine' in Waterford. A military tribunal tried the men for the charge of promoting, encouraging and advocating the non-payment of rates in October 1933.[70] When the tribunal returned a verdict of not guilty on all charges, the nine men were immediately released, and the next day, Bridget Redmond and Nicholas Wall hosted a reception for them in Leinster House, attended by most of their party colleagues. She travelled with the nine men by train to Waterford the following day, where a large crowd of supporters greeted them; the deputy told the men that 'they were all with them in their tribulation and in their hour of need'.[71]

A friend and supporter of General Eoin O'Duffy, Bridget Redmond was actively engaged in the Blueshirt movement. The organisation stemmed from the ACA, which comprised ex-members of the National Army and had been established in 1932 in opposition to the Fianna Fáil government.[72] The ACA offered physical protection to members of Cumann na nGaedheal amidst a turbulent political climate. Political meetings regularly descended into bitter clashes and acts of violence between the ACA and republicans who supported Fianna Fáil. In July 1933, General O'Duffy became the leader of the Blueshirts, renaming the ACA the National Guard.⁷³ A former leader in the IRA and National Army General in the Irish Civil War, he was dismissed as the Garda Commissioner by Éamon de Valera on 22 February 1933 (O'Duffy had begun 'to canvass support for a *coup d'état*' in the run up to 1932 election, and rumours among senior police and army figures persisted after de Valera took power).⁷⁴ Initially an all-male entity, the Blueshirts soon admitted women as members. Within a year, the Blue Blouses — the women's auxiliary – marked a significant development, becoming the country's largest women's political group, with 628 branches nationwide and a presence in every county.⁷⁵ The majority of members came from rural locales, particularly counties in the southeast that were severely affected by the economic war. Notably, the Blue Blouses had a broader geographical presence compared to contemporaneous women's organisations, including the republican Cumann na mBan.⁷⁶ Like analogous shirted movements across Europe⁷⁷, the Blue Blouses did not challenge prevailing gender norms regarding women's involvement in public affairs. Leadership predominantly confined women to segregated roles aligned with domesticity, such as organising social events, fundraising and canvassing.⁷⁸ Despite these limitations, women featured prominently in Blueshirt public gatherings and assemblies, exemplified by Bridget Redmond, who adorned a military-style blue blouse as a public marker of her affiliation.⁷⁹ Newspaper reports from this period demonstrate that she regularly participated and spoke at Blueshirt events in Waterford and neighbouring counties.⁸⁰

There has been considerable scholarly debate on whether the Blueshirts should be classified as a fascist organisation. While General O'Duffy undoubtedly identified himself and his movement with the rising fascist ideology in Europe and the Blueshirts displayed certain similarities with fascist groups, such as the inclusion of ceremonial elements, several members outwardly rejected the leadership's views.⁸¹ Akin to many Cumann na nGaedheal TDs, Bridget Redmond's affiliation with the Blueshirts stemmed from her opposition to Fianna Fáil and the IRA and the ongoing repercussions of the economic war, 'rather than from any explicit endorsement of European fascist figures'.⁸² She openly espoused the principles of constitutionalism, free speech and non-violence – values directly at odds with fascist ideology – despite her proximity to political actors like General O'Duffy.⁸³ The United Ireland Party/Fine Gael was established after a merger between Cumann na nGaedheal, the Centre Party and the Blueshirts in September 1933.⁸⁴ Former Blue Blouses wishing to stay politically active likely transitioned into the ranks of this new political party. However, only a select few, such as Bridget Redmond and her party colleague Senator Kathleen Browne (who wore the paraphernalia in the Seanad),⁸⁵ would ever reach the level of parliament. Her dedication to expanding the Fine Gael party's influence in Waterford was evident in her grassroots organisational efforts, and she is credited with fostering considerable membership growth in East Waterford.⁸⁶

Bridget Redmond as a Legislator, 1933–52

Despite her shy demeanour, Bridget Redmond was regarded by her contemporaries as a talented orator who participated in thoughtful and measured discussions. Following her seventh successful election in 1951, the *Irish Independent* profiled her:

> But when she stands up in public or private debate and sets out her ideas or claims in her

crisp, clear voice, the years of parliamentary experience at once begin to weigh the scale in her favour.[87]

Her physical presence as a woman in a patriarchal party and parliament was significant, as was the case for her small number of female colleagues – these 'space invaders' acted to subtly challenge the political norm of male dominance, even if they did not perceive of themselves in this way.[88] Her obituary in the *Cork Examiner* suggested that as a woman TD, she employed a more effective style of parliamentary discourse than her male colleagues:

> Mrs Bridget Redmond will be missed from Leinster House, to which she brought a breath of femininity and grace to the assembly. She was always in fashion, and her smart appearance always caught the eye. Since she came to the House 19 years ago to continue the traditional representation of Waterford by the Redmond family, she was popular and she had the ear of Ministers, no matter which side of the House their party happened to be. Mrs Redmond never wasted words and she could say in a quarter of an hour what some male Deputies would take an hour to get around. In recent years she seldom intervened in debates, but when she did so it was to voice sound reason, of which only a woman seems capable when the men have tied themselves into knots with their own cloudy verbiage.[89]

Nonetheless, modern historians have come to different conclusions regarding her effectiveness as a legislator.[90] For this chapter, an analysis of the Oireachtas record revealed that she spoke in the Dáil on 84 occasions – this includes contributions to committees. While this may seem relatively low for a career spanning two decades, a comprehensive comparison with her female and male contemporaries is required to draw a definitive conclusion. Bridget Redmond's ideological approach has been described as a 'curious mixture of liberal and conservative guiding principles'.[91] Her affiliation with the Blueshirts represented the most right-leaning aspect of her political career; as discussed, not from a fascist viewpoint but in reaction to the perceived threats of Fianna Fáil and the IRA. Like other backbench TDs, her legislative priorities stemmed primarily from her constituents' pressing needs and concerns in the context of severe economic and social challenges in Ireland and Europe. She emphasised common themes like improving living standards, ensuring access to adequate housing and fostering employment opportunities within her constituency. For example, she addressed the Minister for Local Government Seán MacEntee in 1947:

> I fully appreciate all that the Minister and the Government have done for the housing of the poorer classes and the middle-class people in the last few years… Now that the war has passed, we hope that things will be speeded up as much as possible… All of us in our constituencies are–I should not say pestered, but it just describes what we are up against, by various people of all kinds asking us to get them a house. They are all genuine cases in their own way and something should be done to have these people saved from the suffering they are undergoing at present. In Waterford City at present there are cases of eight in a family living in two rooms. In the year 1947, that is not what any of us would wish.[92]

She also grounded her legislative agenda in her own personal experiences. For instance, she opposed the introduction of a betting tax in 1945, contributing to the discussion on the Bill on four separate occasions. Her apprehension for the future of the horse racing industry in Ireland was evident, underscoring her own involvement and familiarity with the sector.

> In my opinion there is no necessity for this interference with racing. As one who has had associations with racing for some years, and my family before me for over 50 years, I would ask the Minister to consider this matter very carefully. I am sure he knows what a big industry racing in Ireland is, and what a big trade there is in the export of horses.[93]

Other contributions focused on addressing the requirements of pig buyers, a demographic identified as key supporters of Redmondism in Waterford City. Her opposition to the Pigs and Bacon Bill of 1937 provides a typical example of her advocacy efforts:

> This Bill does away with competition. The pig dealer, no matter what anybody may say in this House, has always been regarded as a decent and honourable man… Why should we hand over their business to people who will have a complete monopoly of the bacon trade?[94]

Bridget Redmond frequently addressed educational matters in the Dáil. Similar to her late husband, she staunchly argued against the mandatory instruction of all academic subjects in the Irish language.[95] This stance diverged from the views of numerous prominent Fine Gael members, including General Richard Mulcahy.[96] As the school leaving age was established at 14, she also argued for additional technical schools, believing that a period of technical education would 'encourage the children to have other interests in addition to book learning'.[97] While boys should receive some agricultural training due to its significance as the leading industry in the country, girls should be instructed in domestic affairs to equip them with the skills necessary to manage a household. As she stated in a 1947 Dáil debate:

> Now that these schools are in existence, I think that an effort should be made to make girls appreciate the subjects taught in these schools which would be very useful to them in after life. Whether they intend to take up a profession or other employment, or whether they intend to stay at home, they will, probably, get married eventually, and be the wives in the future Ireland. It will be a bad day for Ireland when the housewives are without adequate technical knowledge of the responsibilities they assume. Long ago, we were proud of our domestic accomplishments.[98]

Most of Bridget Redmond's legislative career was spent on the opposition benches. Only between 1948 and 1951 did she experience being a government party member, when the country's first coalition government was established between five political parties, with Fine Gael as the largest party and John A. Costello as Taoiseach.[99] The defining moments of the First Inter-Party Government revolved around two significant issues: the declaration of the Republic of Ireland in 1948, announced unexpectedly by the Taoiseach during a visit to Canada that summer, surprising many; and the crisis surrounding the 'Mother and Child Scheme' in 1951.

Regarding the Republic of Ireland Bill 1948, Bridget Redmond expressed her support for the legislation, which formalised the Taoiseach's earlier announcement. She contributed to the parliamentary debate: 'I stand for what he [an Taoiseach] did because he has put us once more on the map as an independent nation'.[100] The *Irish Times* praised her speech, which also expressed the constitutional position long associated with her marital name.[101]

Bridget Redmond did not publicly express any views on the controversial 'Mother and Child Scheme' in 1951, nor did any of her female counterparts in the Dáil. Dr Noel Browne's efforts to implement the non-means-tested service faced strong opposition from the medical profession, the Catholic hierarchy and even fellow government members. The crisis highlighted the vulnerability of the Irish democratic system when challenged and contributed to the downfall of the government. Following a general election in May 1951, Bridget Redmond returned to the opposition benches with her Fine Gael colleagues.

A 'Silent Sister'? Representation of Women's Issues

Historians have lamented how the second generation of women TDs nearly 'always placed party before sex'[102] and seldom made substantial feminist or gender-based contributions to parliamentary debates, despite the backdrop of diminishing women's rights. Reflecting on the results of the 1943 general election, where Bridget Redmond secured re-election alongside her Fine Gael colleague Mary Reynolds and Bridget Mary Rice for Fianna Fáil, Hanna Sheehy Skeffington stated that:

> The net result was that the same three women previously elected – Mrs Rice, Mrs Redmond and Miss Reynolds, called often 'the three R's', also 'Silent Sisters', were returned. All are widows of former TDs… They are obedient party women and have never shown any interest in questions affecting women.[103]

One of Ireland's most prominent feminist activists with a background in the suffrage, nationalist and labour movements, Hanna Sheehy Skeffington had unsuccessfully contested the 1943 general election alongside three other independent women as part of a women's equality platform, with the ultimate aim of establishing a women's political party.[104] However, the national results suggested little appetite amongst women voters for feminist agendas in electoral politics, as all four lost and only one retained her deposit.[105] Like men, most women electors voted for established party candidates who worked to protect and further the interests of their constituency – in that sense, Bridget Redmond and other female backbench TDs were more representative of ordinary women than prominent feminists.

The efforts of women TDs must be placed 'in a context of a social and political life that was inimical to the participation of women'.[106] Women deputies prioritised constituency-related matters as opposed to issues of national concern – reflected in their lengthy political careers and notable electoral successes – but so did most male backbenchers.[107] These TDs provided a service that was expected of them by locals at a time when the Irish welfare state was still in development. The dearth of archival papers and personal correspondence that have survived from women TDs of this period means that scholars cannot quantify the impact of their constituency casework, but it is reasonable to assume that such efforts held significance in the everyday lives of many individuals and families. Despite not aligning with feminist concerns, they were likely attuned to the unique challenges that women living in their constituencies faced, including economic hardship and the bureaucratic hurdles in accessing public services. In relation to Bridget Redmond, the *Sunday Independent* made the following observation after she was returned by voters in the 1937 general election:

> Mrs Redmond – one of the two lady TDs in the new Dáil – topped the poll in Waterford. A great many TDs of other parties and not a few public servants were pleased with the people of Waterford for doing what they did. It was not that they were in favour of women on politics or anything like that. It was merely because Mrs Redmond's family [the Redmond dynasty] possesses certain specialised knowledge of interest to a numerous public and that Mrs Redmond is not adverse from assisting with advice when consulted.[108]

Historians have noted that none of the women TDs elected in the 1933 general election contributed to the debate about the Criminal Law (Amendment) Bill 1934, which addressed the issues of prostitution, contraception and the age of consent. Nor did they contribute to deliberations about the Conditions of Employment Bill 1935, which extended the marriage bar to the entire civil service (except for workers in the lower, highly feminised posts such as cleaners) and gave the government power to limit the number of women employed in any given industry.[109] Bridget Redmond did participate in the debates surrounding the new Constitution in 1937. Feminist campaigners denounced the document as 'sinister and retrogressive' regarding women's rights.[110] Among several concerning constitutional provisions[111], feminists feared that Section 16 could be used to justify the disenfranchisement of women based on 'incapacity' or 'disability'. Éamon de Valera stated that he had removed the phrase 'without the distinction of sex' (as in the 1922 Constitution) because he regarded it as a marker of women's previous inferiority as citizens, which he maintained no longer existed in the draft Constitution.[112] Deputations from women's organisations, including the Women Graduates' Association (WGA) and the Joint Committee of Women's Societies and Social Workers, met with the President of the Executive Council and the three women TDs to lobby for amendments.[113] The President of the Executive Council eventually re-inserted the clause into Article 16 after Bridget Redmond proposed an amendment for that purpose, but he believed it was redundant.[114] The Dáil debate suggests that she did so largely in response to the pressure exerted by the women's movement, rather than stemming from her own personal motivations.

> I thought it well to put down the amendment because certain fears were aroused amongst women's associations and amongst women generally throughout the country. Certainly, if nothing was meant by leaving it out, there is no reason why it should not be put in. I am glad the President has seen his way to accept it.[115]

Her amendment to Article 9 (that no citizen shall be placed by law under any such disability or incapacity by reason of sex, class, or religion) failed. She expressed a willingness to table further amendments, if necessary, to meet the points put to her by activists.[116] Margaret Ward describes her as 'a half-hearted fighter', and she made only short contributions to the debates; furthermore, most of the arguments in favour of her amendments were made by Dr Robert Rowlette who was an independent TD.[117] Nonetheless, Bridget Redmond was the only woman TD to propose amendments to the Constitution. Margaret Pearse of Fianna Fáil was 'present as voting fodder' only.[118] Her party colleague Helena Concannon, a member of the WGA, raised some of the women's concerns with de Valera but declared that she was assured by his explanations. However, she stressed the importance of including female voices in the constitutional debate.[119] As a member of the opposition, Bridget Redmond likely had more institutional capacity, if still highly constrained, to respond to feminist concerns than women TDs on the government benches. Helena Concannon informed the WGA that 'as a disciplined member of the Fianna Fáil party, she could not propose any amendments to the draft Constitution'.[120]

Electoral Record

Bridget Redmond, like her late father-in-law and husband, opted not to live in Waterford, maintaining her primary residence in Dublin. In contrast to many female colleagues in the Dáil, she did not pursue a local government seat. She made regular visits to the constituency, with a heightened presence during election campaigns, and played a role in maintaining the Redmond family's connections in the city. She successfully contested seven consecutive general elections, initially as a candidate for Cumann na nGaedheal in 1933, and subsequently as a Fine Gael nominee from 1937 to 1951, topping the poll on four occasions (see Table 1). Throughout Bridget Redmond's political career, the Fine Gael vote in Waterford consistently surpassed the party's national average. Her strongest electoral performance was in 1951, securing 24.6 per cent of the first preference vote in a contest with six candidates, all men, running for four seats – it would be her final election campaign. McDermott summarises the significance of her electoral success over two decades, particularly as a woman TD. She was, therefore, the highest vote-catcher of all the Waterford TDs during her twenty years as a public representative there. She was also the highest vote-catcher, and the youngest when first elected, of all the women elected to Dáil Éireann during the same period.[121]

Table 1: Bridget Redmond's electoral record in Waterford, 1933–52[128]

Date	Election	Party	Seat	Votes	% Share
1933	8th Dáil	Cumann na nGaedheal	1	6,864	17.72%
1937	9th Dáil	Fine Gael	3	8,254	20.43%
1938	10th Dáil	Fine Gael	2	7,514	18.12%
1943	11th Dáil	Fine Gael	2	7,765	19.59%
1944	12th Dáil	Fine Gael	1	8,061	21.61%
1948	13th Dáil	Fine Gael	1	6,810	19.63%
1951	14th Dáil	Fine Gael	1	8,372	24.59%

Conclusion: More than a Redmond

Bridget Redmond passed away on 3 May 1952 at her mother's home in Athgarvan, county Kildare. She was 47 and had been ill in the previous two years but kept this information private.[122] She had not spoken in the Dáil for over a year. There was an outpouring of grief in Waterford upon the news of her death, and, as was tradition, men from Ballybricken were pallbearers at her funeral. With no children to succeed her, Bridget Redmond's passing marked the conclusion of the Redmond dynasty in Waterford, which spanned six decades of dedicated public service by the family. This chapter illustrates that she recognised the great symbolism attached to her election, actively working to nurture this local political heritage.

However, historical research has often tended to downplay the contributions of the 'Dáil widows', such as Bridget Redmond, by construing them solely as successors to men's political legacies with a narrow on constituency matters. For example, McElroy describes the women TDs of this period as 'honorary men'[123] and Manning, drawing on Mac Curtain's assessment, similarly concludes that:

> Thus, in the half century of independence, the impact of women on Irish politics in both numerical representation and quality of that representation has been slight. Indeed, it is difficult to ignore the judgment of one leading feminist and historian, Dr Margaret Mac Curtain, who wrote in 1978: 'Irish women in post-revolutionary Ireland did not make political traditions; they inherited them from fathers, husbands and brothers'.[124]

Both Sinéad McCoole and McGing have advocated for a re-appraisal of women parliamentarians during the early decades of the Irish state, arguing that they had to negotiate a political system that was becoming increasingly localised and patriarchal.[125] Women TDs who represented dynasties found themselves in dual roles, serving as political insiders because of a family connection and outsiders due to their gender identity; their lineage allayed some of the tensions surrounding the participation and representation of women in public life.[126]

As discussed, the fact that so little archival documentation has survived about these women suppresses their visibility further. This detailed examination of one of the women, Bridget Redmond, demonstrates that she was a multifaceted politician, surpassing the role of solely a torchbearer for the Redmond dynasty. Despite her lack of political experience before 1932, she successfully carved out a space for herself in politics by straddling the ideological divide and actively participating in the redevelopment of her constituency party organisation. Though often overlooked by modern historians, her peers acknowledged her as a talented and measured orator. Her parliamentary contributions encompassed various issues, primarily focused on advancing society for the lower and middle classes. Bridget Redmond infrequently advocated for gender equality, much to the disappointment of feminist campaigners, but her perspectives on women's roles likely mirrored the prevailing conservative attitudes within Irish society. Like other deputies in the house, female and male, she placed a strong emphasis on constituency casework. While this work may not be quantifiable in the same way as parliamentary debates, it is this aspect of her role where she likely had the most significant impact on the everyday lives of her constituents. Her assiduous record of local service saw her continuously re-elected, even as her political party's fortunes waxed and waned. As an obituary in the *Leinster Leader* remarked:

> The extent of her good work in Waterford and Kildare will perhaps never be measured but there are many in both counties who can thank the good offices of the late Mrs Redmond for something which had helped to ease the burden of life. It would be idle, too, to attempt to

measure the value of her presence in the Dáil. She figured little in the reports of debates but on all sides of the House she was recognised as a most able deputy and one who served her constituents to the maximum.[127]

Further in-depth studies examining Bridget Redmond's female counterparts in the Oireachtas, especially the widows, would be very instructive; they were elected during a 'dark age' for women's political and social equality yet cultivated long political careers. In recent years, commemorative events to mark the birth and formative years of the Irish Free State have raised important questions regarding the rollback of women's citizenship rights in the new state. As part of this endeavor, there is a need to re-evaluate the contributions of the early generations of women politicians, and this chapter has assisted with this reassessment.

CHAPTER 9

THE CONTRADICTIONS OF REDMONDISM

Paul Bew

The conventional dismissal of John Redmond has disappeared from mainstream attitudes and assumptions. Not that long ago, Charles Haughey in his speech to Ógra Fianna Fáil, referred to the Irish Parliamentary Party 'so degrading the political process that no man or woman of sensitivity or idealism could have any part of it'.[1] It is amusing to think of Haughey being an arbiter of men and women of sensitivity and idealism and their involvement in the political process. However, he also went on to say, and I will return to this point later, because this is a real point of substance, to ask this question: 'Did the utmost conciliation of John Redmond, for instance, make any difference to the Ulster Unionists?'[2]

The title of this chapter is 'The Contradictions of Redmondism', and what I want to say about that is that the contradictions of Redmondism, in many respects, mirror the contradictions of Parnellism. On the 150th anniversary of Parnell's birth, I wrote a piece for the *Sunday Tribune*, and the very snappy editor, Joe Jordan, put a title on the piece, much snappier than anything in my article, in which he said 'The Chief: a Republican Revolutionary or a Tory Landlord'. I am one of those historians who has emphasised the conservative streak in Parnell's political makeup, especially after 1882 and after his period of imprisonment.[3] I don't resile from that, but there is also a revolutionary side to Parnellism, and that's a real part of the tradition as well, and of the contradictions of Redmondism, particularly in the early phase of Redmond's career — 'Redmond the Parnellite', as Dermot Meleady quite correctly calls volume one of his excellent two-volume biography.[4] The contradictions of Redmond's career embody, to some degree, reproductions of contradictions in Parnell's career. When Parnell becomes involved in the Land Question, most moderate nationalists, and this certainly includes the Redmond family and Redmond's father, regard him with horror as a disconnected young Protestant 'who does not get it'. They think that Parnell is hanging out with some very hard guys indeed and it is not just a matter of association with neo-Fenian/Fenian types rather than respectable politicians, but that he is caught up in a strategy. These people (the neo-Fenians) are not interested just in the Land Question, they are interested in having a very militant agitation on the Land Question, which will then raise the National Question, and possibly lead to insurrection or at least a withdrawal of Irish MPs from Parliament, and that, by the way, was very much the view of the Redmond family. John and Willie Redmond, with some difficulty, broke with this in the early 1880s. John's mother, Mary, in particular, of course, a Protestant who converted to Catholicism, did not convert to nationalism. This is the whole point about Parnell; indeed, one will not understand Parnell and his significance if one does not understand why the owner of the *Freeman's Journal*, in April 1880, a moderate Catholic nationalist, regarded him with horror. It is because of his entanglement, not just with a certain type of person, but with a well-advertised political project.[5]

I argued, and Patrick Maume subsequently produced further documentary evidence of the sort,[6] for the possibility at least that Parnell did swear himself or was sworn into the IRB, in a very kind of notional way, at a point when he was, as it were, trying to move to the right, but reassure hard men of his intentions on the eve of the Phoenix Park Murders. But, while there is significant evidence that this could well have happened, I do not think it happened as an endorsement of radical republicanism. It happened as an attempt, to borrow a phrase from the Northern Ireland Peace Process, as 'a confidence building measure'. According to the account we have, Parnell insisted his membership would remain secret. But nonetheless Parnell also, it is clear, did seek, and intensely sought during the negotiations with Gladstone on the first Home Rule bill, to find a way out for Irish landlords. His vision more broadly was, that if you could solve the Land Question, you might get more landlords and more people like himself, of respectability, joining the nationalist movement. If that happened it would certainly be a good thing for the nationalist movement, and indeed would create a greater possibility of the actual concession of Home Rule on a sound basis.[7] Redmond reproduced many of these assumptions. Some correspondence of Harold Spender, the pro-Home Rule journalist, are reproduced in Meleady's selection of Redmond's letters.[8] Spender wrote this just shortly after Redmond's death: 'Like all landlords, Redmond could not put aside entirely the clan feeling for his own class. There he was a true follower of Parnell. Right through the heart of the nationalist fight, Parnell was always held back by a strain of sympathy for the landlords'.[9]

This becomes particularly clear in Parnell's various speeches on the Land Question in the last year of his political career, and at that point nationalists openly said, 'well there you are, you see that he is, at the end of the day, just a landlord publicist'.

Redmond, in my view, is correctly summed up by Harold Spender. As the 1880s move on, into the 1890s, it is perfectly clear and 'Redmond the Parnellite' (to use Meleady's phrase)[10] echoes these themes, the revolutionary themes, for example. Parnell's last speech in Parliament was a plea, even at the end, for amnesty for those involved in Irish dynamite activities. That is his very last speech. In 1893, John Morley, who has just become Chief Secretary, wrote to Redmond, 'What can I do, to get a peaceful winter in Ireland?', and Redmond replied, sorry, 'to deal with the dynamite question?', 'Amnesty — Amnesty — Amnesty!'.[11] So there is an echo there of that side of the Parnellite tradition.

The Spectator, for example, in 1894, quite respected Redmond, in London, noted 'Parnellism is pure separatism' and that is all it is. But it is not all it is, and we can see this very clearly in the characteristic positions Redmond starts to take up. There is a hint of this already in 1886 when Redmond, who has married into an Irish-Australian family, said during the Home Rule debate, that he 'thinks it would be a sad thing if the councils of Ireland are ever completely withdrawn from that of the Empire, to which the Irish have done so much to build up', and that is because he knew from his first wife's family, how successful and important Irish-Australians have become. There is a hint there, of what then is more marked in the 1890s, a move away from something that you could call, in the *Spectator*'s phrase, pure 'separatism'.[12] This is shown by his support for and involvement in Horace Plunkett's Recess Committee, when he worked with unionists on common matters concerned, particularly about agricultural policy. The Recess Committee is a very important moment, as is Redmond's attitude when the Second Home Rule bill is thrown out. At that point, it would have been quite a natural thing for Irish nationalists to say 'well, we should ally with the English democracy and radicals to destroy the House of Lords, which alone has stopped Home Rule being implemented. We should ally with those people'. Redmond took the position that the real problem is not the House of Lords, the real problem is the division of the Irish people, and that's the pressing question that has to be addressed. He follows this up in 1897/1898, when Irish local government is democratised by the Tories, and Redmond says; 'Look, in most parts of Ireland we can ensure the election of nationalist candidates, but actually we should not use our vote solely for this purpose, where there are local figures who have a public spirited record, even though they are not nationalists, we should actually vote for them, and allow some of those people to be elected and be part of the new local government system in Ireland, and it's how we should use our democratic weight'.[13] It was known as the policy of toleration — not popular with most nationalists, not even actually popular among some Parnellites, and it is one of the policy positions which leads to the erosion of Redmond's position as the independent leader of the Parnellite minority.

The big thing that really leads to the erosion of his position is William O'Brien launching the United Irish League in 1898. O'Brien siphons off families like the Haydens (who were still close to Redmond by 1914), but they all feel that they must join William O'Brien, the Fitzgibbons, rural Parnellites, not Dublin Parnellites, which is the biggest single element. Rural Parnellism is siphoned off by William O'Brien's United Irish League, and Parnellism as an independent national force, really ceased to exist in 1900, and it is one of the reasons why the Parnellites are prepared to cast around for unity, because the possibility that they might become the hegemonic force in parliamentary nationalism has gone forever, and therefore some compromised unity is going to occur, some compromise candidate. In the end it is Redmond who becomes Chairman of the Party, in a situation when probably, the loyalty of perhaps almost 40 MPs, is as much to Dillon than it is to Redmond, but this is the compromise that has been reached. It was always a difficult management task running that party. When the Wyndham Land Act comes in in 1903, Redmond thinks it is wonderful. This is the end of this awful Land Question which has divided Ireland, and the chance again, to bring landlords and the upper classes over to the nationalist side. He immediately enters into dialogue with leading figures in landlord opinion. His correspondence is exultant, that this is wonderful benign reform which will take the Land Question out of Irish politics. The problem is that the majority of Irish MPs have made their political careers in movements like the Land League and the United Irish League, and they are very reluctant to give up the Land Question, and they are very reluctant to say that it is substantially solved, and they insist, they insist that there are also remaining areas of genuine grievance. The problem with that is, that the Land Question is sufficiently solved with the Wyndham Land Act of 1903, that any further attempt to maintain agitation on the Land Question in the countryside will set nationalists against nationalists. It is no longer going to be as clear-cut as a campaign against the landlord class, because the landlord class is clearly on the way out, and the issues now become the amount of land any good nationalist should be legitimately allowed to control. And so, when the party decides to maintain the Land War, it is an understandable decision, but it is not without its downside, and it is not without its divisive side, for the cohesive functioning of Irish nationalism.[14] Redmond did not want to go down that road, of what became the Ranch War,[15] but he was effectively dragged, reluctantly, down that road.

In 1907, when devolution was on offer, there is equally no doubt that Redmond is tempted by working with the grain of that Liberal concession, and equally no doubt that, in the end, he puts in a motion, feeling the mood of the convention, and this is found in Laurence Ginnell's diary, one of the great radical ranch warriors of this period. Redmond puts down a motion rejecting the Irish Council Bill.[16] It is obvious that Redmond was personally very sympathetic to it. In all this time, Redmond continues to make speeches. There are occasionally flashes of a return to the Redmond who said 'Amnesty, Amnesty, Amnesty' for the dynamitards, but mostly the tone of what he is saying is one of conciliation with Britain and with the British polity. It is very clear that his vision of Home Rule assumes that Irish MPs should remain at Westminster, and that this is not the worst outcome — that is a good outcome in his view. In other words, it is effectively the solution that Scotland has had in the last decade and a half or more since Tony Blair brought in devolution. Scottish MPs have remained in the London Parliament, but also have their own Parliament. For Redmond, and this is very important also for his views on how the north might be solved, this is a positive thing, not a failure to Home Rule or a blight. The retention of Irish MPs at Westminster would be fundamentally a good thing, reflecting the connections that truly exist, because he thinks that Home Rule is a debt owed to history. As he says, 'we must be a truthful and honourable people'.[17] I am not sure it is a very good thing to advise an Irish audience that it must be truthful and honourable, and say we are a truthful and honourable people, but we have got the land back, we have got education reforms. This is what he says in 1915: we have got these things. What we have not got yet is self-government, and that is a debt owed to history that must be paid. Once it is paid, the conflict with English democracy is over. Full stop. Finished. The conflict with Britain is over. Finished.

That is not how many people in Ireland naturally viewed it. But that is how he naturally viewed this question. It is a debt owed to history, it must be resolved, but once resolved you are in a totally new situation, including if the Irish Party should disappear. So, when people said to Redmond 'you know your party members are all, sort of, nasty hacks and agrarian agitators and not very talented people. Where are the businessmen? Where are the scientists of Ireland? Where are the really creative people in Ireland in your party? They are not there'. Redmond said 'I agree. Yeah, they are a bit like that. It's a party machine. You've got to build it up. That's what party machines are like. They're run by people like that. But once we achieve self-government, the people who govern Ireland, will all be, once they're reconciled to it, like the fine minds in the Royal Irish Academy and so on'. They are the people who run the country. Redmond's discussion of the proposed Upper House in home rule polity led D. P. Moran to say, 'is the end of home rule to be that the Unionists are to run the country?'.[18] But Redmond is absolutely clear: the Irish Party shall disappear. You can say it is likely to be as much of a myth as the disappearance of the state in Marxist theory, but he did believe in the disappearance of the party upon the achievement of Home Rule.[19]

In his interviews with A. G. Gardiner, it is perfectly clear the way in which the balance of his thinking is: that there is no racial agenda of any sort, there is no sense that any further long-term grievance of history which justifies Anglophobia.[20] This is the clue to his approach to the Home Rule crisis and it is, of course, his approach to the decision, in the end fatal, to support the British war effort.

Redmond's cast of mind is unambiguous as time goes on, and the balance between that, and the occasional flashback to what you might call Parnellite republicanism, is rare. There is a moment, he is reported, as late as November 1910 in the *Irish World*, 'we can get Home Rule and then we can go get more', and F. E. Smith makes a big fuss about this.[21] There is a controversy in English papers. And Redmond is really upset about this claim. Now he had said things like that in the 1890s, but that he would have said in 1910, is something which obviously, the claim that he had said it as late as that, sends him completely crazy, and he says things like 'there is not a syllable of truth in this claim that I said this in 1910'. Because his vision is that what you are moving into is a different phase, and it is a vision of Home Rule not unlike the Scottish vision of a century later.

It is often said about this period 'if only we'd had Home Rule, we'd have avoided the Troubles and the violence and the sectarianism, and if only the unionist position… was different' — a position Roy Foster suggested 'ludicrously extreme in retrospect' in opposing the moderate demand for Home Rule.[22] However, Foster wrote that in 1988. Today when we have had experience of Scottish devolution, we know two things: devolution does not automatically siphon off people demanding full independence, and pushing very hard for it, number one. And secondly: the actual basis of Scottish nationalism, which I do not wish to insult, is different. The real grievances flowing into it are trivial, compared to the deeper historical basis of Irish nationalism. So, we know that in the case of Scottish nationalism, where fundamentally, for example, one could make the case that Irish Catholics got something out of empire, but they certainly did not get anything as much as Scots did, in general, out of empire. So, there is no question, that the broad historical weight of grievance of Irish nationalism is far stronger, than that that feeds into Scottish nationalism. Even so, the Scottish Referendum of 2014 was a close-run thing.

It is quite important when you look at what Carson and the unionists say, and what W. F. Monypenny says, as well as what other unionist writers and thinkers of this period say. They say there is no guarantee, if you concede a Dublin Parliament, we suddenly enter a world of harmony. Redmond said we will, but it is perfectly obvious, and Wheatley is very clear on this – Redmond's conciliatory discourse is not the discourse of mainstream nationalism, even before the change of 1916.[23]

I want to conclude by saying a few things about what is living and what is dead in the thinking of John Redmond. In the early 1990s, mid-90s even, I was trying to say in my book, *Ideology and the Irish Question* and the Redmond biography,[24] I was of the view that it was an inadequate way to look at Redmond, to say that the era of Redmond closed with his death in 1918, or indeed at the point in which the Irish Parliamentary Party was eclipsed.[25] I believe, myself, it was alive and well on the eve of the Easter Rising, but it was dead at the end of Easter week. It is as simple as that. There are so many reasons for saying this. The by-elections between the outbreak of war and the Easter Rising were not good performances in nationalist Ireland for the Parliamentary Party, but every single one was run by someone claiming to be a Redmondite.[26] So it is not impressive, and there was evidence of radicals doing quite well, but every single one before the Easter Rising is won by somebody called a Redmondite. The common perception may be that Redmond was betrayed by everybody: the Ulster Unionists, the English Liberals. Redmond at the beginning of 1916, even after the amount of slaughter that there had already been. The loss of, really, the flower of a lot of Dublin moderate nationalism and unionism at Gallipoli, really a lot of chaps who had been the core of either a moderate nationalist or moderate unionist disposition, at Gallipoli.[27] Even after huge losses like that, Redmond is still sitting there, talking to Michael MacDonagh,[28] as a man who is sure he is on a road to victory, that the policy is right, there was no alternative to the policy — as every Constitutional National leader has said, you must give Home Rule to Ireland because we will back you in an international crisis, and then he had not backed England in an international crisis, what would that have said? Not just for his own word, but the word of the constitutional movement over several decades. He had no doubt the Germans were wrong, having a niece who was a nun in Catholic Belgium was part of this, but he had absolutely no doubt that the honour of the rationalist movement required support for the British war effort, and if you allowed the unionists, simply, to garner all the credit for coming to support that war effort, you would therefore insure yourself, when the war was over, whatever the final compromise was, the worst possible terms that you would actually get.

It is very important to understand that point. It is very important that Redmond felt strong enough to turn down the offer of a position in the cabinet. This is what is so striking, in 1915 when people talk about the Coalition Government and Carson coming in and saying it is unbalanced, it is an insult to Catholic Ireland. They offered Redmond a position in the Cabinet. It is such a striking moment: some young man is sent down to Aghavannagh, breathlessly pounding down to the lodge castle,[29] bangs on the door, and the cook runs in to the back and says 'Mr Redmond! Mr Redmond! They've come to arrest you!' and he says, 'No, actually, I don't think so, let him in', and the chap comes in hot and bothered and says 'Will you serve in the cabinet?', and he says 'No' because it is a Parnellite principle, that until Home Rule is actually granted, rather than promised on the statute book, then you won't actually serve in a cabinet.[30] D. P. Moran always said it was a mistake, because what it meant was, that Redmond had the apparent responsibility for the conduct of the war effort, and all the downsides, the insults to nationalist sentiment, or apparent insults to nationalist sentiment.[31] There was a feeling that Wheatley referred to as the unionists being held back from the worst of the fighting at the front.[32] Even when unionists were slaughtered at the Somme, nationalist sentiment did not change. Nobody ever said in the Dublin newspapers 'Oh we were wrong about that one, they were not holding them back so that they could just be ready to fight us in Belfast at a later date'. They were just slaughtered, that was it. It is very important to notice, opinions form about what is happening, then when it turns out it was something else. In the wider world people do not really change their mind about it. But the point is, there was a feeling that the war was being conducted in a way which was insensitive to nationalist Ireland, and Redmond lost, Moran rightly says, the ability to be seen to be influencing it, or be closer to this, by turning down the position.[33] But this shows Redmond would have felt strong, and it is up until the eve of Easter Week he feels the by-elections are just about okay, they are not perfect.

One reason it was not perfect is the Land Question is largely solved, and it was the farmers who gave the United Irish League branches their vitality. So, you are just not going to get so many people turning up to meetings. And he took that as normal, and not that worrying. This was the situation for Redmond, who is destroyed by the Easter Rising, and it became commonplace to say, 'that's the end of his story'. I argued in the 1990s that it is not as simple as that. To take one point in case, Redmond's proposed solution for partition was, in the end, to accept some form of partition. Now, he probably did this too slowly—that's Stephen Gwynn's argument, 'Do the big thing in Ireland. Make the big generous offer upfront, quick, and if you do it, you will impress people'.[34] What happened to Redmond is that he was dragged into accepting what we call 'the principle of consent' in 1914. So, Stephen Gwynn's argument in his great book on Redmond's last years, was that Redmond, in April 1914, should have just called Carson's bluff and said 'okay, I accept'. What Redmond then eventually said, in Parliament, openly in the middle of September 1914, that he, 'did not believe that any county in Ireland which had a majority against the Dublin Parliament, should be forced to go under a Dublin Parliament', which he eventually said publicly.[35] Had he said this earlier, you then open a debate about exactly what is the size of the excluded area? Six counties, in the end, is not the happy solution, because many nationalists were included where they did not want to be, and also in the case in certain parts of Donegal, many unionists were included in a place that they did not want to be. You open up the possibility of a compromise agreement. Much more subtle. And in Redmond's vision it would, of course, have been direct rule. This is what he was discussing with the Liberal Government of the day. It would have been direct rule, supervised by the Irish MPs, possibly members of the Irish cabinet who remain at Westminster, and therefore the fairest possible deal for the Catholic minority in the north. And you can say Redmond failed on partition but, as John Bruton pointed out so eloquently,[36] for one 100 years, other traditions have taken over and they have still failed. So that is not a killing point against Redmond. Redmond was not offering a solution to partition; he was offering the best possible and most benign and fairest compromise to the rights that exist on all sides. And that is what his thinking was. My argument in the early 90s was that, in a way, the Anglo-Irish Agreement of 1985,[37] in some ways reproduced that model – it was 'Direct Rule with a green tinge',[38] the Anglo Irish-Agreement had an Irish nationalist input into the operation of Direct Rule, and this is probably, from the point of view of a northern nationalist identity, the fairest thing that you could do. My argument then was that Redmondism in that way was not dead, but actually alive.

But now we are in a new moment. Brexit has changed things. In 1996, there was a vigorous *Irish Times* editorial defence of John Bruton, for being associated with the Redmond tradition, and the editorial stated, 'the things that Redmond brought to the table, of moderation, pragmatism, these are the skills which are required if we are going to achieve accommodation'.[39] These are the skills which are actually required, so it's entirely right that John Bruton had this interest in John Redmond. There is a tradition here you can draw upon. And then I look at Serjeant A. M. Sullivan saying, about Redmond, 'He was slow, cautious, cynical, with a prejudice in favour of truth that was almost English'.[40] And ironically of all the *Irish Times* editorials about Brexit in 2017 and 2018 none expressed classic Redmondite respect for English respect for truth. In that moment, by definition, the English political class lost truth after Brexit, as anyone who reads large sections of the Irish media will have discovered. And I understand the temper on this — I was a Remain voter myself, but we are now at a very dangerous point with this. This is now, very, very advanced. So let me explain why.

The *Irish Times* was right, in the mid-90s, right in the first place. Redmond's virtues are appropriate. The avoidance of Anglophobia on a massive scale, which Irish nationalism can easily fall into, is desirable and defensible. Redmond, as a man, had an intuition here that is to be defended. But, most of all, the Agreement itself, and the process of David Trimble's leading into a phase that could only have been constructed, in part, because John Bruton was Taoiseach, and because there was a Cabinet there which opened up lines of communication to the north. I say this with all respect to Bertie Ahern, who also did an excellent job when he became Taoiseach in 1997. However, without the steps that John Bruton took in the first place, you would not actually have got a Good Friday Agreement.[41] The essence of this was, what Trimble called 'ending the Cold War between North and South'.[42] Now the danger, at the moment, we are in, and this is why I wonder whether the time of Redmond is now over and dead, is that the cold war between North and South has reopened to an incredible degree as a side effect of Brexit. Not totally to my surprise, and I understand aspects of this, but it is extremely dangerous. Far more dangerous than hypothetical issues about this or that, or ongoing arguments concerning Brexit arrangements and the Irish border. Far too much talk about that as a problem, and not enough talk about the profound danger, which is that the cold war is being reopened in a way that it was not since the mid-90s between North and South. That is the real danger, and that is the position that we are now in, and I understand completely, the frustrations which exist about Brexit, and that are bound to exist within Irish public opinion.

In conclusion, there is a defence of Redmondism surviving after its substantive political execution in the Easter Rising, and the defence was easy enough to make in the 1990s. The European Union did other things for Ireland that Redmond wanted Britain to do. One was to subsidise it. It did, for some considerable time, provide financial support. When Redmond stands behind Churchill in Belfast in February 1912, Churchill gets up and he says, Britain was 'at the moment paying on the balance... a subsidy to Ireland ... which equals the sum of £2,000,000 a year' including paying for the old age pensions.[43] He then goes on to say, 'the separation of Ireland from Great Britain is absolutely impossible. The interests and affairs of the two islands are eternally interwoven. The whole tendency of things. The whole inevitable drift of things, is towards a more intimate association'.[44] Is that true today? I do not think so. Not when I pick up any Irish newspaper. 'The whole tendency of things. The whole inevitable drift of things is towards a more intimate association. The economic dependence of Ireland on England is absolute and quite apart from moral, military, and constitutional arguments, the two nations are bound together till the end of time, by the national force of circumstance'.[45] That's what Churchill said, but Redmond gets up and says 'I accept every word of it' and 'I accept all that he has said, and with reference to the safeguards that he has announced will be inserted into the Home Rule bill, I accept every one of them'.[46] There's a logic here. Who is going to pay for the old age pensions after Home Rule unless it is the British Treasury? And so on. It is perfectly obvious. There is a logic here, but are we living in this moment? There is another problem, of course, that there always has been a consistent republican tradition against this, but it is one that genuinely believed in the case of Connolly or Casement, that Germany represented something more progressive, more civilised, more advanced. Now actually, that is a logical position to hold against Redmond's position. Redmond would have regarded such a view as patently absurd. Redmond could hardly have given that argument even a serious thought. But Connolly believed it and gave it plenty of serious thought, and so did Casement. The real question for Ireland now is, in the moment that it is in, is it going to give it a serious thought? Because there is one thing to be Anglophobic, and another thing to actually endorse more positively the leadership of Europe and different alliances for Ireland than those it has effectively had for much of the recent decades.

Notes

INTRODUCTION

1. Nicholas Mansergh, 'John Redmond' in Conor Cruise O'Brien (ed.), *The Shaping of Modern Ireland* (London, 1960) cited in Diana Mansergh (ed.) *Nationalism and Independence: Selected Irish Papers by Nicholas Mansergh* (Cork, 1997), p. 31.
2. Dermot Meleady, *John Redmond: The National Leader* (Dublin, 2013), p. 456.
3. Michael Laffan, 'Illustrious corpses: Burying Irish nationalist heroes', in Wolfgang Marx (ed.), *Who Telleth a Tale of Unspeaking Death? Dublin Death Studies II* (Dublin, 2017), pp 7–30.
4. Martin O'Donoghue, 'The renewal of a pledge of faith? John Redmond days in the south-east in the 1920s', *History Ireland*, vol. 23, no. 1 (2015), pp 38–41.
5. Mansergh, 'John Redmond', p. 23.
6. While the first volume of Meleady's biography characterised Redmond as 'the Parnellite', detailed comparative studies have not abounded with Parnell alternatively compared with Daniel O'Connell or Edward Carson, R. F. Foster and Alvin Jackson, 'Men for all seasons? Carson, Parnell, and the limits of heroism in modern Ireland', *European History Quarterly*, vol. 39, no. 3 (2009), pp 414–36; Oliver MacDonagh, 'O'Connell and Parnell' in Joep Leerssen (ed.), *Parnell and his Times* (Cambridge, 2021), pp 21–35. On a comparison between Isaac Butt and Redmond, see Pauline Collombier-Lakeman, 'Comparing Isaac Butt and John Redmond', *Review of Irish Studies in Europe* vol. 3, no. 2 (2020), pp 6-23.
7. Simon Carswell, 'The shape of the 33rd Dáil: Gender and age', *Irish Times*, 14 February 2020 https://www.irishtimes.com/news/politics/the-shape-of-the-33rd-dail-gender-and-age-1.4172965 (12 Feb. 2023). See also the work of Claire McGing, in particular; Lisa Keenan and Claire McGing, '"An unfinished democracy": Gender and political representation in the Republic of Ireland', *Irish Political Studies*, vol. 37 (2022), pp 467–76.
8. James McConnel, *The Irish Parliamentary Party and the Third Home Rule Crisis* (Dublin, 2013); Conor Mulvagh, *The Irish Parliamentary Party at Westminster, 1900*–1918 (Manchester, 2016); Paul Bew, *Ideology and the Irish Question: Ulster Unionism and Irish Nationalism, 1912-1916* (Oxford, 1994); Martin O'Donoghue, *The Legacy of the Irish Parliamentary Party in Independent Ireland, 1922–1949* (Liverpool, 2019); Pat McCarthy, *The Redmonds and Waterford: A Political Dynasty, 1891–1952* (Dublin, 2018); Colin Reid, *The Lost Ireland of Stephen Gwynn: Irish Constitutional Nationalism and Cultural Politics, 1864–1950* (Manchester, 2011); Michael Wheatley, *Nationalism and the Irish Party: Provincial Ireland, 1910–1916* (Oxford, 2005); and Paul Bew, *Ancestral Voices in Irish Politics: Judging Dillon and Parnell* (Oxford, 2023). Most recently, how people envisaged what a home rule 'future' would look like was the subject of Pauline Collombier's monograph, *Imagining Ireland's Future: Home Rule, Utopia, Dystopia* (London, 2023).
9. F. S. L. Lyons, *Ireland Since the Famine* (London, 1971); *The Irish Parliamentary Party, 1890–1910* (London, 1951); *John Dillon: A Biography* (London, 1968); *Charles Stewart Parnell* (Dublin, 2005); T. W. Moody, *Davitt and Irish Revolution, 1846–82* (Oxford, 1981); Paul Bew, *Conflict and Conciliation in Ireland, 1890–1910: Parnellites and Radical Agrarians* (Oxford, 1987); D. S. Jones, *Graziers, Land Reform and Political Conflict in Ireland* (Washington, D.C., 1995). While much of this work was published in the second half of the twentieth century, more recent work on Davitt has also appeared: Laurence Marley, *Michael Davitt: Freelance Radical and Frondeur* (Dublin, 2007) and Carla King, *Michael Davitt after the Land League* (Dublin, 2016).
10. As Colin Reid discusses later in this volume, Isaac Butt has been relatively neglected; however, prior to Reid's recent work, Butt was the subject of study by Terence de Vere White, *The Road of Excess* (Dublin, 1946) and David Thornley, *Isaac Butt and Home Rule* (London, 1964).
11. Alvin Jackson, *Home Rule: An Irish History* (London, 2003).
12. Senia Pašeta, '1798 in 1898: The politics of commemoration', *The Irish Review*, 22 (Cork), pp 46–53, pp 49–50.

13. James McConnel, '"Fenians at Westminster": The Edwardian Irish Parliamentary Party and the legacy of the New Departure', *Irish Historical Studies*, vol. 34, no. 133 (May 2004), pp 42–64. Gerard MacAtasney, *Tom Clarke: Life, Liberty, Revolution* (Sallins, 2013), pp 41–2.

14. MacAtasney, *Tom Clarke*, p. 50. See also Letter from John Redmond M.P. to Tom Clarke, supporting Clarke's candidacy for the clerkship in Rathdown Union, 26 May 1899, National Library of Ireland (NLI) Tom Clarke and Kathleen Clarke Papers MS 49,354/5/4. Thanks to Brian Hanley for suggesting this source.

15. *Freeman's Journal*, 5 September 1907. Thanks to Brian Hanley for pointing out this source.

16. O'Brien was driven out of the party after attack from AOH members at the infamous 'Baton Convention' of the UIL in 1909. The AOH also attacked a Sunday school party at Castledawson during the Ulster crisis in 1912, see Martin O'Donoghue, '"Faith and Fatherland?" The Ancient Order of Hibernians, Northern Nationalism and the Partition of Ireland', *Irish Historical Studies*, vol. 46, no. 169 (May 2022), pp 77–100, pp 82–3.

17. Jackson, this volume, p. 49. See also Meleady, *Redmond: The Parnellite*, p. 121.

18. Brian Farrell (ed.), *The Irish Parliamentary Tradition (with Three Essays on the Treaty by F. S. L. Lyons)* (Dublin, 1973).

19. Conor Cruise O'Brien, *Parnell and his Party 1880–90* (Oxford, 1957).

20. For earlier work, see Stephen Gwynn, *John Redmond's Last Years* (London, 1919); Denis Gwynn, *The Life of John Redmond* (London, 1932); Paul Bew, *John Redmond* (Dundalk, 1996).

21. On O'Connell, see Patrick Geoghegan's magisterial two-volume biography, *King Dan: The Rise of Daniel O'Connell, 1775–1829* (Dublin, 2008); *Liberator: The Life and Death of Daniel O'Connell, 1830–1847* (Dublin, 2010); Seán McMahon, *Daniel O'Connell* (Dublin, 2000); Leslie A. Williams, *Daniel O'Connell, The British Press and The Irish Famine: Killing Remarks* (London, 2003); R. V. Comerford and Enda Delaney (eds), *National Questions: Reflections on Daniel O'Connell and Contemporary Ireland* (Dublin, 2000). On Parnell, see Alan O'Day, *Charles Stewart Parnell* (Dundalk, 1998); Bew, *Enigma: A New Life of Charles Stewart Parnell* (Dublin, 2011); Bernadette Whelan, 'The transatlantic world of Charles Stewart Parnell (1846-91)', *Journal of Transatlantic Studies*, vol. 14, no. 3 (2016), pp 293–308; and Eugenio Biagini; Patrick Geoghegan, Hugh Hanley, Aneirin Jones, and Huw Jones, 'From sentiment to style: Charles Stewart Parnell's rhetoric in the first crisis of the UK', *Digital Scholarship in Humanities*, vol. 38, no. 2 (2023), pp 492–500.

22. R. B. McDowell, *Grattan: A Life* (Dublin, 2001). For a discussion of Grattan's memory and a call to reassert his importance, see Charles Lysaght, 'Henry Grattan looms large over modern Ireland', *Irish Times*, 4 June 2020.

23. Meleady, *John Redmond: The National Leader*; Meleady, *Redmond the Parnellite* (Cork, 2008); Joseph Finnan, *John Redmond and Irish Unity, 1912–1918* (NY, 2004); Paul Bew, *John Redmond* (Dundalk, 1996); Alvin Jackson, *Judging Redmond and Carson: Comparative Irish Lives* (Dublin, 2018). However, for a recent collection of thematic essays relating to the Parnell era, see Leerssen, *Parnell and his Times* (Cambridge, 2021).

24. Stephen Howe, *Ireland and Empire* (Oxford, 2000); For one of the best overviews of the debates, see Gearóid Ó Tuathaigh, 'Exemplar, outlier, impostor?: A reflection on Ireland and the discourses of colonialism', in Róisín Healy and Enrico dal Lago (eds), *The Shadow of Colonialism on Europe's Modern Past* (Basingstoke, 2014), pp 36–56. And most recently, Caoimhe Nic Dháibhéid, Shahmima Akhtar, Dónal Hassett, Kevin Kenny, Timothy McMahon and Jane Ohlmeyer, 'Round table: Decolonising Irish history? Possibilities, challenges, practices', in *Irish Historical Studies*, 159 (2021), pp 303–32.

25. James Doherty, *Irish Liberty, British Democracy: The Third Irish Home Rule Crisis, 1909–14* (Cork, 2019) and Ronan Fanning, *Fatal Path: British Government and Irish Revolution, 1910–1922* (London, 2013).

26. George Dangerfield, *The Strange Death of Liberal England* (London, 1935).

27. Eugenio Biagini, *British Democracy and Irish Nationalism 1876–1906* (Cambridge, 2007); Patricia Jalland, *The Liberals and Ireland: The Ulster Question in British Politics to 1914* (Sussex, 1980).

28. Mulvagh, *The Irish Parliamentary Party at Westminster*, p. 259.

29. O'Callaghan, this volume, pp [??].

30. Paul Townend, *The Road to Home Rule: Anti-Imperialism and the Irish National Movement* (Madison, WI, 2016). Mid-century Fenians had displayed a sense of the Irish as a conquered people though not necessarily 'colonised' as the idea of an Irish nation survived, Matthew Kelly, 'The *Irish People* and the disciplining of dissent' in James McConnel and Fearghal McGarry (eds), *The Black*

Hand of Republicanism: Fenianism in Modern Ireland (Dublin, 2009), pp 34-54.; 'Irish nationalist opinion and the British Empire in the 1850s and 1860s', *Past & Present*, no. 204 (2009), pp 127–54.
31. Speech of Isaac Butt, 'Proceedings of the Home Rule Conference held at the Rotunda, Dublin, on 18th, 19th, 20th, and 21st November 1873' (Dublin, 1874), p. 28.
32. Mansergh, 'John Redmond', p. 30. In reference to Louis Botha (1862–1919), first prime minister of the Union of South Africa, he had personally captured Winston Churchill during the Second Boer War. He became the first prime minister and later played full role in Empire.
33. John E. Redmond, 'Introduction' to Michael MacDonagh, *The Irish at the Front* (London, New York, Toronto, 1916), pp 1–14.
34. Wheatley, *Nationalism and the Irish Party: Provincial Ireland, 1910–1916* (Oxford, 2005); James McConnel: 'John Redmond and Irish Catholic Loyalism', *English Historical Review*, vol. 125, no. 512 (Feb. 2010), pp 83–111; Michael Wheatley, 'John Redmond and Federalism in 1910', *Irish Historical Studies*, vol. 32, no. 127 (May 2001), pp 343–64.
35. On this wider experience, see Timothy McMahon, Michael de Nie and Paul Townend (eds), *Ireland in an Imperial World: Citizenship, Opportunity and Subversion* (Basingstoke, 2017).
36. Michael Laffan, 'Redmond, John Edward', *Dictionary of Irish Biography* https://www.dib.ie/biography/redmond-john-edward-a7602 (10 Mar. 2023). On the concept of a 'revolutionary generation', see R. F. Foster, *Vivid Faces: The Revolutionary Generation in Ireland, 1890–1923* (London, 2014).
37. In James McConnel's view, the party was effectively 'petit bourgeois' for most part – despite provincial middle-class men in Ireland appearing poor in Britain. There were some working-class members from the 1880s, but the town tenants' organisations linked to the party still favoured small businesses, James McConnel, 'The Irish Parliamentary Party, industrial relations and the 1913 Dublin Lockout', *Saothar*, vol. 28 (2003), pp 25–36, pp 26–28.
38. Padraig Yeates, *Lockout: Dublin 1913* (Dublin, 2000), pp 573–6; Ciarán Wallace, 'Joseph P. Nannetti Lord Mayor 1906–08: A rather mild sort of rebel', in Lisa-Marie Griffith and Ruth McManus (eds), *Leaders of the City: Dublin's First Citizens, 1500–1950* (Dublin, 2012). Wheatley has shown regional variation e.g. in Sligo, many Hibernian-Labour followers went into Sinn Féin, Wheatley, *Nationalism and the Irish Party*, p. 111.
39. For example, see David Fitzpatrick, *Politics and Irish Life, 1913–21: Provincial Experience of War and Revolution* (Aldershot, 1977); Fergus Campbell, *Land and Revolution: Nationalist Politics in the West of Ireland 1891–1921* (Oxford, 2005); Marie Coleman, *County Longford and the Irish Revolution, 1910–1923* (Dublin, 2003); John Borgonovo, *The Dynamics of War and Revolution: Cork City 1916–1918* (Cork, 2013); Elaine Callinan, *Electioneering and Propaganda in Ireland, 1917–1922* (Dublin, 2020).
40. This point was made in respect of Redmond by Patrick Maume, 'Review of Meleady, *Redmond: The Parnellite*', *Irish Historical Studies*, vol. 36, no. 2 (November 2008), pp 283–4.
41. O'Donoghue, *The Legacy of the Irish Parliamentary Party*. See also Redmond's inclusion in Ciarán Brady (ed.), *Worsted in the Game? Losers in Irish History* (Dublin, 1989), and Finnan, *John Redmond and Irish Unity*.
42. Edward Madigan and John Horne (eds), *Towards Commemoration: Ireland in War and Revolution, 1912–1923* (Dublin, 2013).
43. 'Agency' has now long been a central concept in 'history from below' approaches that seek to broaden historical narratives beyond the powerful. Redmond though ostensibly powerful and a political leader faced 'constraints', as shown by O'Callaghan, occasioned by circumstances at home and Ireland's unusual position within the United Kingdom politically. On Thompson's use of the term and a recent commentary, see E. P. Thompson, *The Making of the English Working Class* (Harmondsworth, 1968); Dipesh Chakrabarty, 'The Lost causes of E. P. Thompson', in *Labour/Le Travail*, vol. 72 (Fall/Automne 2013), pp 207–12; Carl Grey Marin and Modhumita Roy, 'Narrative resistance: A conversation with historian Marcus Rediker', in *Workplace: A Journal For Academic Labor*, vol. 30 (2018), pp 54–69.
44. See for example, Samuel Moyn, 'Fantasies of federalism', *Dissent*, vol. 62, no.1 (Winter 2015), pp 145–51. For discussions on federalist thought in South Asia, Sarath Pillai, 'Fragmenting the nation: Divisible sovereignty and Travancore's quest for federal independence', in *Law and History Review*, vol. 34, no. 3 (2016), pp 743–82, and Priyasha Saksena, *Sovereignty, International Law and the Princely States of Colonial South Asia* (Oxford, 2023), especially chapters 4–5. On decolonisation and federalist

thought more generally, Michael Collins, 'Decolonisation and the "federal moment"', in *Diplomacy & Statecraft*, vol. 24, no.1 (2013), pp 21–40, and Adom Getachew, *Worldmaking after Empire: The Rise and Fall of Self-Determination* (Princeton, NJ, 2019).
45. Emmet Larkin, 'Church, state and nation in modern Ireland', in Larkin, *The Historical Dimensions of Irish Catholicism* (Washington DC, 1976), p. 110. Article first published in the *American Historical Review*, vol. 80 (1975), 1244–1276.
46. J. J. Lee, 'On the birth of the modern Irish state: The Larkin thesis' in Stewart J. Brown and David W. Miller (eds), *Piety and Power in Ireland, 1760–1960* (South Bend, IN, 2000), pp 130–57. Under Redmond's leadership in 1901, the Irish Party did, however, resist 'an attempt to remove the exemption from inspection of Irish convent laundries – the Magdalen laundries', Meleady, *Redmond: The National Leader*, p. 26. On the chairman/chief dichotomy in Irish politics, see Brian Farrell (ed.), *Chairman or Chief?: The Role of Taoiseach in Irish Government* (Dublin, 1971).
47. Ward, this volume, p. 64.
48. Alice McDermott, 'Bridget Redmond: The keeper of the Redmondite flame in Waterford' in *Decies*, 66 (2010) pp 87–102; McCarthy, *The Redmonds and Waterford*.
49. Bew, 'The contradictions of Redmondism', this volume, p. 111.
50. Paul Bew, 'John E. Redmond, 1856–1918', *Oxford Dictionary of National Biography* (Oxford, 2004). In 1996, Bew had referred to them as the 'great prickly personalities', *John Redmond*, pp 24–5; Michael Laffan, *DIB* entry republished in Laurence White and James Quinn (eds), *1916: Portraits and Lives* (Dublin, 2015), pp 271–87. See more recently Conor Mulvagh, 'A souring of friendships?: Internal divisions in the leadership of the Irish Parliamentary Party in the aftermath of the Easter Rising', in Diarmaid Ferriter and Susanah Riordan (eds), *Years of Turbulence: The Irish Revolution and its Aftermath* (Dublin, 2015), pp 85–105; in particular, p. 85: 'Redmond, as chairman, was the titular leader of the party. However, Redmond was not a chief in the way Charles Stewart Parnell had been in the 1880s'. Though the leadership did present a united front in the years of the Home Rule Crisis (1912–14).

CHAPTER 1: JOHN REDMOND, IRISH PASTS, AND IMPERIAL ACTUALITIES:
CONTEXTS OF AND CONSTRAINTS ON HIS BATTLE FOR HOME RULE

* This chapter is dedicated to the memory of Frank Callanan, SC (1956–2021). I would like to thank my husband, Dr James McGeachie, for his help and advice.
1. A partial version of this narrative is contained in Paul Bew, *John Redmond* (Dundalk, 1996). Also, a view promulgated by John Bruton, former Taoiseach. See too Alvin Jackson, *Judging Redmond and Carson: Comparative Irish Lives* (Dublin, 2018), p. 222.
2. For these years see Dermot Meleady, *Redmond: The Parnellite* (Cork, 2008).
3. Dermot Meleady, John *Redmond: The National Leader* (Dublin, 2013).
4. Margaret O'Callaghan, *British High Politics and a Nationalist Ireland: Criminality, Land and the Law under Forster and Balfour* (Cork, 1994).
5. Margaret O'Callaghan, 'Franchise reform: "First past the post" and the strange case of unionist Ireland', in *Parliamentary History*, vol. 16, no. 1 (1997), pp 85–106.
6. Alvin Jackson, *Home Rule: An Irish History, 1800–2000* (Oxford, 2003). For Redmond and his later unionist protagonist see also Jackson, *Judging Redmond and Carson*.
7. Correspondence on John Redmond as 'Jack', see Jackson, *Judging Redmond and Carson*, p. 8.
8. Meleady, *Redmond: The Parnellite*.
9. Frank Callanan, *The Parnell Split, 1890–91* (Cork, 1992).
10. From William Butler Yeats' poem, 'Two Songs from a Play' in *The Tower* (1928).
11. A supporter of Young Ireland and a participant in the 1848 Rebellion, McManus died in San Francisco in January 1861. His body was re-interred in Glasnevin that November in a huge affair orchestrated by the Fenians, see Owen McGee, 'McManus, Terence Bellew', *Dictionary of Irish Biography*, https://www.dib.ie/biography/mcmanus-terence-bellew-a5267 (8 Mar. 2024).
12. Callanan, *Parnell Split* and the same author's *Tim Healy* (Cork, 1996).
13. Meleady, *Redmond: The National Leader*, p. 117.
14. Ibid.

15. Donal P. McCracken, *Inspector Mallon: Buying Irish Patriotism for a Five-Pound Note* (Dublin, 2009).
16. Meleady, *Redmond: The Parnellite*. p. 315.
17. Ibid.
18. On Healy's admiration for the Tory Chief Secretary Gerald Balfour, see Callanan, *Healy*, pp 428.
19. See for example Jackson, *Judging Redmond and Carson*, pp 81–2 on Redmond's enthusiasm for the March 1898 Irish Local Government Bill on what he describes as Parnellite and Fenian grounds.
20. Jackson, *Judging Redmond and Carson*, pp 76–90.
21. For further discussion of Dicey's writings, see O'Callaghan, 'Franchise reform', p. 89, fn 19. See also James Kirby, 'A. V. Dicey and English Constitutionalism', *History of European Ideas* vol. 45, no. 1 (2019), pp 33–46.
22. O'Callaghan, 'Franchise reform', *passim*.
23. Donald Horowitz, *A Democratic South Africa? Constitutional Engineering in a Divided Society* (Berkeley and Oxford, 1991); Arend Lijphart, *Democracy in Plural Societies: A Comparative Exploration* (New Haven, 1977).
24. Eugenio F. Biagini, *British Democracy and Irish Nationalism 1876–1906* (Cambridge, 2007).
25. H. C. G. Matthew, 'William Ewart Gladstone, 1809–1898', *Oxford Dictionary of National Biography* (Oxford, 2004).
26. Margaret O'Callaghan, 'Richard Pigott', *Dictionary of Irish Biography*. See too Margaret O'Callaghan, 'Richard Pigott, the Fringe-Fenian Press and the politics of Irish Nationalist transition to Parnellism', in Fearghal McGarry and James McConnel (eds), *The Black Hand of Republicanism: Fenianism in Modern Ireland* (Dublin, 2009), pp 149–59.
27. O'Callaghan, *British High Politics and a Nationalist Ireland*.
28. O'Callaghan. 'Franchise reform', *passim*, 'New ways of looking at the state apparatus and the state archive in nineteenth-century Ireland: "Curiosities of that strange phonetic museum": Royal Irish Constabulary reports and their political uses, 1879–91', in *Proceedings of the Royal Irish Academy: Archaeology, Literature, Culture*, vol. 104C, no. 2 (2004), pp 37–56; See also O'Callaghan, 'Political formation in pre-First World War Ireland: The politics of the lost generation and the cult of Tom Kettle', in Caoimhe Nic Dháibhéid and Colin Reid (eds), *From Parnell to Paisley: Constitutional and Revolutionary Politics in Modern Ireland* (Dublin, 2010), pp 56–72.
29. Maurice Cowling, *1867: Disraeli, Gladstone and Revolution: The Passing of the Second Reform Bill* (Cambridge, 1967).
30. A. B. Cooke and John Vincent, *The Governing Passion: Cabinet Government and Party Politics in Britain, 1885–6* (Brighton, 1974).
31. Meleady, *Redmond: The Parnellite*.
32. Jackson, *Judging Redmond and Carson*, p. 12.
33. O'Callaghan, 'Parnellism and crime: Constructing a Conservative strategy of containment 1887–1891', in Donal McCartney (ed), *Parnell and the Politics of Power* (Dublin 1991), pp 102-124; see also O'Callaghan, *British High Politics and a Nationalist Ireland*.
34. Paul Bew, *Ideology and the Irish Question: Ulster Unionism and Irish Nationalism, 1912–1916* (Oxford, 1994); see also, Bew, *Ancestral Voices in Irish Politics: Judging Parnell and Dillon* (Oxford, 2023), pp 157–83.
35. James Joyce, 'Home Rule comes of age', in Kevin Barry (ed.), *James Joyce: Occasional Critical and Political Writings* (Oxford, 2000), pp 142–4.
36. Tom Garvin, *Nationalist Revolutionaries in Ireland 1858–1928* (Dublin, 2014).
37. Ronan Fanning, *Fatal Path: British Government and Irish Revolution 1910 to 1922* (London, 2013), chapters 2–3.
38. Alvin Jackson, *Home Rule: An Irish History 1800–2000* (London, 2003), pp 84–6.
39. In the second general election of December 1910.
40. T. P. O' Connor, *Memoirs of an Old Parliamentarian*, 2 vols (London, 1929) pp 2–3.
41. Cooke and Vincent, *The Governing Passion*.
42. For a wider perspective, see Margaret O'Callaghan, 'Ireland, Empire, and British foreign policy: Roger Casement and the First World War', in *Breac: A Digital Journal of Irish Studies* (2016): https://breac.nd.edu/articles/ireland-empire-and-british-foreign-policy-roger-casement-and-the-first-world-war/ (accessed Mar. 2024)
43. Fanning, *Fatal Path: British Government and Irish Revolution*, pp 61–2.

44. Reference to Dickens's character. Wilkins Micawber, clerk in *David Copperfield*. Meaning one who is poor but lives in optimistic expectation of better fortune.
45. Deirdre McMahon, (ed.), 'The Irish settlement meeting of the unionist party', 7 July 1916, in *Annalecta Hibernica*, vol. no. 41 (2009), pp 203–70, p. 201.
46. R. B. McDowell, *The Irish Convention, 1917–18* (London, 1970). See also Report of the Proceedings of the Irish Convention (Dublin, 1917–1918).
47. Irish Landowners Convention, *The Case of the Irish Landlords by one of them with the Resolutions and Statements on the Irish Land Purchase Question Adopted by the Irish Landowners' Convention on 10 October, 1902, and the Report of the Irish Land Conference* (London and Dublin, 1903).
48. A. C. Hepburn, 'The Irish Council Bill and the fall of Sir Antony MacDonnell, 1906–07', in *Irish Historical Studies*, vol. 17, no. 68, pp 470–98; Patrick Maume, 'Sir Antony MacDonnell', *DIB*. See also Patrick Maume, *The Long Gestation: Irish Nationalist Life, 1891–1918* (Dublin, 1999).
49. Eunan O'Halpin, *The Decline of the Union: British Government in Ireland, 1892-1920* (Dublin, 1987).
50. Jackson, *Home Rule*.
51. McDowell, *The Irish Convention*.
52. Michael Laffan, *The Resurrection of Ireland: The Sinn Féin Party, 1916-1923* (Cambridge, 1999).
53. For Milner and his circle, see Margaret O'Callaghan, '"Old parchment and water": The Irish Boundary Commission of 1925 and the copper fastening of the Irish border', in *Bullán: an Irish Studies Journal*, vol. 4, no. 2 (Nov., 2000), pp 27–55. The Round Table, formed in 1909, sought to foster closer relations between Britain and its colonies. Members expressed interest in schemes of imperial federation and 'home rule all around'. J. J. Horgan would become Irish correspondent for its journal, see also John Kendle, *The Round Table Movement and Imperial Union* (Toronto, ON, 1975).
54. Brian Harrison, 'Adams, William George Stewart', *ODNB;* John Turner, *Lloyd George's Secretariat* (London, 1980).
55. Andrew Boyle, *The Riddle of Erskine Childers* (London, 1977).
56. Lawrence William White and Aideen Foley, 'O'Brien, Francis Cruise', *DIB*.
57. Trevor West, *Horace Plunkett: Co-operation and Politics an Irish Biography* (Gerrards Cross, 1986).
58. Callanan, *Healy*, p. 542.

CHAPTER 2: ISAAC BUTT'S LEGACY: THE IRISH PARLIAMENTARY PARTY, 1879–1918

1. The important work of Paul Bew in the 1990s set the tenor of our current understanding of John Redmond. See his *Ideology and the Irish Question: Ulster Unionism and Irish Nationalism, 1912–1916* (Oxford, 1994) and *John Redmond* (Dundalk, 1996).
2. *Irish Times*, 15 March 2016. The four chosen leaders were: Henry Grattan, Daniel O'Connell, Charles Stewart Parnell, and John Redmond.
3. Terence de Vere White, *The Road of Excess* (Dublin, 1946).
4. David Thornley, *Isaac Butt and Home Rule* (London, 1964); Lawrence J. McCaffrey, 'Irish federalism in the 1870s: A study in conservative nationalism', in *Transactions of the American Philosophical Society*, vol. 52, no. 6 (1962), pp 1–58.
5. McCaffrey, 'Irish federalism', passim; Thornley, *Isaac Butt*, p. 20.
6. Joseph Spence, 'Isaac Butt, Irish nationality and the conditional defence of the Union, 1833–70', in D. George Boyce and Alan O'Day (eds), *Defenders of the Union: A Survey of British and Irish Unionism Since 1801* (London, 2001), pp 65–89; Colin W. Reid, '"An experiment in constructive unionism": Isaac Butt, Home Rule and federalist political thought during the 1870s', *English Historical Review*, vol. 129, no. 537 (2014), pp 332–61.
7. See, for example, Conor Mulvagh, *The Irish Parliamentary Party at Westminster, 1900–1918* (Manchester, 2016); Michael Wheatley, *Nationalism and the Irish Party: Provincial Ireland, 1910–1916* (Oxford, 2005); Dermot Meleady, *John Redmond: The National Leader* (Dublin, 2013).
8. Alan O'Day, *Irish Home Rule, 1867–1921* (Manchester, 1998), p. 52.
9. L. G. Redmond-Howard, *John Redmond: The Man and the Demand* (London, 1910), p. 257.
10. R. F. Foster, *Words Alone: Yeats and his Inheritances* (Oxford, 2011), p. 87.
11. Paul Bew, *Enigma: A New Life of Charles Stewart Parnell* (Dublin, 2011), p. 37.
12. Spence, 'Isaac Butt', pp 65–89.

13. Reid, 'An experiment in constructive unionism', pp 332–61.
14. Charles Read and T. P. O'Connor (eds), *The Cabinet of Irish Literature: Selections from the Chief Poets, Orators and Prose Writers of Ireland*, four vols (London, 1878–80), vol. iv, pp 165–7. For an arresting overview of the *Cabinet*, see Margaret Kelleher, 'The Cabinet of Irish Literature: A historical view of Irish anthologies', *Eire-Ireland*, vol. 38, no. 3–4 (2003), pp 68–89.
15. Michael Davitt, *The Fall of Feudalism in Ireland: Or the Story of the Land League Revolution* (London, 1904), p. 81.
16. Isaac Butt, *Land Tenure in Ireland: A Plea for the Celtic Race* (Dublin, 1866), p. 92.
17. Reid, 'An experiment in constructive unionism', p. 359.
18. Butt, *Land Tenure*, p. 42.
19. Butt, *The Irish People and the Irish Land: A Letter to Lord Lifford* (Dublin, 1867), p. 91.
20. Ibid., p. 246.
21. Ibid., p. 118.
22. Butt, *The Irish Querist: A Series of Questions Proposed for the Consideration of all who Desire to Solve the Problem of Ireland's Social Condition* (Dublin, 1867), p. 31.
23. For Lalor, see Marta Ramón's introduction to James Fintan Lalor, *'The Faith of a Felon' and Other Writings*, ed. Marta Ramón (Dublin, 2012), pp 1–51.
24. The classic overview was provided by A. M. Sullivan, in *New Ireland: Political Sketches and Personal Reminiscences of Thirty Years of Irish Public Life*, sixteenth edn (London, 1877), pp 344–5. For more recent scholarly interpretations of the Association, see Alvin Jackson, *Home Rule: An Irish History, 1800–2000* (London, 2003), pp 24–7; Jennifer Regan-Lefebvre, *Cosmopolitan Nationalism in the Victorian Empire: Ireland, India and the Politics of Alfred Webb* (Basingstoke, 2009), pp 66–74; J. J. Golden, 'Protestant influence on the origins of the Home Government Association, 1861–71', in *English Historical Review*, vol. 128, no. 535 (2013), pp 1,483–516.
25. Sullivan, *New Ireland*, pp 344–5.
26. Quoted in Butt, *Irish People*, p. 6.
27. Paul Bew, *Enigma*, pp 73–7.
28. James Collins, *Life in Old Dublin* (Cork, 1978; first published 1913), pp 182–3. For Collins as Butt's illegitimate son, see Pat Holland, with Máire Ni Giolla Bhridghe, *Isaac Butt, Father of Home Rule: The Great Tribune of Donegal* (Ballybofey, 2013), chapter 19.
29. *Irish Book Lover*, vol. 5, September 1913, pp 21–3.
30. *Irish Independent*, 5 September 1913.
31. *Irish Examiner*, 16 April 1913.
32. *Donegal News*, 24 July 1920.
33. F. Hugh O'Donnell, *Paraguay on Shannon: The Price of a Political Priesthood* (London, 1908), p. ix.
34. F. Hugh O'Donnell, *The Stage Irishman of the Pseudo-Celtic Drama* (London, 1904), p. 8.
35. O'Donnell, *History of the Irish Parliamentary Party*, two vols (London, 1910), vol. i, p. 321.
36. Ibid., vol. i, p. 250.
37. Ibid., vol. i, p. 4.
38. Ibid., vol. i, pp 237–8.
39. *Irish Times*, 21 March 1910.
40. White, *Road of Excess*, p. 370.
41. *Irish Times*, 21 March 1910.
42. *Freeman's Journal*, 18 March 1913.
43. *Irish Examiner*, 2 January 1914.
44. For a rather more nuanced take, see John Bew, *The Glory of Being Britons: Civic Unionism in Nineteenth-Century Belfast* (Dublin, 2009). For the anti-democratic charge, see Colin W. Reid, 'Democracy, sovereignty and unionist political thought during the revolutionary period in Ireland, c.1912–1922', in *Transactions of the Royal Historical Society*, vol. 27 (2017), pp 211–32, 216–18.
45. For Butt's unionism, see Reid, 'An experiment in constructive unionism', p. 334.
46. J. G. Swift MacNeill, *What I Have Seen and Heard* (London, 1925), p. 120.
47. Although Stephen Gwynn, another Protestant member of the Irish Party, believed it was an advantage for a prospective parliamentarian to be non-Catholic. Colin W. Reid, *The Lost Ireland of Stephen Gwynn: Irish Constitutional Nationalism and Cultural Politics, 1864–1950* (Manchester, 2011), p. 74.

48. J. G. Swift MacNeill, 'Isaac Butt, father of Home Rule', in *Fortnightly Review*, vol. 94, no. 561 (1913), pp 448-59, pp 450–1.
49. Ibid., p. 450.
50. Ibid., p. 457.
51. *Irish Examiner*, 2 January 1914.
52. Reid, 'An experiment in constructive unionism', p. 360.
53. The most thorough account of this period is provided in Dermot Meleady, *Redmond: The Parnellite* (Cork, 2008).
54. For an overview of the waxing and waning of federalism within British and imperial intellectual life, see John Kendle, *Federal Britain: A History* (London, 1997).
55. *Freeman's Journal*, 18 March 1913.
56. Warre B. Wells, *John Redmond: A Biography* (London, 1919), p. 31.
57. Townend, *The Road to Home Rule*, p. 73.
58. Quoted in James McConnel, 'John Redmond and Irish Catholic loyalism', in *English Historical Review*, vol. 125, no. 512 (2010), pp 83–111, p. 95.
59. *Hansard*, series 4, vol. 230, 30 June 1876, c. 749. For the original quotation, see *Macbeth*, Act 5, Scene 3, pp 40–6.
60. Stephen Gwynn, *John Redmond's Last Years* (London, 1919), p. 6.
61. *Hansard*, series 4, vol. 11, 13 April 1893, c. 251. See also R. Barry O'Brien (ed.), *Home Rule Speeches of John Redmond, MP* (London, 1910), p. 58.
62. For which, see Malcolm Campbell, 'John Redmond and the Irish National League in Australia and New Zealand, 1883', in *History*, vol. 86, no. 283 (2001), pp 348–62.
63. John Redmond, *Historical and Political Addresses, 1883–1897* (Dublin, 1898), p. 183.
64. Ibid., p. 184.
65. F. S. L. Lyons, 'The political ideas of Parnell', in *The Historical Journal*, 16, no. 4 (1973), pp 749–75, p. 758.
66. *Nation*, 24 January 1885.
67. Isaac Butt, *Home Government for Ireland: Irish Federalism! Its Meaning, its Objects, and its Hopes* (4th edn, Dublin, 1874), p. v.
68. Redmond, *Historical and Political Addresses*, p. 326.
69. Ibid., p. 325.
70. Ibid., pp 325–6.
71. *Leader*, 22 October 1910.
72. Michael Wheatley, 'John Redmond and federalism in 1910', in *Irish Historical Studies*, vol. 32, no. 127 (2001), pp 343–64, *Express* quote on p. 355.
73. John E. Redmond, *The Home Rule Bill* (London, 1912), p. 67.
74. Ibid., pp 71–2.
75. Alvin Jackson, *Judging Redmond and Carson: Comparative Irish Lives* (Dublin, 2018), pp 143–4; Reid, *Lost Ireland*, p. 179; Michael Burgess, *The British Tradition of Federalism* (London, 1995), p. 121.
76. Vernon Bogdanor, *Beyond Brexit: Towards a British Constitution* (London, 2019), pp 187–8.
77. Charles Gavan Duffy, *Young Ireland: A Fragment of Irish History, 1840–1850* (London, 1880), p. 577.
78. John E. Redmond, 'Readjustment of the Union: The nationalist plan', in *Nineteenth Century*, vol. 32, no. 188 (1892), pp 509–23, p. 523.
79. Quentin Skinner, *The Foundations of Modern Political Thought*, 2 vols (Cambridge, 1978), vol. i, pp 109–10.
80. The intergenerational tension of the revolutionary period in Ireland is a central theme of R. F. Foster, *Vivid Faces: The Revolutionary Generation in Ireland, 1890–1923* (London, 2014).

CHAPTER 3: THE CHAIRMAN AND THE CHIEF: JOHN REDMOND AND CHARLES STEWART PARNELL

1. *Irish Times*, 2 October 1911; *Freeman's Journal*, 2 October 1911.
2. *Irish Times*, 2 October 1911.

3. On Parnell's legacy, in particular, see Patrick Maume, *The Long Gestation: Irish Nationalist Life, 1891–1918* (Dublin, 1999); Matthew Kelly, *The Fenian Ideal and Irish Nationalism, 1882–1916* (Suffolk, 2006); and more recently Paul Bew, *Ancestral Voices in Irish Politics: Judging Dillon and Parnell* (Oxford, 2023).
4. Francis Cruise O'Brien, 'John Redmond', *The Leader*, 29 Feb. 1910, quoted in Paul Bew, *John Redmond* (Dundalk, 1996), p. 4.
5. Kelly, *The Fenian Ideal and Irish Nationalism*, p. 74.
6. In contrast, Paul Bew's recent study of Parnell and John Dillon demonstrates how radically different Parnell and Dillon were. Bew, *Ancestral Voices in Irish Politics*.
7. J. J. Horgan, *Parnell to Pearse* (Dublin, 1949 & 2009), pp 321–2.
8. R. Barry O'Brien, *The Life of Charles Stewart Parnell* (London, 1898), vol. I, pp 213–14.
9. *Wexford Independent*, 10 November 1880; Dermot Meleady, *Redmond: The Parnellite* (Cork, 2008), p. 37.
10. Barry O'Brien, *The Life of Charles Stewart Parnell*, vol. I, pp 74–5; James Bryce, *Studies in Contemporary Biography* (London, 1903), pp 241–2; John Morley, *Recollections* (London, 1917), vol. I, p. 241; T. P. O'Connor, *The Parnellite Movement* (London, 1886), pp 237–8. On Parnell as a political speaker, see Pauric Travers 'Reading between the lines: The political speeches of Charles Stewart Parnell', in Donal McCartney & Pauric Travers, *The Ivy Leaf: The Parnells Remembered* (Dublin, 2006).
11. Justin McCarthy, *British Political Leaders* (London, 1903), pp 231–4.
12. *Daily News*, 19 December 1925; W. T. Stead, *Coming Men on Coming Questions* (London, 1905), p. 65; Horgan, *Parnell to Pearse*, pp 321–2.
13. John Morley, *Life of Gladstone* (London, 1903), vol. III, p. 313 & 337.
14. Michael Davitt, *The Fall of Feudalism in Ireland* (London, 1904), p. 494.
15. *Hansard* series 3, vol. 305, 13 May 1886, cc 96–74, 13 May 1886; *Freeman's Journal*, 13 May 1886.
16. *Freeman's Journal*, 18 May 1886. On Parnell and the Ulster Question, see F. S. L. Lyons, 'The political ideas of Parnell', in *The Historical Journal*, vol. XVI, no. 4 (1973), pp 749–75, pp 768–9; Paul Bew, *C. S. Parnell* (Dublin, 1980), pp 140–2 & *Enigma: A New Life of Charles Stewart Parnell* (Dublin, 2011), pp 181–5, 195–9; Conor Cruise O'Brien review, *Irish Historical Studies*, vol. 20, no. 80 (1977), p. 518; and P. Travers, 'Parnell and the Ulster question', in Donal McCartney (ed.), *Parnell: The Politics of Power* (Dublin, 1991), pp 57–71.
17. *Northern Whig*, 23 May 1891.
18. On the legislature proposed in the First Home Rule Bill, see A. J. Ward, *The Irish Constitutional Tradition: Responsible Government and Modern Ireland, 1782–1992* (Dublin, 1994), pp 67–8.
19. *Irish Times*, 2 Oct. 1911.
20. Ibid.
21. Kelly, *The Fenian Ideal and Irish Nationalism*, p. 74.
22. Barry O'Brien, *The Life of Charles Stewart Parnell*, vol. I, p. 99.
23. Michael MacDonagh, *The Life of William O'Brien: The Irish Nationalist* (London, 1928), p. 228.
24. Stead, *Coming Men on Coming Questions*, p. 65.
25. Bew, *John Redmond*, p. 16.
26. *Weekly Freeman's Journal*, 9 March 1918.
27. *Freeman's Journal*, 19 November 1890.
28. Ibid.
29. Morley, *Life of Gladstone*, vol. III, p. 447.
30. *Freeman's Journal*, 2 December 1890.
31. Francis Cruise O'Brien, *The Leader*, 26 Feb. 1910, quoted in Bew, *Redmond*, p. 15.
32. *Freeman's Journal*, 2 December 1890.
33. Barry O'Brien, *The Life of Charles Stewart Parnell*, vol. II, pp 257–66.
34. For an insightful reading of the manifesto, see Donal McCartney, 'Parnell's Manifesto 'To the people of Ireland', 29 November 1890: Causes, content and consequences', in McCartney & Travers (eds), *Parnell Reconsidered* (Dublin, 2013), pp 197–203.
35. On negotiations in France, see Barry O'Brien, *The Life of Charles Stewart Parnell*, vol. 2, pp 310–29 and Callanan, *The Parnell Split*, pp 80–109.
36. *Freeman's Journal*, 5 November 1891.

37. Winston Churchill, *Lord Randolph Churchill* (London, 1906), vol. II, pp 437–8.
38. Redmond to Revd Patrick Furlong, 7 December 1890, NLI Redmond Papers MS 28,894(A).
39. *Freeman's Journal*, 25 February 1891.
40. Ibid., 11 May 1891.
41. Ibid., 21 September & 23 October 1891; Meleady, *Redmond: The Parnellite*, p. 193 & 370.
42. Katharine O'Shea, *The Uncrowned King of Ireland* (London, 2005), p. 287. On the Parnell funeral, see Pauric Travers, 'Our Fenian dead: Glasnevin Cemetery and the genesis of the republican funeral', in James Kelly & Uaitear MacGearailt, *Dublin and Dubliners* (Dublin, 1990), pp 52–72.
43. *National Press*, 23 September 1891; Frank Callanan, *The Parnell Split, 1890–91*, p. 151.
44. *Freeman's Journal*, 18 March 1892.
45. Ibid., 1 September 1893; *Irish Times*, 10 October 1893.
46. On the Parnellite movement after Parnell, see Maume, *The Long Gestation*, pp 14–40.
47. Kelly, *The Fenian Ideal and Irish Nationalism*, pp 93–4.
48. On Ivy Day, see Pauric Travers, '"The thurible as a weapon of war": Ivy Day', in McCartney & Travers, *The Ivy Leaf*, pp 140–7.
49. *Irish Times*, 9 October 1899
50. Nicholas Mansergh, 'John Redmond', in Conor Cruise O'Brien, *The Shaping of Modern Ireland* (London, 1960), p. 40.
51. Arthur Lynch, *My Life Story* (London, 1924), p. 263.
52. Kelly, *The Fenian Ideal and Irish Nationalism*, p.73. See also his 'Radical nationalisms, 1882–1916', in Thomas Bartlett (ed.), *The Cambridge History of Ireland*, vol. IV, pp 44–5 and '"Parnell's old brigade": The Redmondite-Fenian nexus in the 1890s', in *Irish Historical Studies*, vol. 33, no. 130 (2002), pp 209–32.
53. Maume, *The Long Gestation*, p. 27.
54. *Irish Times*, 8 October 1899.
55. *Freeman's Journal*, 2 Oct. 1911; *Sinn Féin*, 7 October 1911.
56. Quoted in Michael Laffan, 'John Redmond and Home Rule', in Ciaran Brady (ed.), *Worsted in the Game: Losers in Irish History* (Dublin, 1989), p. 137.
57. Quoted in Mansergh, 'John Redmond', p. 39. On Parnell's 'Ne Plus Ultra' speech, see, Pauric Travers, 'The march of the nation: Parnell's *ne plus ultra* speech', in McCartney & Travers, *Parnell Reconsidered*, pp 179–96.
58. Mansergh, 'John Redmond', p. 47.
59. 'Fifteen years in the House of Commons', in John Redmond, *Historical and Political Addresses, 1883–1897* (Dublin, 1898), p. 11.
60. Horgan, *Parnell to Pearse*, p. 322.

CHAPTER 4: JOHN REDMOND & EDWARD CARSON: BLOODSHED, BORDERS, AND THE UNION STATE

1. An earlier version of this text was delivered as a Royal Irish Academy Discourse (Public Lecture) on 6 March 2018 (introduced by the then Taoiseach, Leo Varadkar TD) and has since appeared as 'Redmond and Carson: Bloodshed, borders and the Union State/ Redmond et Carson: l'affrontement, les frontières et l'Union' in the *Revue Française de Civilisation Britannique*, vol. 24, no. 2 (2019). Some of the themes of the article are developed at greater length in Alvin Jackson, *Judging Redmond and Carson: Comparative Irish Lives* (Dublin, 2018) and in Alvin Jackson, *United Kingdoms: Multinational Union States in Europe and Beyond, 1800–1925* (Oxford, 2023). For an acute reflection on the task of comparing the two men see Frank Callanan, 'Out with the old, in with the new', in *Dublin Review of Books*, 26 Nov. 2018 https://www.drb.ie/blog/comment/2018/11/27/out-with-the-old-in-with-the-new, accessed 2019.
2. For Carson and federalism see Jeremy Smith, 'Federalism, devolution and partition: Sir Edward Carson and the search for a compromise on the third Home Rule Bill', in *Irish Historical Studies*, vol. 35, no. 140 (Nov. 2007), pp 496–518; for Redmond and federalism see Michael Wheatley, 'John Redmond and federalism in 1910', in *Irish Historical Studies*, vol. 32, no. 127 (May 2001), pp 343–64, and the chapter by Colin Reid in this volume.
3. Harry Carson and Louis Redmond-Howard, 'An Irishman's home or the crisis: A topical play on the Ulster question' (London, 1914). This has been reprinted by the Aubane Historical Society in

2006 together with *Six Days of the Irish Republic* (original edition: London, 1916) and other works by Louis Redmond-Howard.

4. Alvin Jackson, 'Shamrock and saltire: Irish Home Rule, independence and the Scottish referendum, 1914–2014', in Senia Pašeta (ed.), *Uncertain Futures: Essays about the Irish Past for Roy Foster* (Oxford, 2016), pp 257–69.

5. For a recent exploration of the federal theme by constitutional lawyers and historians see Robert Schütze and Stephen Tierney (eds), *The United Kingdom and the Federal Idea* (London, 2018). In 2016, the Parliamentary Constitution Reform Group, convened by the seventh Marquis of Salisbury, proposed a new, federal, act of union for the nations of the United Kingdom.

6. Jackson, 'Shamrock and saltire', p. 259. For a reflection on the analogy by Iain Macwhirter: *The Herald*, 21 December 2014 see: https://www.heraldscotland.com/opinion/13194391.salmond-and-parnells-precedent/ (accessed 2019).

7. Dermot Meleady, *Redmond: The Parnellite* (Cork, 2008), p. 25.

8. 'Notes of a conversation with Mrs St George Robinson (sister of Lord Carson), supplemented by Lady Carson', 22 July 1950, Public Record Office of Northern Ireland (PRONI), H. M. Hyde Papers, D.3084/H/3/9). The evidence is inconclusive, but suggests that Edward Carson senior, who died on 14 February 1881, left some assets but little cash (*Wills and Administrations 1881*, p. 97).

9. Anna Debenham to Hyde, 12 November 1951, PRONI, Hyde Papers, D.3084/H/2/91. For Asquith's attitude to Carson see (for example), H. H. Asquith (Earl of Oxford and Asquith), *Memories and Reflections, 1852–1927* (two vols, London, 1928), vol. i, p. 102.

10. For a fuller discussion see Alvin Jackson, *United Kingdoms: Multinational Union States in Europe and Beyond, 1800–1925* (Oxford, 2023).

11. See Rosebery's provocative 'predominant partner' speech of March 1894: *Hansard*, series 4, vol. 12, House of Commons, 13 March 1894, col. 185.

12. There is an extensive debate on Ireland's relationship with empire. For a starting point see Stephen Howe, *Ireland and Empire: Colonial Legacies in Irish History and Culture* (Oxford, 2000); see also Michael Hechter, *Internal Colonialism: The Celtic Fringe in British National Development, 1536–1966* (London, 1975). For a very comprehensive fresh examination of the theme see Brendan O'Leary, *A Treatise on Northern Ireland* (3 vols, Oxford, 2019).

13. K. Theodore Hoppen, *Governing Hibernia: British Politicians and Ireland, 1800–1921* (Oxford, 2016).

14. Steven Beller, *Francis Joseph* (Harlow, 1996), p. 161.

15. Quoted in Ronan Fanning, *Fatal Path: British Government and Irish Revolution* (London, 2013), pp 88–9.

16. See, for example, Redmond to Churchill, 4 August 1914, Churchill College Cambridge, Winston Churchill Papers, CHAR 2/64/10.

17. Redmond to Dillon, 22 July 1908, TCD, John Dillon Papers, 6748/377.

18. Edward Marjoribanks and Ian Colvin 1932–6, *Life of Lord Carson* (London, 1932–6), vol. iii, p. 27; Stephen Gwynn, *John Redmond's Last Years* (London, 1919), p. 147.

19. See Oszkár Jászi, *The Dissolution of the Habsburg Monarchy* (Chicago, 1929); see also Pieter Judson, *The Habsburg Empire: A New History* (Cambridge, MA, and London, 2016).

20. Even for the Norwegian patriot, Fridtjof Nansen, the great antiquity of the monarchy in Norway meant that 'fidelity to their Royal House has therefore always been particularly characteristic of the Norwegian peasantry': Fridtjof Nansen, *Norway and the Union with Sweden* (London, 1905), p. 5.

21. In terms of Habsburg historiography alone, see, for example, Laurence Cole and Daniel Unowsky (eds), *The Limits of Loyalty: Imperial Symbolism, Popular Allegiances, and State Patriotism in the late Habsburg Monarchy* (Oxford and New York, 2009); Pieter Judson, *Exclusive Revolutionaries: Liberal Politics, Social Experience, and National Identity in the Austrian Empire, 1848–1914* (Ann Arbor, 1996); idem, *Guardians of the Nation? Activists on the Language Frontiers of Imperial Austria* (Cambridge MA, 2006); idem, *The Habsburg Empire: A New History* (Cambridge Mass., 2016); idem and Marsha Rozenblit (eds), *Constructing Nationalities in East Central Europe* (New York and Oxford, 2005); Jeremy King, *Budweisers into Czechs and Germans? A Local History of Bohemian Politics, 1848–1948* (Princeton, 2002).

22. For the general theme, see Richard Dunphy, *The Making of Fianna Fáil Power in Ireland, 1923–48* (Oxford, 1995).

23. Meleady, *Redmond: The Parnellite*, p. 121.

24. Redmond to O'Callaghan, 3 April 1908 (copy), TCD, John Dillon Papers, 6747/291.
25. This is a key theme and argument of Alvin Jackson, *The Ulster Party: Irish Unionists in the House of Commons, 1884–1911* (Oxford, 1989).
26. Jackson, *Judging Redmond and Carson*, p. 162.
27. Alvin Jackson, *Home Rule: An Irish History, 1800–2000* (London, 2003), pp 124–5.
28. '"Illustrious Leader": Mr John Dillon's Eloquent Tribute', in *Freeman's Journal*, 10 March 1924, TCD Dillon Papers, 6749/706.
29. Carson to F. S. Oliver, 12 February 1918, National Library of Scotland (NLS), F. S. Oliver Papers, MS 24856, f.36.
30. Carson to Oliver, 5 September 1922, NLS, Oliver Papers, MS 24856, f.157.
31. Quoted in H. M. Hyde, *Carson: The Life of Sir Edward Carson, Lord Carson of Duncairn* (London, 1953), p. 486, and Jackson, *Judging Redmond and Carson*, p. 203.
32. Sir Charles Biron, *Without Prejudice: Impressions of Life and Law* (London, 1936), pp 215–16 – later quoted by the Ulster nationalist leader, T. J. Campbell, in *Fifty Years of Ulster, 1890–1940* (Belfast, 1941), p. 240.
33. This theme is explored in Alvin Jackson, 'Unionist myths, 1912–85', in *Past & Present*, no. 136 (August, 1992), pp 164–85.

CHAPTER 5: THE IRISH PARTY: RECRUITMENT AND THE GREAT WAR, c.1914–1915

1. Arthur C. Murray, *Master and Brother: Murrays of Elibank* (London, 1945), p. 108.
2. See Catriona Pennell, *A Kingdom United: Popular Responses to the Outbreak of the First World War in Britain and Ireland* (Oxford, 2012); Niamh Gallagher, *Ireland and the Great War: A Social and Political History* (London, 2020); Dermot Meleady, *John Redmond: the National Leader* (Sallins, 2013); James McConnel, *The Irish Parliamentary Party and the Third Home Rule Crisis* (Dublin, 2013); James Doherty, *Irish Liberty, British Democracy: The Third Home Rule Crisis, 1909–14* (Cork, 2019); Conor Mulvagh, *The Irish Parliamentary Party at Westminster, 1900–18* (Manchester, 2016); Timothy Bowman, William Butler and Michael Wheatley, *The Disparity of Sacrifice: Irish Recruitment to the British Armed Forces, 1914–1918* (Liverpool, 2020).
3. An account of long-term decline from the fall of Parnell was provided in F. S. L. Lyons, *The Irish Parliamentary Party, 1890–1910* (London, 1951).
4. See Doherty, *Irish Liberty, British Democracy*, p. 206.
5. *Irish Independent*, 12 October 1914, cited by McConnel in *The Irish Parliamentary Party and the Third Home Rule Crisis*, p. 299.
6. *Wicklow People*, 8 August 1914.
7. *Dundalk Democrat*, 8 August 1914.
8. *Freeman's Journal*, 3 August 1914.
9. For the evolution of public opinion across Europe in the months immediately prior to the outbreak of war and in the war's early months, read Michael S. Neiberg, *The Dance of the Furies* (Cambridge, Mass., 2011). For the impact of the first months of the war on British opinion, read Adrian Gregory, *The Last Great War: British Society and the First World War* (Cambridge, 2008); concerning both British and Irish public opinion see Pennell, *A Kingdom United*.
10. Monthly report of the RIC Roscommon County Inspector, August 1914, TNA CO 904/94.
11. See Pennell, *A Kingdom United*, pp 163–77.
12. Mulvagh, *The Irish Parliamentary Party at Westminster, 1900–18*, p. 267.
13. Stephen Gwynn, *John Redmond's Last Years* (London, 1919), p. 182.
14. McConnel, '"Après la Guerre": John Redmond, the Irish Volunteers and Armed Constitutionalism, 1913–1915', *English Historical Review*, vol. 131, no. 553 (December 2016), pp 1445–70.
15. *Wicklow People*, *Dundalk Democrat*, 8 August 1914.
16. McConnel, *The Irish Parliamentary Party and the Third Home Rule Crisis*, p. 305.
17. *Cork Free Press*, 18 March 1915. A 'fugleman' is best defined as a leader or spokesman, one at the forefront of a movement. See also Bowman, Butler and Wheatley, *The Disparity of Sacrifice*, pp 47–50.
18. Dillon to O'Connor, 5 September 1914, TCD Dillon Papers. MS 6740/225.
19. Bowman, Butler and Wheatley, *The Disparity of Sacrifice*, pp 53–4.

20. McConnel, *The Irish Parliamentary Party and the Third Home Rule Crisis,* pp 305–13; Bowman, Butler and Wheatley, *The Disparity of Sacrifice,* pp 54–6.
21. On this organisation and its decline, see Tony King, *Home Rule from a Transnational Perspective: The Irish Parliamentary Party and the United Irish League of America, 1901–1918* (Wilmington, DE, 2021).
22. TNA NATS 1/397. The 'South and West' is defined as Ireland excluding the army recruiting districts of Belfast, Armagh, and Omagh.
23. *Irish Times,* 7 November 1914.
24. See Redmond speaking in Tuam on 6 December 1914 (*Western Nationalist, Wicklow People,* 12 December 1914).
25. Redmond speaking in Wexford on 4 October (*Leitrim Advertiser,* 8 October); Waterford on 11 October (*Southern Star,* 17 October); Dublin on 18 October (*Dundalk Democrat,* 23 October) and Tuam on 6 December 1914, (*Western Nationalist,* 12 December 1914).
26. Conor Mulvagh has written of a private rift between Dillon and Redmond, in March 1915, over Redmond's futile pursuit of War Office cooperation. By May 1915, however, Dillon could write to O'Connor that 'Redmond and I are thoroughly agreed on policy'. See Mulvagh, *The Irish Parliamentary Party at Westminster,* pp 124–6.
27. Redmond speaking in Thurles, Co. Tipperary on 3 August 1915 (*Longford Leader,* 8 August 1915).
28. Redmond speaking in London, 23 November 1915, cited in D. G. Boyce, *Nationalism in Ireland,* (London, 1982) p. 284.
29. *Westmeath Independent,* 8 August 1914; 5 June 1915.
30. Maurice Moore to Redmond, 24 September 1915, NLI, Redmond Papers MS 15206.
31. See *Anglo-Celt,* 3 April; *Sligo Champion,* 19 June; *Clare Champion,* 24 June; *Westmeath Independent,* 26 June; *Dundalk Democrat,* 10 July; *Longford Leader,* 24 July; *Sligo Nationalist,* 23 October 1915.
32. Dillon speaking at Limerick in July 1915 (*Western Nationalist,* 31 July 1915).
33. Doris speaking to the Westport UIL in December 1915 (*Connaught Telegraph,* 11 December 1915).
34. *Strokestown Democrat,* 29 May; *Leitrim Observer, Roscommon Herald,* 5 June; *Longford Independent, Strokestown Democrat,* 12 June 1915.
35. *Longford Leader,* 5 June 1915.
36. Farrell speaking to the South Longford UIL executive in November 1916 (*Longford Leader,* 25 November 1916).
37. Dillon to O'Connor, 1 July 1915, quoted in F. S. L. Lyons, *John Dillon: A Biography* (London, 1968), p. 365.
38. Birrell to Redmond, 19 December 1915, NLI, Redmond Papers MS 15169.
39. See Wheatley, '"Irreconcilable Enemies" or "Flesh and Blood": The Irish Party and the Easter Rebels, 1914–16' in Gabriel Doherty and Dermot Keogh (eds), *1916: The Long Revolution* (Cork, 2007), pp 61–86.
40. Patrick Maume, *The Long Gestation: Irish Nationalist Life, 1891–1918* (Dublin, 1999), pp 203–5.
41. See Adrian Gregory, '"You might as well recruit Germans": British public opinion and the decision to recruit the Irish in 1918' in Adrian Gregory and Senia Pašeta (eds), *Ireland and the Great War: A War to Unite us all?* (Manchester, 2002), pp 113–32.
42. Wheatley, *Nationalism and the Irish Party: Provincial Ireland, 1910–1916* (Oxford, 2005), p. 266.
43. I am indebted to Timothy Bowman of the University of Kent and William Butler of UK National Archives, my co-authors of *The Disparity of Sacrifice: Irish Recruitment to the British Armed Forces, 1914–1918* (Liverpool, 2020) which has underpinned much of the work undertaken for this chapter.

CHAPTER 6: WOMEN'S SUFFRAGE, JOHN REDMOND, AND THE IRISH PARLIAMENTARY PARTY

1. Senia Pašeta, *Irish Nationalist Women 1900–1918* (Cambridge, 2013), p. 64.
2. Ibid., p. 67.
3. *Irish World,* 5 August 1882.
4. Maud Gonne, *A Servant of the Queen* (London, 1974), p. 117.
5. Ibid., p. 291.

6. Senia Pašeta, *Before the Revolution: Nationalism, Social Change and Ireland's Catholic Elite 1879–1922* (Cork, 1999), p. 64.
7. Hanna Sheehy Skeffington, 'Women and the National Movement', 19 February 1909, included in Margaret Ward (ed.), *Hanna Sheehy Skeffington, Suffragette and Sinn Féiner, Her Memoirs and Political Writings* (Dublin, 2017), pp 48–9.
8. Ibid., pp 50–1.
9. Ibid., p. 57.
10. James and Margaret Cousins, *We Two Together* (Madras, 1950), p. 128.
11. *Irish Citizen*, 3 August 1912.
12. *Votes for Women*, 24 December, 1909.
13. Dermot Meleady, *John Redmond: The National Leader* (Dublin, 2013), pp 176–7.
14. Hanna Sheehy Skeffington, 'Reminiscences of an Irish Suffragette' in Ward (ed.), *Hanna Sheehy Skeffington,* p. 73.
15. Ibid.
16. Ibid.
17. Constance Rover, *Women's Suffrage and Party Politics in Britain 1866–1914* (London, 1967), p. 125.
18. Ibid., p. 127.
19. *Votes for Women*, 27 January 1911.
20. Ibid., 12 May 1912.
21. *Hansard*, series 5, vol. 25, 5 May 1911, col. 807.
22. Rover, *Women's Suffrage and Party Politics*, p. 130.
23. Cliona Murphy, *The Women's Suffrage Movement and Irish Society in the Early Twentieth Century* (Hertfordshire, 1989), p. 188.
24. Sylvia Pankhurst, *The Suffragette Movement* (London, 1977), p. 403.
25. Oldham's sister Alice Oldham (1850–1907) taught at Alexandra College, Dublin, and became well known for her efforts to get women admitted to TCD. His younger sister, Edith (1865–1950), was an honorary member of the Royal College of Music in London and the wife of Richard Irvine Best, Celticist. See C. J. Woods, 'Best, Richard Irvine', *Dictionary of Irish Biography*, https://www.dib.ie/biography/best-richard-irvine-a0635 [12 July 2023].
26. *Freeman's Journal*, 2 April 1912.
27. Quoted in *Votes for Women*, 31 March 1912.
28. Hanna Sheehy Skeffington, 'Reminiscences of an Irish Suffragette' in Ward (ed.), *Hanna Sheehy Skeffington*, p. 74.
29. *Irish Citizen*, 20 July 1912.
30. Cousins, *We Two Together*, p. 168.
31. *Freeman's Journal*, 18 April 1912.
32. *Votes for Women*, 12 April 1912.
33. *Freeman's Journal*, 18 April 1912.
34. Ibid., 23 April 1912.
35. Ibid. O'Farrelly later presided over the inaugural meeting of Cumann na mBan, the nationalist women's organisation, in April 1914.
36. Ibid., 24 April 1912.
37. Tom Kettle to Hanna Sheehy Skeffington, n.d. (1912) (NLI Sheehy Skeffington papers MS 22,663).
38. Patrick Maume, *The Long Gestation: Irish Nationalist Life, 1891–1918* (Dublin, 1999), p. 122.
39. Joyce Padbury, *Mary Hayden: Historian and Feminist, 1862–1942* (Dublin, 2021), p. 203.
40. *Irish Citizen*, 8 June 1912.
41. *Suffragette*, 1 November 1912.
42. *Hansard*, series 5, vol. 43, 5 November 1912 cc1060-131
43. Diane Urquhart, *Women in Ulster Politics, 1890–1940* (Dublin, 2000), p. 30.
44. *Irish Citizen*, 16 November 1912.
45. *Suffragette*, 8 November 1912.
46. Ibid., 15 November 1912.
47. Ibid.
48. Ibid., 28 November 1912.

49. Ibid., 15 November 1912.
50. Ibid., 1 November 1912.
51. Denis Gwynn, *The Life of John Redmond* (London, 1932), p. 225.
52. Many more details of discrepancies in treatment are included in the poster, *Men and Women. Note these Facts: 1912–1915*, Women's Social and Political Union, Museum of London prints.
53. Ibid., 20 June 1914.
54. *Irish Citizen*, 5 July 1913.
55. *Hansard*, series 5, vol. 52, 6 May 1913, c.2003.
56. *Irish Citizen*, 8 May 1913.
57. Ibid., 10 August 1912.
58. Ibid., 23 May 1914.
59. Ibid.
60. Gywnn, *John Redmond*, p. 354.
61. Cliona Murphy, 'Humour and the fight for Irish women's suffrage', in Louise Ryan and Margaret Ward (eds), *Irish Women and the Vote: Becoming Citizens* (Dublin, 2007, reprinted 2018), p. 108.
62. Murphy, *The Women's Suffrage Movement*, p. 195.

CHAPTER 7: THE IRISH PARLIAMENTARY PARTY AND ITS SUCCESSORS

1. *Irish Times*, 7 August 1940.
2. Eunan O'Halpin, *Defending Ireland: The Irish State and its Enemies since 1922* (Oxford, 1999), p. 105.
3. Peter Mair, *The Changing Irish Party System: Organization, Ideology and Electoral Competition* (London, 1987). On the 1918 moment globally, see the influential Erez Manela, *The Wilsonian Moment: Self-determination and the International Origins of Anticolonial Nationalism* (Oxford, 2007) and for a counter-point to Manela: Hussein A. H. Omar, 'The Arab Spring of 1919', *London Review of Books*, 4 April 2019, https://www.lrb.co.uk/blog/2019/april/the-arab-spring-of-1919%20 [19 April 2022].
4. Mel Farrell, *Party Politics in a New Democracy* (Basingstoke, 2017), pp 292–7.
5. Michael Davitt, 'The Irish National Assembly (session of 1910)', *The Independent Review*, vol. 5 (April 1905), pp 284–98, p. 284 cited in James McConnel, 'The Franchise Factor in the defeat of the Irish Parliamentary Party, 1885–1918', *The Historical Journal*, vol. 47, no. 2 (June 2004), pp 355–77, p. 361. For an interesting contemporary imagining of an Irish House of Commons, see Dermot Meleady, *John Redmond: National Leader* (Dublin, 2014), epilogue.
6. Speech by Thomas Condon, 17 March 1914 cited in Martin O'Donoghue, *The Legacy of the Irish Parliamentary Party in Independent Ireland, 1922–1949* (Liverpool, 2019), p. 1. The statistics on politicians with Irish Party heritage referred to here are based on research undertaken for the book.
7. David Fitzpatrick, *Politics and Irish Life, 1913–21: Provincial Experience of War and Revolution* (Aldershot, 1977), pp 128–130.
8. David S. Jones, 'The cleavage between graziers and peasants in the land struggle, 1890–1910', in Samuel Clark and James S. Donnelly (eds), *Irish Peasants: Violence and Political Unrest, 1780–1914* (Madison, WI, 1986), pp 374–419.
9. Ciarán Wallace, 'Early Sinn Féin — the anti-corruption party', *History Ireland*, vol. 21, no. 5 (September/October 2013), pp 36–7.
10. On the relationship between labour politics and nationalism in the AFIL's support base, see Patrick Murphy, 'The banshee's kiss: conciliation, class and conflict and the All for Ireland League', unpublished PhD thesis (University of Liverpool, 2019).
11. Martin O'Donoghue, '"Ireland's Independence Day": the 1918 election campaign in Ireland and the Wilsonian moment', *European Review of History: Revue européenne d'histoire*, vol. 25, no. 5 (2019), pp 834–54.
12. MPs were, however, arrested up to the 1900s. Willie Redmond for example spent the Christmas of 1902 in prison due to fiery platform speeches; see Terence Denman, *A Lonely Grave: The Life and Death of William Redmond* (Dublin, 1995).
13. Michael Laffan, *The Resurrection of Ireland: The Sinn Féin Party, 1916–1923* (Cambridge, 2004).

14. On the Nation League providing a stopping point for Irish Party supporters drifting towards Sinn Féin, see Laffan, *The Resurrection of Ireland*, pp 62–4.
15. Michael Wheatley, *Nationalism and the Irish Party: Provincial Ireland, 1910–1916* (Oxford, 2005), p. 111.
16. Mary Harris, *The Catholic Church and the Foundation of the Northern Irish State* (Cork, 1993).
17. Fergus Campbell, *Land and Revolution: Nationalist Politics in the West of Ireland, 1891–1921* (Oxford, 2005), pp 223–5, 231, 308–11. On suffrage, see Senia Pašeta,'Feminist political thought and activism in revolutionary Ireland *c.*1880–1918', *Transactions of the Royal Historical Society*, vol. 27 (2017), pp 193–209 and the previous chapter in this volume by Margaret Ward.
18. Tom Garvin, *The Evolution of Irish Nationalist Politics* (Dublin, 1981), pp 151–8.
19. T. P. O'Connor to John Dillon, January 1919, TCD John Dillon Papers 6743/593; James O'Neill to Dillon 16 April 1919, TCD John Dillon Papers 6786/1906.
20. For Dillon's views on MPs putting down amendments without consulting colleagues, see Dillon to O'Connor, 4 April 1920, TCD John Dillon Papers 6743/754.
21. Colin Reid, 'Stephen Gwynn and the failure of constitutionalism in Ireland, 1919–1921', *The Historical Journal*, vol. 53, no. 3 (2010), pp 723–45, p. 724.
22. Reid, 'Stephen Gwynn and the failure of constitutionalism in Ireland', pp 729–32. For reactions among the Dublin UIL and IPP leaders, see committee meeting UIL Metropolitan branch, 28 January 1919, NLI O'Donnell Papers MS 16,185; Devlin to Dillon, 26 May 1919, TCD John Dillon Papers, 6730/ 229.
23. Fitzpatrick, *Politics and Irish Life*, pp 113–44.
24. Eamon Phoenix, *Northern Nationalism: Nationalist Politics, Partition and the Catholic Minority in Northern Ireland* (Belfast, 1994), p. 142; *Hibernian Journal*, January 1920, p. 128.
25. Phoenix, *Northern Nationalism*, p. 96.
26. Laffan, *The Resurrection of Ireland*, p. 339.
27. Phoenix, *Northern Nationalism*, pp 114–19. Hepburn, *Catholic Belfast and Nationalist Ireland in the era of Joe Devlin, 1871–1934* (Oxford, 2008), pp 224–5.
28. Alvin Jackson, *Home Rule: An Irish History, 1800–2000* (London, 2003).
29. Hepburn, *Catholic Belfast*, pp 234–6.
30. Phoenix, *Northern Nationalism*, p. 193.
31. National Secretary's report, Meeting of AOH National Board, 11 March 1924: AOH collection, NAI, LOU 13/1/3(a). The AOH reported 4,769 male members and 603 members of its Ladies' Auxiliary in Northern Ireland.
32. Public Record Office of Northern Ireland (PRONI) Reports on meetings of the Ancient Order of Hibernians HA/32/1/321 and CAB/9/B/182.
33. Hepburn, *Catholic Belfast*, p. 257.
34. Secretary's report, AOH National Board Meeting, 14 July 1931: NAI LOU 13/1/3 (a); *Hibernian Journal*, August 1928, p. 55.
35. Conor Mulvagh, *The Irish Parliamentary Party at Westminster* (Manchester, 2016), pp 52–6.
36. *Irish Independent*, 21, 24 June 1924; cf. Joseph P. O'Kane, *The Canker of Partition* (Belfast, 1924).
37. *Hibernian Journal*, January 1928, p. 3.
38. Michael Farrell, *Northern Ireland: The Orange State* (London, 1976), p. 115.
39. Brendan Lynn, 'The Irish Anti-Partition League and the political realities of partition, 1945–9', *Irish Historical Studies*, vol. 34, no. 135 (2005), pp 321–32, p. 323.
40. Michael Foy, 'The Ancient Order of Hibernians: An Irish political-religious pressure group 1884–1975' (unpublished MA thesis, Queen's University, Belfast, 1976), p. 150. Opened in 1932, the Stormont building was home to both houses of parliament in Northern Ireland until its suspension in 1972, Alan Greer, 'Sir James Craig and the construction of parliament buildings at Stormont', *Irish Historical Studies*, vol. 31, no. 123 (May 1999), pp 373–88.
41. Byrne, Cosgrave, and Redmond have been categorised as 'vestigial independents' in the Dáil, Liam Weeks, *Independents in Irish Party Democracy* (Manchester, 2017).
42. Charles Callan and Barry Desmond, *Irish Labour Lives: A Biographical Dictionary of Irish Labour Party Deputies, Senators, MPs and MEPs* (Dublin, 2010).
43. Tony Varley, 'Gaining ground, losing ground: the politics of land reform in twentieth-century Ireland', in Fergus Campbell and Varley (eds), *Land Questions in Modern Ireland* (Manchester, 2013). p. 48.

44. Varley, 'Irish Farmers' Parties, nationalism and class politics in the twentieth century' in Liam Weeks and Alastair Clark, *Radical or Redundant? Minor Parties in Irish Political Life* (Dublin, 2012), p. 161.
45. Fitzpatrick, *Politics and Irish Life*, pp 274–5.
46. Quoted in John Shepherd, 'The flight from the Liberal Party: Liberals who joined Labour, 1914–1931', *Journal of Liberal History*, 67 (Summer 2010), pp 24-34, p. 25.
47. Catherine Ann Cline, *Recruits to Labour: The British Labour Party 1914–1931* (New York, 1963), p. 134, n. 26 and appendix, pp 149–78; Shepherd, 'The flight from the Liberal Party'; Robert E. Dowse, 'The entry of the Liberals into the Labour Party 1910–1920', *Bulletin of Economic Research*, vol. 13, no. 2 (November 1961), pp 78–87.
48. On the longer-term legacies of 'Liberal Britain', see Vernon Bogdanor, *The Strange Survival of Liberal Britain: Politics and Power Before the First World War* (London, 2022).
49. Ciara Meehan, *The Cosgrave Party: A History of Cumann na nGaedheal, 1923–33* (Dublin, 2010), p. xi.
50. See James McConnel, *The Irish Parliamentary Party and the Third Home Rule Crisis* (Dublin, 2013), chapter 10.
51. Anne Dolan, *Commemorating the Irish Civil War: History and Memory, 1923–2000* (Cambridge, 2003), pp 57–121.
52. Jason Knirck, *Afterimage of the Revolution: Cumann na nGaedheal and Irish Politics, 1922–1932* (Madison, WI, 2014), pp 141–213; Hugh Hanley, 'Monarchism, international relations, and the continuing Irish revolution, 1926–29', *The Journal of Imperial and Commonwealth History*, vol. 49, no. 1 (2021), pp 93–117. On republicanism, see Seán Donnelly, 'Republicanism and civic virtue in Treatyite political thought, 1921–3', *The Historical Journal*, vol. 63, no. 5 (December 2020), pp 1257–80.
53. Frank Callanan, *T. M Healy* (Cork, 1996), pp 595–605; John M. Regan, *The Irish Counter-Revolution, 1921–1936: Treatyite Politics and Settlement in Independent Ireland* (Dublin, 2001), pp 232–3, 244, 265.
54. Mulvagh, *The Irish Parliamentary Party*, p. 1; Wheatley, *Nationalism and the Irish Party*.
55. For critiques of the Free State government by O'Donnell and Dillon, see F. S. L. Lyons, *John Dillon: A Biography* (London, 1968) and J. Anthony Gaughan, *A Political Odyssey: Thomas O'Donnell, MP for West Kerry, 1900–1918* (Dublin, 1983).
56. O'Donoghue, *The Legacy of the Irish Parliamentary Party*, pp 36–7.
57. O'Donoghue, *The Legacy of the Irish Parliamentary Party*, p. 86.
58. Edward C. Walsh to B. C. Hackett, 3 September 1926, NLI O'Donnell Papers MS 15,461(3).
59. O'Donoghue, *The Legacy of the Irish Parliamentary Party*, p. 102.
60. See. for example, letter from Capt. Redmond and Tom O'Donnell, 19 August 1927, NLI, O'Donnell papers, MS 15,465 (7).
61. Patrick Maume, *The Long Gestation: Irish Nationalist Life, 1891–1918* (Dublin, 1999), p. 219.
62. O'Donoghue, *The Legacy of the Irish Parliamentary Party*, p. 127.
63. Farrell, *Party Politics*.
64. Paul Bew, Ellen Hazelkorn and Henry Patterson, *The Dynamics of Irish Politics* (London, 1989).
65. *Seanad Debates*, vol. 15, cc 557–8, 28 January 1932; *Irish Independent*, 14 January 1933; Reports and correspondence of honorary secretaries 1926–32, UCD Archives (UCDA) Fianna Fáil Archives, P176/352.
66. *Irish Independent*, 6 January 1933. The Free-thinking Democratic League in the Netherlands (VDB) produced a poster in 1922 depicting the ship of state sailing between the rocks of revolution and reaction. In the twenty-first century, the image has been revived, including by Neoliberal opponents of left and right political movements, https://cnliberalism.org/store/p/steer-clear-of-the-populist-tides-poster [12 February 2024]. For a discussion of Free State politics in a European context, see Farrell, *Party Politics*, pp 54–7.
67. Meehan, *The Cosgrave Party*.
68. Mike Cronin, 'The Blueshirt movement, 1932–5: Ireland's Fascists?', *Journal of Contemporary History*, vol. 30, no. 2 (1995), pp 311–32; Maurice Manning, *The Blueshirts* (Dublin, 1970).
69. *Irish Independent*, 2 September 1933. Heads of Policy, minutes of meeting of the General Purposes Committee of Fine Gael, 9 November 1933, UCDA Fine Gael Papers, P39/MIN 2. Other policies

included settling the economic dispute with Britain, remission of Annuities, anti-communism, opposition to proportional representation and reform of local government.

70. Ciara Meehan, 'Fine Gael's uncomfortable history: the legacy of Cumann na nGaedheal', *Éire-Ireland*, vol. 43, nos 3–4 (2008), pp 53–66.
71. O'Donoghue, *The Legacy of the Irish Parliamentary Party*, p. 172.
72. Christopher Norton, *The Politics of Constitutional Nationalism in Northern Ireland, 1932–70: Between Grievance and Reconciliation* (Manchester, 2016). For an example of its diversity, see circular letter from Cahir Healy 20 February 1939, PRONI Cahir Healy Papers D2991/A/5/42.
73. Farrell, *Northern Ireland: The Orange State*, p. 170.
74. Manning, *James Dillon: A Biography* (Dublin, 1999), pp 173–4.
75. Lynn, 'The Irish Anti-Partition League'; Bob Purdie, *Politics in the Streets: The Origins of the Civil Rights Movement in Northern Ireland* (Belfast, 1990), p. 41.
76. Éamon de Valera speech at Parnell centenary quoted in *Irish Independent*, 30 December 1946.
77. David McCullagh, *The Reluctant Taoiseach: A Biography of John A. Costello* (Dublin, 2010), pp 21–2.
78. *Dáil Debates*, vol. 113, cols. 644–5 and 848, 26 November and 1 December 1948; Manning, *James Dillon*, pp 241–6; Mel Farrell, 'Cumann na nGaedheal: "a new national party"?', in Mel Farrell, Jason Knirck and Ciara Meehan (eds), *A Formative Decade: Ireland in the 1920s* (Dublin, 2015), p. 38.
79. Arthur Balfour quoted in Sydney H. Zebel, *Balfour: A Political Biography* (Cambridge, 1973), p. 186.
80. Eoin MacNeill to Maurice Moore, 11 September 1916, NLI Moore Papers MS 10,561 (27).
81. Basil Chubb, *The Government and Politics of Ireland* (London, 1992); Michael Gallagher and Lee Komito, 'The constituency role of TDs' in John Coakley and Michael Gallagher (eds), *Politics in the Republic of Ireland* (London, 2009), pp 230–62.
82. David Fitzpatrick, 'Ireland and Empire', in Andrew Porter (ed.) *The Oxford History of the British Empire: Volume III: The Nineteenth Century* (Oxford, 1999), pp 494–521; Mulvagh, *The Irish Parliamentary Party*, p. 1.
83. Stephen Legg, 'Dyarchy: Democracy, autocracy, and the scalar sovereignty of interwar India', *Comparative Studies of South Asia, Africa and the Middle East*, vol. 36, no 1 (May 2016), pp 44–65, p. 62. The Irish Party had talks with Dadabhai Naoroji about becoming an Irish Party MP in 1883 and Alfred Webb was President of the Indian National Congress in its earlier form in 1894, Jennifer Regan-Lefebvre, *Cosmopolitan Nationalism in the Victorian Empire: Ireland, India and the Politics of Alfred Webb* (Cambridge, 2009); John R. McLane, *Indian Nationalism and the Early Congress* (Princeton, NJ, 1977), pp 99, 123, 128.
84. Mulvagh, *The Irish Parliamentary Party*, p. 260.
85. Steven P. Erie, *Rainbow's End: Irish-Americans and the Dilemmas of Urban Machine Politics, 1840–1985* (Berkeley, CA, 1990).
86. Home rulers dominated local government from the foundation of county councils in 1899 while AOH rhetoric often centred on Catholic advancement. On the favourable treatment received by larger farmers at local level in Galway, Fergus Campbell, 'Land purchase and radicalisation in county Galway, c.1881–1931', *Irish Studies Review*, vol. 28, no. 1 (2020), pp 20–42.
87. James McConnel, 'The view from the backbench: Irish Nationalist MPs and their work, 1910–1914', PhD thesis (University of Durham, 2002), pp 278–82.
88. Brendan Lynn, *Holding the Ground: The Nationalist Party in Northern Ireland, 1945–1972* (Farnham, 1997).
89. Regan, *The Irish Counter-Revolution*, pp 150, 214, 218–19.
90. Farrell, 'Cumann na nGaedheal: a new national party?', p. 44.
91. Regan, *The Irish Counter-Revolution*, pp 231, 312; Brian Reynolds, 'The formation and development of Fianna Fáil, 1926–33', PhD thesis, (Trinity College Dublin, 1976), pp 422–3; McConnel, 'The view from the backbench', p. 129.
92. Richard Dunphy, *The Making of Fianna Fáil Power in Ireland, 1923–1948* (Oxford, 1995), p. 49.
93. Reynolds, 'The formation and development of Fianna Fáil', pp 187–190; Meehan, *The Cosgrave Party*, p. 160; Sarah-Jane Delany, Richard Sinnott and Niall O'Reilly, 'The Extent of Clientelism in Irish Politics: evidence from classifying Dáil questions on a local-national dimension', *AICS: Proceedings of the 21st Conference on Artificial Intelligence and Cognitive Science*, NUI Galway (2010).
94. Manning, *James Dillon*, pp 202–10.

95. Dillon delivered a lecture on the subject in the Irish Club in London, *Cork Examiner*, 9 February 1966; *Roscommon Herald*, 28 February 1986; *Irish Times*, London letter, TCD James Dillon papers MS 10541/95.
96. 'Former Taoiseach says Easter Rising "unnecessary"', *Irish Times*, 4 August 2014.
97. Norton, *The Politics of Constitutional Nationalism in Northern Ireland*.
98. Sarah Campbell, *Gerry Fitt and the SDLP – 'in a minority of one'* (Manchester, 2015).
99. James McConnel, *The Irish Parliamentary Party and the Third Home Rule Crisis* (Dublin, 2013), conclusion; Maurice Manning, 'Houses of the Oireachtas: background and early development' in Manning and Muiris MacCarthaigh (eds), *The Houses of the Oireachtas: Parliament in Ireland* (Dublin, 2010), pp 15–17.

Chapter 8: The Parliamentary Career of Bridget Redmond TD, 1933–52: A Gendered Analysis

1. A TD or Teachta Dála is a member of Dáil Éireann, the lower house of the Oireachtas (the Irish Parliament). It is equivalent to an MP or Member of Parliament.
2. He had previously been MP for East Tyrone from 1910 to 1918.
3. Alice McDermott, 'Bridget Redmond: the keeper of the Redmondite flame in Waterford', *Decies*, 66 (2010), pp 87–102, p. 87.
4. Maebhbh McNamara and Paschal Mooney, *Women in Parliament: Ireland, 1918–2000* (Dublin, 2000), p. 28.
5. Karen Beckwith, 'A common language of gender?', *Politics and Gender*, vol, 1, no. 1N (2005), pp 128–37, p. 131.
6. Maryann Gialanella Valiulis, 'The politics of gender in the Irish Free State, 1922–1937', *Women's History Review*, vol. 20, no. 2, pp 569–78, p. 570.
7. Claire McGing, 'Without distinction of sex: The roles of women in the 1923 general election' in Elaine Callinan, Mel Farrell and Thomas Tormey (eds), *Vying for Victory: The 1923 General Election in the Irish Free State* (Dublin, 2022), pp 87–98, p. 91.
8. *Cork Examiner*, 17 November 1922.
9. Thomas Mohr, 'The rights of women under the constitution of the Irish Free State', *Irish Jurist*, vol. 41, no. 3 (2006), pp 20–59, p. 56.
10. *Irish Independent*, 28 September 1922 and 30 September 1922.
11. Maryann Gialanella Valiulis, 'Power, gender and identity in the Irish Free State', *Journal of Women's History*, vol. 7, no. 1 (1995), pp 117–36, p. 118.
12. Caitriona Beaumont, 'After the vote: Women, citizenship and the campaign for gender equality in the Irish Free State' (1922–43) in Louise Ryan and Margaret Ward (eds), *Irish Women and the Vote: Becoming Citizens* (Dublin, 2018), pp 231–49, p. 233.
13. Valiulis, 'Power, gender and identity in the Irish Free State', p. 122.
14. Alpha Connelly, 'Women and the constitution in Ireland' in Yvonne Galligan, Eilís Ward and Rick Wilford (eds), *Contesting Politics: Women in Ireland, North and South* (Oxford, 1999), pp 18–37, p. 19.
15. Tom Garvin, 'Continuity and change in Irish electoral politics, 1923–1926', *Economic and Social Review*, vol. 3, no. 3 (1972), pp 359–72, p. 362.
16. Claire McGing, 'Women's political representation in Dáil Éireann in revolutionary and post-revolutionary Ireland' in Linda Connolly (ed.), *Women and the Irish Revolution: Feminism, Activism, Violence* (Dublin, 2020), pp 85–100, p. 96.
17. P. S. O'Hegarty, *The Victory of Sinn Féin: How it won it, and how it used it* (Dublin, 1924), p. 104.
18. McGing, 'Without distinction of sex', p. 90.
19. McGing, 'Women's political representation in Dáil Éireann', p. 78.
20. McDermott, 'Bridget Redmond', pp 87–102.
21. Pat McCarthy, *The Redmonds and Waterford: A Political Dynasty, 1891–1952* (Dublin, 2018).
22. McNamara and Mooney, *Women in Parliament*, p. 95.
23. McDermott, 'Bridget Redmond', p. 99.
24. Ibid.; Maria Hegarty and Martina Murray, *Proud to Serve: The Voices of the Women of Cumann na nGaedheal and Fine Gael* (Dublin, 2021), p. 41.

25. Marie Coleman, 'Redmond, William Archer', in *Dictionary of Irish Biography* (Dublin, 2009). Available at: https://www.dib.ie/biography/redmond-william-archer-a7608, accessed 10 July 2018.
26. *Irish Times*, 22 November 1930.
27. McDermott, 'Bridget Redmond', p. 91.
28. Alice McDermott, 'The heart of the matter: an analysis of the most significantly influential factors in the creation of Redmondism in Waterford city from 1891–1918', *Decies*, 69 (2013), pp 139–53.
29. McDermott, 'The heart of the matter', p. 142.
30. McDermott, 'Bridget Redmond', p. 93.
31. Ibid.
32. Information sourced from https://electionsireland.org, accessed 6 July 2018.
33. McDermott, 'Bridget Redmond', p. 95.
34. *Cork Examiner*, 13 December 1930.
35. Mel Farrell, *Party Politics in a New Democracy: The Irish Free State* (Basingstoke, 2017), p. 155.
36. Farrell, *Party Politics in a New Democracy*, p. 78.
37. McDermott, 'Bridget Redmond', p. 99.
38. Eleanor Lowe, 'To keep it in the family: Spouses, seat inheritance and parliamentary elections in post-suffrage Britain 1918–1945', *Open Library of Humanities*, vol. 6, no. 2 (2020), pp 1–33, p. 28.
39. *Irish Press*, 18 April 1932.
40. Ibid.
41. *Munster Express*, 22 April 1932.
42. Ibid.
43. Ibid.
44. *Munster Express*, 13 May 1932.
45. *Waterford Standard*, 23 April 1932.
46. *Kerry News*, 25 April 1932.
47. Ibid.
48. McCarthy, *The Redmonds and Waterford*, p. 143.
49. *Irish Independent*, 20 July 1932.
50. McCarthy, *The Redmonds and Waterford*, p. 143.
51. McDermott, 'Bridget Redmond', p. 96; Mooney and McNamara, *Women in Parliament*, p. 16.
52. *The Watchword*, 30 April 1932.
53. McCarthy, *The Redmonds and Waterford*, pp 142–6.
54. Ibid., p. 144.
55. For example, *Evening Echo*, 16 December 1932; *Irish Press*, 16 December 1932.
56. *Cork Evening Echo*, 19 December 1932.
57. McCarthy, *The Redmonds and Waterford*, p. 145.
58. *Dublin Evening Mail*, 19 December 1932.
59. *Munster Express*, 23 December 1932.
60. Ibid., 13 January 1933.
61. Farrell, *Party Politics in a New Democracy*, p. 14.
62. *Cork Examiner*, 17 January 1933; *Irish Independent*, 18 January 1933.
63. McCarthy, *The Redmonds and Waterford*, p. 144.
64. *Irish Press*, 23 January 1933.
65. *Cork Examiner*, 17 January 1933.
66. McCarthy, *The Redmonds and Waterford*, p. 147.
67. Ibid., p. 149.
68. *Cork Examiner*, 31 July 1933.
69. *Munster Express*, 30 June 1933.
70. Ibid., 27 October 1933.
71. Ibid.
72. Maurice Manning, *The Blueshirts* (Dublin, 2006), pp 21–5.
73. When the organisation was banned, the Young Ireland Association emerged in September 1933. In December 1933, the YIA was banned, and O'Duffy and Fine Gael set up the League of Youth.
74. Manning, *The Blueshirts*, pp 61–2; Fearghal McGarry, *Eoin O'Duffy: A Self-Made Hero* (Oxford, 2007), pp 189–97.

75. Dale Montgomery, 'No Suggestion of Suffragettism: The Blue Blouses in Ireland, 1933–1936', *Women's History Review*, vol. 23, no. 5 (2014), pp 776–92, p. 781.
76. Ibid.
77. Kevin Passmore, 'Europe' in Kevin Passmore (ed.), *Women, Gender, and Fascism in Europe, 1919–45* (New Brunswick, 2003), pp 235–68, p. 257.
78. Montgomery, 'No Suggestion of Suffragettism', p. 257.
79. *Munster Express*, 6 April 1934.
80. For example, *Munster Express*, 23 March, 1934; *United Ireland*, 16 December 1933.
81. Manning, *The Blueshirts*, p. 238; Mike Cronin, 'The Blueshirt Movement, 1932–5: Ireland's Fascists?', *Journal of Contemporary History*, vol. 30, no. 2 (1995), pp 311–32, p. 331.
82. McDermott, 'Bridget Redmond', p. 101.
83. *Irish Press*, 21 July 1933.
84. Mel Farrell, 'From Cumann na nGaedheal to Fine Gael: the foundation of the United Ireland Party in September 1933', *Éire-Ireland*, vol. 49, nos 3–4 (2014), pp 143–71, p. 143.
85. Pauric J. Dempsey and Shaun Boylan, 'Brown, Kathleen Anne', in *Dictionary of Irish Biography* (Dublin, 2009). Available at: https://www.dib.ie/biography/browne-kathleen-anne-a1036, accessed 21 July 2019.
86. McCarthy, *The Redmonds and Waterford*, p. 152.
87. *Irish Independent*, 16 June 1951.
88. Joni Lovenduski, *Feminizing Politics* (Cambridge, 2005), p. 48.
89. *Cork Examiner*, 5 May 1952.
90. Clancy, 'Shaping the nation', p. 207; McCarthy, *The Redmonds and Waterford*, p. 162; McDermott, 'Bridget Redmond', p. 100; McNamara and Mooney, *Women in Parliament*, p. 96, Margaret Ward, *Unmanageable Revolutionaries:Women and Irish Nationalism* (London, 1983), p. 241.
91. McDermott, 'Bridget Redmond', pp 100–1.
92. Dáil Éireann debates, Committee on Finance – Local Government (Resumed), vol. 106, no. 10, 3 June 1947.
93. Dáil Éireann debates, Committee on Finance – Racing Board and Racecourses Bill – Financial Resolution, vol. 96, no. 10, 8 March 1945.
94. Dáil Éireann debates, Committee on Finance – Pigs and Bacon Bill – Financial Resolution, vol. 67, no. 4, 14 May 1937.
95. McNamara and Mooney, *Women in Parliament*, p. 96.
96. McCarthy, *The Redmonds and Waterford*, p. 160.
97. Hegarty and Murray, 'Proud to Serve', p. 42.
98. Dáil Éireann debates – Office of the Minister for Education (Resumed) – vol. 106, no. 3, 20 May 1947.
99. The five parties were Fine Gael, the Labour Party, Clann na Poblachta, Clann na Talmhan and the National Labour Party – and one independent TD, James Dillon (a former member of Fine Gael).
100. Dáil Éireann debates, The Republic of Ireland Bill, vol. 113, no. 5, 26 November 1948.
101. *Irish Times*, 27 November 1948. See also McCarthy, *The Redmonds and Waterford*, p.164.
102. Maurice Manning, 'Women in Irish National and Local Politics, 1922–1977' in Margaret MacCurtain and Donnacha Ó Corráin (eds), *Women in Irish Society: The Historical Dimension* (Dublin, 1978), pp 92–102, p. 96.
103. Hanna Sheehy Skeffington, 'Women in politics', *The Bell*, 7 November 1943, cited in Margaret Ward (ed.), *Hanna Sheehy Skeffington: Suffragette and Sinn Féiner: Her Memoirs and Political Writings* (Dublin, 2017), p. 385.
104. Margaret Ward, *In Their Own Voice: Women and Irish Nationalism* (Cork, 1995), pp 188–9.
105. Ibid.
106. McNamara and Mooney, *Women in Parliament*, p.17.
107. Mary Daly, 'The 'women element' in politics: Irish women and the vote, 1918–2008' in Esther Breitenbach and Pat Thane (eds), *Women and Citizenship in Britain and Ireland in the Twentieth Century* (London, 2010), pp 79–94, p. 81.
108. *Sunday Independent*, 18 July 1937.
109. McCarthy, *The Redmonds and Waterford*, p. 160.
110. Maria Luddy, 'A "sinister and retrogressive" proposal: Irish women's opposition to the 1937 draft constitution', *Transactions of the RHS*, 15 (2005), pp 175–95.

111. Connelly, 'Women and the constitution in Ireland', pp 18–37.
112. Luddy, 'A "sinister and retrogressive" proposal', p. 184.
113. *Irish Press*, 15 May 1937.
114. Ibid.
115. Dáil Éireann debates, Bunreacht na hÉireann, vol. 67, no. 10, 28 May 1937.
116. *Irish Press*, 20 May 1937.
117. Ward, *Unmanageable Revolutionaries*, pp 240–1.
118. Ibid., p. 241.
119. Luddy, 'A "sinister and retrogressive" proposal', p. 183.
120. Ibid.
121. McDermott, 'Bridget Redmond', p. 101.
122. McCarthy, *The Redmonds and Waterford*, p. 165.
123. Gail McElroy, 'The impact of gender quotas on voting behaviour in 2016' in David Farrell, Michael Marsh and Theresa Reidy (eds), *The Post-Crisis Irish Voter: Voting Behaviour in the Irish 2016 General Election* (Manchester, 2018), pp 165–89, p. 166.
124. Maurice Manning, 'Women and the elections' in Howard R. Penniman and Brian Farrell (eds) *Ireland at the Polls: 1981, 1982 and 1987* (North Carolina, 1987), pp 156–66, p. 158.
125. Sinéad McCoole, 'Debating not negotiating: the female TDs of the second Dáil' in Liam Weeks and Mícheál Ó Fathartaigh (eds), *The Treaty: Debating and Establishing the Irish State* (Dublin, 2018), pp 136–59, p. 155; McGing, 'Women's political representation in Dáil Éireann', p. 99.
126. Lowe, 'To keep it in the family', p. 3.
127. *Leinster Leader,* 10 May 1952.
128. Information sourced from https://electionsireland.org, accessed 15 August 2018.

Chapter 9: The Contradictions of Redmondism

1. Martin Mansergh (ed.), *The Spirit of the Nation: The Speeches and Statements of Charles J. Haughey* (Cork, 1986), p. 310.
2. Ibid., p. 259.
3. Paul Bew, *Enigma: A New Life of Charles Stewart Parnell* (Dublin, 2011), p. 189.
4. Dermot Meleady, *Redmond: The Parnellite* (Cork, 2008).
5. The owner Edmund Dwyer Gray was born a Protestant but converted to Catholicism prior to marriage, Felix M. Larkin, 'A great daily organ': the *Freeman's Journal*, 1763–1924, *History Ireland*, vol. 14, no. 3 (May/June 2006), pp 44–9.
6. Patrick Maume, 'Parnell and the IRB Oath', *Irish Historical Studies*, vol. 29, no. 115 (1995), pp 363–70.
7. Paul Bew, *Enigma*; Harold Spender, 'John Redmond: An impression', *Contemporary Review*, vol. 113 (April 1918), pp 375–6.
8. Dermot Meleady (ed.), *John Redmond: Selected Letters and Memoranda, 1880–1918* (Dublin, 2018), p. 272.
9. Spender, 'John Redmond: an impression', pp 375–6.
10. Meleady, *Redmond: The Parnellite*.
11. Meleady, *Selected Letters*, p. 49.
12. For this section, see Paul Bew, *John Redmond* (Dublin, 1996), chapters 2 and 3. See also, Paul Bew, *Conflict and Conciliation in Ireland, 1890–1910: Parnellites and Radical Agrarians* (Oxford, 1987).
13. Spender, 'John Redmond: An impression', pp 375–6.
14. David S. Jones, *Graziers, Land Reform and Political Conflict in Ireland* (Washington, DC, 1995). See also review of by Bew, *History Ireland*, vol. 4, no. 2 (Summer issue, 1996), pp 55–6 and Jones, 'The cleavage between graziers and peasants in the land struggle, 1890–1910', in Samuel Clark and James S. Donnelly (eds), *Irish peasants: violence and political unrest, 1780–1914* (Madison, WI, 1986), pp 374–419.
15. The Ranch War 1906–9 was a campaign of direct action (cattle drives, boycotts, intimidation) by smallholders to gain more land, see Bew, *Conflict and Conciliation*.

16. 'The diaries of Laurence and Alice Ginnell', in Michael Wheatley, *Nationalism and the Irish Party* (Oxford, 2005), Appendix C, p. 254, entry for 2 May 1907. I am indebted to Michael Wheatley for signposting this, and to his important book.
17. Bew, *Ideology and the Irish Question: Ulster Unionism and Irish Nationalism, 1912–1916* (Oxford, 1994), p. 120.
18. D. P. Moran, *The Leader*, 1 March 1913 quoted in Bew, *John Redmond*, p. 34.
19. Compare with Michael Davitt, 'The Irish National Assembly (session of 1910)', *Independent Review*, no. 5 (1905), pp 284–98.
20. Bew, *Redmond*, p. 30, reference to May 1908 interview with A . G. Gardiner, *Irish People*, 26 May 1908.
21. *Irish World*, 26 November 1910, where the *IW* reported that Redmond gave a speech at Syracuse in New York where he quoted Parnell and said 'Let us get this first and then demand more'.
22. R. F. Foster, *Modern Ireland, 1600–1972* (London, 1988), p. 470.
23. Wheatley, *Nationalism and the Irish Party*.
24. Bew, *Ideology and the Irish Question*.
25. Bew, *Ideology and the Irish Question*; *John Redmond*.
26. Bew, *Ideology and the Irish Question*, pp 148–50.
27. See Paul Bew, *Churchill and Ireland* (Oxford, 2016), pp 85–6.
28. For Michael MacDonagh, *The Irish at the Front* (London, 1916), with an introduction by John Redmond.
29. Aghavannagh, Co Wicklow, the location of Redmond's home and had previously been Parnell's shooting lodge.
30. Bew, *Ideology and the Irish Question*, p. 138.
31. Patrick Maume, *The Long Gestation: Irish Nationalist Life*, 1891-1918 (Dublin, 1999), p. 157.
32. Wheatley, chapter 5 in this volume.
33. Maume, *The Long Gestation*, p. 157.
34. This argument is developed in Stephen Gwynn, *John Redmond's Last Years* (London, 1919).
35. Bew, *John Redmond*, p. 35.
36. John Bruton remarks at Redmond Centenary Symposium, 6 March 2018.
37. Frank Sheridan (ed.), *The Making of The Anglo-Irish Agreement of 1985: A Memoir by David Goodall* (Dublin, 2021).
38. Bew, Gibbon and Patterson, *Northern Ireland 1921–1996 Political Forces and Social Classes* (1996), pp 217–224.
39. *Irish Times*, 22 April 1996: 'The Hardening of Fianna Fáil'.
40. A. M. Sullivan, *Old Ireland: Reminiscences of an Irish K.C.* (London, 1927), p. 137.
41. Paul Bew, *The Making and Remaking of the Good Friday Agreement* (Dublin, 2007).
42. See Trimble comments on the British-Irish Council, *Irish Times*, 15 December 1999.
43. Churchill quoted in Bew, *Churchill and Ireland* (Oxford, 2016), p. 56.
44. *Belfast News-Letter*, 9 February, 1912.
45. Ibid.
46. Ibid.; Bew, *Churchill and Ireland*, p. 58.

Select Bibliography

Bew, Paul, *Conflict and Conciliation in Ireland, 1880–1910: Parnellites and Radical Agrarians* (London, 1987).
Bew, Paul, *Ideology and the Irish Question: Ulster Unionism and Irish Nationalism, 1912–1916* (Oxford, 1994).
Bew, Paul, *John Redmond* (Dundalk, 1996).
Bew, Paul, 'Moderate nationalism and the Irish revolution, 1916–1923', in *The Historical Journal*, vol. 42, no. 3 (1999), pp 729–49.
Bew, Paul, 'Redmond, John Edward (1856–1918)', in *Oxford Dictionary of National Biography* (2004–05).
Bew, Paul, *Ireland: The Politics of Enmity, 1789–2006* (Oxford, 2007).
Bew, Paul, *Enigma: A New Life of Charles Stewart Parnell* (Dublin, 2011).
Bew, Paul, *Ancestral Voices in Irish Politics: Judging Dillon and Parnell* (Oxford, 2023).
Biagini, Eugenio, *British Democracy and Irish Nationalism 1876–1906* (Cambridge, 2007).
Biagini, Eugenio, Patrick Geoghegan, Hugh Hanley, Aneirin Jones, and Huw Jones, 'From sentiment to style: Charles Stewart Parnell's rhetoric in the first crisis of the UK', in *Digital Scholarship in Humanities*, vol. 38, no. 2 (2023), pp 492–500.
Boyce, D. G., *Nationalism in Ireland* (Dublin, 1982).
Brady, L. W., *T. P. O'Connor and the Liverpool Irish* (London, 1983).
Brady, Ciarán (ed.), *Worsted in the Game? Losers in Irish History* (Dublin, 1989).
Bull, Philip, 'The United Irish League and the reunion of the Irish Parliamentary Party, 1898–1900'. in *Irish Historical Studies*, vol. 26, no. 101 (1988), pp 51–78.
Butt, Isaac, *Home Government for Ireland: Irish Federalism! Its Meaning, Its Objects, and Its Hopes* (Dublin, 1874).
Callanan, Frank, *The Parnell Split, 1890–91* (Cork, 1992).
Callanan, Frank, *T. M. Healy* (Cork, 1996).
Collombier-Lakeman, Pauline, 'Ireland and the Empire: The ambivalence of Irish constitutional nationalism', in *Radical History Review*, no. 104 (2009), pp 57–76.
Collombier-Lakeman, Pauline, 'Nationality and citizenship in the Irish home rule debates of 1886', in *Revue Française de Civilisation Britannique* (2016), pp 1–16.
Collombier-Lakeman, Pauline, *The Home Rule Question (1870–1914)* (Paris, 2018).
Collombier-Lakeman, Pauline, 'Comparing Isaac Butt and John Redmond', in *Review of Irish Studies in Europe* 3, no. 2 (2020), pp 6–23.
Collombier, Pauline, *Imagining Ireland's Future: Home Rule, Utopia, Dystopia* (London, 2023).
Dangerfield, George, *The Strange Death of Liberal England* (London, 1935).
Davitt, Michael, *The Fall of Feudalism in Ireland: Or the Story of the Land League Revolution* (London, 1904).
Denman, Terence, *A Lonely Grave: The Life and Death of Willie Redmond* (Dublin, 1995).
De Vere White, Terence, *The Road of Excess* (Dublin, 1946).
Doherty, Erica, 'T. P. O'Connor and the Irish Parliamentary Party, 1912–24', Unpublished PhD thesis, Queen's University Belfast, 2012.
Doherty, Gabriel (ed.), *The Home Rule Crisis, 1912–14: Cork Studies in the Irish Revolution* (Cork, 2014).
Doherty, James, *Irish Liberty, British Democracy: The Third Irish Home Rule Crisis, 1909–14* (Cork, 2019).
Fanning, Ronan, *Fatal Path: British Government and Irish Revolution, 1910–1922* (London, 2013).

Farrell, Brian (ed.), *Chairman or Chief? The Role of Taoiseach in Irish Government* (Dublin, 1971).
Farrell, Brian (ed.), *The Irish Parliamentary Tradition (With Three Essays on the Treaty by F. S.L. Lyons)* (Dublin, 1973).
Ferriter, Diarmaid, *The Transformation of Ireland, 1900–2000* (London, 2004).
Finnan, Joseph P., *John Redmond and Irish Unity: 1912–1918* (New York, 2004).
Fitzpatrick, David, *Politics and Irish Life: Provincial Experiences of War and Revolution* (Aldershot, 1977).
Foster, R. F., *Charles Stewart Parnell: The Man and His Family* (London, 1977).
Foster, R. F., *Modern Ireland, 1600–1972* (London, 1987).
Foster, R. F., and Alvin Jackson, 'Men for all seasons? Carson, Parnell, and the limits of heroism in modern Ireland,' in *European History Quarterly*, vol. 39, no. 3 (2009), pp 414–36.
Foster, R. F. *Vivid Faces: The Revolutionary Generation in Ireland, 1890–1923* (London, 2015).
Fyfe, Hamilton, *T. P. O'Connor* (London, 1934).
Garvin, Tom, *The Evolution of Irish Nationalist Politics* (Dublin, 1981).
Garvin, Tom, *1922: The Birth of Irish Democracy* (Dublin, 1996).
Gaughan, J. A., *A Political Odyssey: Thomas O'Donnell, MP for West Kerry, 1900–1918* (Dublin, 1983).
Gwynn, Denis, *The Life of John Redmond (London, 1932)*.
Gwynn, Stephen, *John Redmond's Last Years* (London 1919).
Harrison, Henry, *Parnell Vindicated: The Lifting of the Veil* (London, 1931).
Harrison, Henry, 'Parnell's vindication', in *Irish Historical Studies*, vol. 5, no. 19 (1947), pp 231–43.
Haslip, Joan, *Parnell: A Biography* (London, 1936).
Healy, T. M., *Letters and Leaders of My Day*, 2 Vols (London, 1929).
Hepburn, A. C., *Catholic Belfast and Nationalist Ireland in the Era of Joe Devlin, 1871–1934* (Oxford, 2008).
Howe, Stephen, *Ireland and Empire: Colonial Legacies in Irish History and Culture* (Oxford, 2002).
Jackson, Alvin, *The Ulster Party: Irish Unionists in the House of Commons, 1884–1911* (Oxford, 1989).
Jackson, Alvin, *Ireland, 1798–1998: Politics and War* (Oxford, 2000).
Jackson, Alvin, *Home Rule: An Irish History* (London, 2003).
Jackson, Alvin, *Judging Redmond and Carson: Comparative Irish Lives* (Dublin, 2018).
Jackson, Alvin, *United Kingdoms: Multinational Union States in Europe and Beyond, 1800–1925* (Oxford, 2023).
Jalland, Patricia, *The Liberals and Ireland: The Ulster Question in British Politics to 1914* (Sussex, 1980).
Kelly, Matthew, '"Parnell's old brigade": the Redmondite–Fenian nexus in the 1890s', in *Irish Historical Studies*, vol. 33, no. 130 (2002), pp 209–32.
Kelly, Matthew, *The Fenian Ideal and Irish Nationalism, 1882–1916* (Woodbridge, 2006).
King, Carla, *Michael Davitt After the Land League, 1882–1906* (Dublin, 2016).
King, Tony, *Home Rule from a Transnational Perspective: The Irish Parliamentary Party and the United Irish League of America, 1901–1918* (Wilmington, DE, 2021).
Laffan, Michael 'Redmond, John Edward', in *Dictionary of Irish Biography*.
Laffan, Michael, *The Resurrection of Ireland: The Sinn Féin Party, 1916–1923* (Cambridge, 1999).
Leerssen, Joep (ed.), *Parnell and His Times* (Cambridge, 2021).
Lubenow, W. C., *Parliamentary Politics and the Home Rule Crisis: The British House of Commons in 1886* (Oxford, 1989).
Lyons, F. S. L., *The Irish Parliamentary Party, 1890–1910* (London, 1951).
Lyons, F. S. L., *John Dillon: A Biography* (London, 1968).
Lyons, F. S. L., *Ireland Since the Famine* (London, 1971).
Lyons, F. S. L., *Charles Stewart Parnell* (London, 1977).
MacAtasney, Gerard, *Tom Clarke: Life, Liberty, Revolution* (Dublin, 2013).
MacDonagh, Michael, *The Irish at the Front* (London, 1916).
Manning, Maurice, *James Dillon: A Biography* (Dublin, 1999).
Manning, Maurice and Muiris MacCarthaigh (eds), *The Houses of the Oireachtas: Parliament in Ireland* (Dublin, 2010).
Mansergh, Nicholas, 'John Redmond', in Conor Cruise O'Brien (ed.), *The Shaping of Modern Ireland* (London, 1960).

Mansergh, Diana, (ed.), *Nationalism and Independence: Selected Irish Papers by Nicholas Mansergh* (Cork, 1997).
Marley, Laurence, *Michael Davitt: Freelance Radical and Frondeur* (Dublin, 2007).
Maume, Patrick, *The Long Gestation: Irish Nationalist Life, 1891–1918* (Dublin, 1999).
McCarthy, Pat, *The Redmonds and Waterford: A Political Dynasty, 1891–1952* (Dublin, 2018).
McCartney, Donal, and Pauric Travers (eds), *The Ivy Leaf: The Parnells Remembered* (Dublin, 2006).
McCartney, Donal and Pauric Travers (eds), *Parnell Reconsidered* (Dublin, 2013).
McConnel, James, 'John Redmond and Irish Catholic Loyalism', in *English Historical Review*, vol. 125, no. 512 (Feb, 2010), pp 83–111.
McConnel, James, *The Irish Parliamentary Party and the Third Home Rule Crisis* (Dublin, 2013).
McConnel, James, 'Out in the cold? The children of the Irish Parliamentary Party and the Irish Free State', in *Irish Historical Studies*, vol. 42, no. 161 (2018), pp 87–114.
McDermott, Alice, 'Bridget Redmond: The keeper of the Redmondite flame in Waterford', in *Decies*, vol. 66 (2010), pp 87–102.
McDermott, Alice, '"The heart of the matter": an analysis of the most significantly influential factor in the creation and configuration of Redmondism in Waterford city from 1891 to 1918', in *Decies*, vol. 69 (2013), pp 139–52.
McDowell, R. B., *The Irish Convention, 1917–18* (London, 1970).
McMahon, Tim, Michael de Nie and Paul Townend (eds), *Ireland in an Imperial World: Citizenship, Opportunity and Subversion* (Basingstoke, 2017).
Meleady, Dermot, *John Redmond: The Parnellite* (Cork, 2008).
Meleady, Dermot, *John Redmond: The National Leader* (Dublin, 2013).
Meleady, Dermot, *John Redmond: Selected Letters and Memoranda, 1880–1918* (Dublin, 2018).
Morrissey, Conor, '"Rotten Protestants": Protestant home rulers and the Ulster Liberal Association, 1906–1918', in *The Historical Journal*, vol. 61, no. 3 (2018), pp 743–65.
Mulvagh, Conor 'A souring of friendships?: Internal divisions in the leadership of the Irish Parliamentary Party in the aftermath of the Easter Rising', in Diarmaid Ferriter and Susanah Riordan (eds), *Years of Turbulence: The Irish Revolution and its Aftermath* (Dublin, 2015), pp 85–105.
Mulvagh, Conor, *The Irish Parliamentary Party at Westminster, 1900–1918* (Manchester, 2016).
Mulvagh, Conor, 'Ulster exclusion and Irish nationalism: consenting to the principle of partition, 1912–1916', in *Revue Française de Civilisation Britannique*, xxiv, no. 2 (2019).
Murphy, William Michael, *The Parnell Myth and Irish Politics, 1891–1956* (New York, 1986).
Nic Dháibhéid, Caoimhe and Colin Reid (eds), *From Parnell to Paisley: Constitutional and Revolutionary Politics in Modern Ireland* (Dublin, 2010).
Nic Dháibhéid, Caoimhe, Shahmima Akhtar, Dónal Hassett, Kevin Kenny, Timothy G. McMahon and Jane Ohlmeyer, 'Round table: Decolonising Irish history? possibilities, challenges, practices', in *Irish Historical Studies*, vol. 159 (2021), pp 303–32.
O'Brien, Conor Cruise, *Parnell and His Party, 1880–90* (Oxford, 1957).
O'Brien, Conor Cruise, *The Shaping of Modern Ireland* (London, 1960).
O'Brien, Conor Cruise, *States of Ireland* (London, 1972).
O'Brien, Joseph, *William O'Brien and the Course of Irish Politics, 1881–1918* (Berkeley, CA, 1976).
O'Brien, R. B., *The Life of Charles Stewart Parnell, 1846–1891* (London, 1899).
O'Brien, R. B. (ed.), *Home Rule: Speeches of John Redmond* (London, 1910).
O'Brien, William, *An Olive Branch in Ireland and Its History* (London, 1910).
O'Brien, William, *The Irish Revolution and how it Came About* (Dublin, 1923).
O'Brien, William, *The Parnell of Real Life* (London, 1926).
O'Connor, T. P., *Memoirs of an Old Parliamentarian*, 2 Vols (London, 1929).
Ó Broin, León, *Parnell: Beathaisnéis* (Baile Átha Cliath, 1937).
O'Callaghan, Margaret, *British High Politics and a Nationalist Ireland: Criminality, Land and the Law under Forster and Balfour* (Cork, 1994).
O'Callaghan, Margaret, '"First Past the Post" and the strange case of unionist Ireland', in *Parliamentary History*, vol. 16 (1997), pp 85–106.
O'Connor Lysaght, D. R., 'The rhetoric of Redmondism', in *History Ireland* (Spring 2003), pp 44–49.
O'Day, Alan, *Irish Home Rule, 1867–1921* (Manchester, 1998).
O'Day, Alan, *Charles Stewart Parnell* (Dundalk, 1998).

O'Donoghue, Martin, *The Legacy of the Irish Parliamentary Party in Independent Ireland, 1922–1949* (Liverpool, 2019).

O'Donoghue, Martin, '"Ireland's Independence Day": The 1918 election campaign in Ireland and the Wilsonian moment', in *European Review of History: Revue Européenne d'Histoire*, vol. 26, no. 5 (2019), pp 834–54.

O'Donoghue, Martin, 'Faith and Fatherland? The Ancient Order of Hibernians, northern nationalism and the partition of Ireland', in *Irish Historical Studies*, vol. 46, no. 169 (May 2022), pp 77–100.

Ó Tuathaigh, Gearóid, 'Exemplar, outlier, impostor? A reflection on Ireland and the discourses of colonialism', in Róisín Healy and Enrico dal Lago (eds), *The Shadow of Colonialism on Europe's Modern Past* (Basingstoke, 2014), pp 36–56.

Pašeta, Senia, '1798 in 1898: The politics of commemoration', in *The Irish Review*, no. 22 (Summer, 1998) pp 46–53.

Pašeta, Senia, *Before the Revolution: Nationalism, Social Change and Ireland's Catholic Elite* (Cork, 1999).

Pašeta, Senia, 'Ireland's last home rule generation: The decline of constitutional nationalism in Ireland, 1916–30', in Mike Cronin and John M. Regan (eds), *Ireland: The Politics of Independence, 1922–49* (Basingstoke, 2000), pp 13–31.

Pašeta, Senia, *Thomas Kettle* (Dublin, 2008).

Pašeta, Senia, *Irish Nationalist Women, 1900–1918* (Cambridge, 2013).

Pašeta, Senia (ed.), *Uncertain Futures: Essays About the Irish Past for Roy Foster* (Oxford, 2016).

Phoenix, Eamon, *Northern Nationalism: Nationalist Politics, Partition and the Catholic Minority in Northern Ireland, 1890–1940* (Belfast, 1994).

Prager, Jeffrey, *Building Democracy in Ireland: Political Order and Cultural Integration in a Newly Independent Nation* (Cambridge, 1986).

Redmond-Howard, Louis, *John Redmond: The Man and the Demand, a Biographical Study in Irish Politics* (London, 1910).

Reid, Colin, *The Lost Ireland of Stephen Gwynn: Irish Constitutional Nationalism and Cultural Politics, 1864–1950* (Manchester, 2011).

Reid, Colin, '"An experiment in constructive unionism": Isaac Butt, home rule and federalist political thought during the 1870s', in *English Historical Review*, vol. 129, no. 537 (2014), pp 332–61.

Reilly, Niamh, 'The many-sided Tom Kettle', in Ciara Boylan, Sarah-Anne Buckley and Pat Dolan (eds), *Family Histories of the Irish Revolution* (Dublin, 2017), pp 84–96.

Thornley, David, 'The Irish Home Rule Party and parliamentary obstruction, 1874–87', in *Irish Historical Studies*, vol. 12, no. 45 (1960), pp 38–57.

Thornley, David, *Isaac Butt and Home Rule* (London, 1964).

Townend, Paul, *The Road to Home Rule: Anti-Imperialism and the Irish National Movement* (Madison, WI, 2016).

Ward. A. J., *The Irish Constitutional Tradition: Responsible Government and Modern Ireland, 1782–1992* (Dublin, 1994).

Ward, Margaret, *Unmanageable Revolutionaries: Women and Irish Nationalism* (London, 1983).

Wells, W. B., *The Life of John Redmond* (London, 1919).

Wheatley, Michael, 'John Redmond and federalism in 1910', in *Irish Historical Studies*, vol. 32, no. 127 (May 2001), pp 343–64.

Wheatley, Michael, *Nationalism and the Irish Party: Provincial Ireland, 1910–1916* (Oxford, 2005).

Whelan, Bernadette, 'The transatlantic world of Charles Stewart Parnell (1846–91)', in *Journal of Transatlantic Studies*, vol. 14, no. 3 (2016), pp 293–308.

Index

1798 Rebellion 6, 12–13
    Commemoration Committee 13
    commemorations 3, 49

abstentionism 78–9, 86
Act of Union (1800) 4, 27, 85
Adams, W.G.S. 19
Æ (George Russell) 19
agrarian radicalism 2, 12, 14, 21–3, 25, 30, 41
Ahern, Bertie 112
All-for-Ireland League 75–6
amnesty campaigns 12–13, 15, 106
Ancient Order of Hibernians (AOH) 4, 7, 42, 54, 59, 66, 75, 77–9, 81, 86
    Ladies' Auxiliary 62
Anglo-Irish Agreement (1985) 9, 111–12
Anglo-Irish relations 7, 9–10
Anglo-Irish Treaty (1921) 11, 79–80, 92, 95
    anti-Treatyites 79–81, 83, 90, 92–3
    Treatyites 80–3, 85, 87
Anglophobia 25, 108, 112–13
Anti-Partition League 84
Army Comrades Association (ACA) 94, 96–7 *see also* National Guard; *see also* Blueshirts
Asquith, H.H. 16–17, 48, 62, 64–5, 80
Austro-Hungarian Empire 48, 51

Balfour, Arthur 17, 19, 84
Ballybricken Pig Buyers' Society 92, 95
Bernadotte monarchy 48
Bew, Paul 4, 15, 21, 36
Biagini, Eugenio 5, 14
Birrell, Augustine 60
Blair, Tony 108
Blue Blouses 89, 97
Blueshirts 9, 83, 96–7
Boer War 5, 13, 16–17, 66
Boundary Commission 9, 78, 81
Brexit 7, 9, 31, 45, 50, 111–12
British Commonwealth 18, 80–1, 83–4, 87
British constitution 14, 16, 45
British Empire 2, 4–5, 13, 15–17, 23, 27–9, 43, 47, 50–1, 53, 81, 85, 106, 109 *see also* imperialism
Browne, Kathleen 97
Browne, Noel 100
Brugha, Caitlín 93
Brugha, Cathal 93
Bruton, John 86, 111–12

Butt, Isaac 1–3, 5–7, 14, 20–31
by-elections 38–9, 58, 60, 109
Byrne, Alfie 79
Byrne, Richard 79, 84

Callanan, Frank 12, 19
Campbell, Fergus 76
Campbell, T.J. 79, 84, 86
Campbell-Bannerman, Henry 42
Carson, Edward 4, 7, 17, 44–52, 55, 62, 110
Carson, Harry 44–5
Casement, Roger 9, 112–13
Cat and Mouse Act (1913) 71
Catholic Church 7, 18, 25–6, 36, 38–9, 90, 100
Catholics 1, 7, 12, 24, 59, 75, 77–8, 109–11
Cecil, Lord Robert 69
Childers, Erskine 19
Church of Ireland 24
Churchill, Lord Randolph 38
Churchill, Winston 17, 112
Civil War 74
Civil War politics 8, 75, 79–81, 83, 86
Clarke, Tom ('Henry Wilson') 4, 13
Cline, Catherine Ann 80
Collins, James 24
Collins, Michael 80
Collins-O'Driscoll, Margaret 96
colonialism 4, 47, 51
Concannon, Helena 96, 101–2
Conciliation Bill (1910) 65–6, 72
Conditions of Employment Bill (1935) 101
Connelly, Alpha 90
Connery, Meg 69
Connolly, James 9, 112–13
conscription 19, 57, 59, 61
Conservative Party 12, 14–17, 48
constitution (1782) 29–30
Cooke, A.B. 15
Cosgrave, James 79, 82
Cosgrave, W.T. 18, 80, 82, 95
Costello, John A. 84, 99
Cousins, Margaret 64, 67
Cowling, Maurice 15
Craig, James 62, 77
Criminal Law (Amendment) Bill (1934) 101
Croatia 51
Crowley, Honor 83
Cumann na nGaedheal 74, 79–81, 83–6, 88–90, 93–7, 102

Dáil Éireann 78–80, 84
    First Dáil 76, 92
    Second Dáil 76
'Dáil widows' 91, 93–5, 100, 103–4
Dangerfield, George 4–5
Davitt, Michael 12, 22, 35, 40, 75, 83
Davitt, Robert Emmet 83
de Valera, Éamon 18, 81–2, 84–5, 95, 97, 101
Decade of Centenaries 2, 6, 9
Democratic Party (USA) 85
democratisation 6, 12–17, 41, 107
Department of Agriculture 41
Devlin, Joe 8, 26–7, 41–2, 41, 57, 63, 76–9, 86–7
devolution 9, 17–18, 27, 29, 31, 50, 108–9
Dicey, Albert Venn 13, 22–3
Dickinson, Willoughby 71
Dillon, James 83–4, 86–7
Dillon, John 15, 17–18, 39, 41–2, 51, 56, 59–60, 65, 70, 76–7, 81–2, 107
Donnelly, Eamon 84
Doris, William 59
Dublin Metropolitan Police 13
Dublin strike and lockout (1913) 5
Dunphy, Richard 85

Easter Rising 4, 8–9, 11, 18–19, 60–1, 75–6, 86, 92, 109–10, 112
economic war 83, 95–6
elections *see* by-elections; general elections; local elections
Elibank, Master of 53
Emerson, Kathleen 69
Esmonde, Thomas Lymbrick 84
Esmonde, Thomas Grattan 77
European Union 9, 112

Fanning, Ronan 17
Farmers' Party 79–80, 82–3
Farrell, Brian 4
Farrell, J.P. 59
Farrell, Mel 83
fascism 83, 97–8
Fawcett, Millicent 65
federalism 6, 19, 20–4, 27–31, 51, 54
Fenianism (Irish Republican Brotherhood) 3–4, 12–13, 23, 42, 48–9, 106
    American 21
    neo-Fenians 105
Fianna Fáil 49, 74, 81–3, 85, 90, 94–8, 100–2
Fine Gael 83–4, 86, 88, 97, 99–100, 102
Finnan, Joseph 4
First World War 7–8, 11, 19, 36, 43, 53–61, 74, 91–2, 109–10
    recruitment 56–8
Fitzgibbon family 107
Fitzpatrick, David 75–6
Foster, Roy 21, 109
free trade 45

Freeman's Journal 105–6
Furlong, Fr Patrick 38

Gaelic League 63
Gardiner, A.G. 34, 108
Garvin, Tom 16, 76
'Gaultier Nine' 96
Gavan Duffy, Charles 31
general elections
    1874: 2
    1906: 42
    1918: 3, 74, 89, 92
    1921: 77, 89
    1929: 78
    1933: 88, 95–6
    1943: 100
German Plot 19
Gilhooley, James 66
Ginnell, Laurence 76, 108
Gladstone, William 11, 13–14, 16–17, 34, 36, 38, 106
Gonne, Maud 63
Good Friday Agreement (1998) 9, 112
Government of Ireland Acts
    1914 (Home Rule Act): 42–3, 55–6, 71
    1920: 9, 77
Grattan, Henry 4
Grattan's parliament 27, 29, 80
Griffith, Arthur 80
gun running 19, 70
Gwynn, Denis 4
Gwynn, Stephen 18, 28, 63, 77, 82, 111

Harbison, Thomas 78
Harrington, Edward 12
Harrison, Sarah Cecilia 67
Haughey, Charles 105
Hayden, Mary 67–8, 72
Hayden family 107
Healy, Cahir 78
Healy, Tim 1, 12–13, 19, 33, 36–7, 40–1, 66, 81
Hoey (Redmond), Mary 1, 105
Hogan, Patrick 81, 93
Home Government Association 23–4, 26
Home Rule 11–12, 14–18, 20–31, 36, 42, 45, 55–6, 79, 85, 110
    in Ulster 77–9
    and women's suffrage 62–73
Home Rule Act *see* Government of Ireland Act (1914)
Home Rule bills 16, 27
    First (1886) 13, 35, 50–1, 106
    Second (1893) 27, 40, 107
    Third (1912) 6–7, 13, 15, 17, 24, 27, 45, 63, 66–8, 73
Home Rule crisis 6–7, 44, 53, 71, 84, 109
Home Rule League 2, 24, 74
Hoppen, K.T. 47

Horgan, J.J. 18, 34, 43
Horowitz, Donald 14
House of Lords 16, 107

Imperial Defence, Committee on 16
imperialism 5–7, 11, 15, 19, 21, 27, 31, 43–5, 47–50 *see also* British Empire; colonialism
Indian National Congress 85
Inghinidhe na hÉireann 63
Inter-Party Government 99
Irish Brigade 58
Irish Citizen 68, 72
Irish Constitution (1937) 90, 101
Irish Convention (1917–18) 17–19
Irish Council Bill (1907) 16–17, 54, 108
Irish diaspora 51
Irish divisions, in the British Army 56–9
Irish Dominion League 77
Irish Farmers Union (IFU) 79
Irish Free State 74, 79, 81, 85
Irish Free State Constitution (1922) 89, 101
Irish Independent 13
Irish Land and Labour Association 79
Irish National Federation 41
Irish Nation League 76
Irish National League 37, 41, 81–3, 93
Irish Parliamentary Party (IPP) 1–3, 12–13, 15–16, 21, 25, 65, 82, 85–6, 108
    achievements 15
    decline 7, 43, 53, 60, 74–80, 92, 109
    and the First World War 53–61
    legacy 74–87
    misogyny 62–4
    reunification 15, 36, 41
    split 2
    and women's suffrage 62–7, 69–71
Irish question 17–18, 31, 35, 39, 49
Irish Republican Army (IRA) 85, 98
Irish Republican Brotherhood (IRB) *see* Fenianism
Irish Unionist Alliance 15
Irish University Question (1908) 42
Irish Volunteers 7, 41, 54–7, 60
Irish Women's Franchise League (IWFL) 64–5, 67–8
Irish World 57
Ivy Day 40–1

Jackson, Alvin 2–4, 78
Jalland, Patricia 5
Jászi, Oszkár 48
Jinks, John 82
Joint Committee of Women's Societies and Social Workers 101
Jordan, Joe 105
Joyce, James 16
Judson, Pieter 48

Kelly, Matthew 41
Kerr, Philip (Lord Lothian) 18
Kettle, Mary Sheehy 65, 82
Kettle, Tom 63–4, 66–8, 71
Kiersey, John 93, 95
Kingston, Lucy 73
Kitchener, Lord 48, 55

Labour Party 62, 79, 82, 94–5
    British 80
    Northern Ireland 79
Ladies' Land League 63, 72
Laffan, Michael 18
Lalor, James Fintan 22–3
Lalor-Fitzpatrick, John 74
Land Conference (1903) 17
Land League 3, 22, 63, 83–4, 107
land purchase 15
land reform 22–3, 41
land question 14, 23–4, 30, 105, 107, 110
land tenure 22–3
Land War 14, 30, 107
Larkin, Emmet 7
Law, Hugh 65, 68–9
Lee, J.J. 7
Leeke, George 78
Lemass, Seán 49
Lennon, Gerry 86
Liberal alliance 12–13, 37–8, 42–3, 50
Liberal Party 11–12, 14–17, 48, 65, 80, 109
Lifford, Lord 24
Lijphart, Arend 14
Lloyd, Maud 66
Lloyd George, David 17–18, 80
local elections (1920) 77
Logue, Cardinal Michael 76, 92
Long, Walter 19
Lothian, Lord (Philip Kerr) 18
Lowe, Eleanor 93
Lynch, Arthur 42
Lyons, F.S.L. 4

McAleer, Hugh 86
McAllister, T.S. 78
MacAtasney, Gerard 4
McCaffrey, Lawrence 20
McCarthy, Justin 34
McCarthy, Pat 91, 94
McConnel, James 55, 85, 87
McCoole, Sinéad 103
McCoubrey, Margaret 71
Mac Curtain, Margaret 103
MacDermot, Frank 83–4, 87
McDermott, Alice 91–2, 102
MacDonagh, Michael 5, 36, 110
MacDonagh, Oliver 42
McDonnell, Sir Antony 17
McDowell, R.B. 4

McElroy, Gail 103
McEntee, Seán 98
Mac Eoin, Sean 94
McGilligan, Patrick 81
McGuinness, Joe 18
McKnight, Thomas 31
MacLysaght, Edward 19
McMahon, Deirdre 17
McManus, Terence Bellew 12
MacNeill, John Gordon Swift 26–7
McSparran, James 84
McSwiney, Mary 72
Mair, Peter 74
Mallick (*née* Sex), Bridget 91
Mallick, John 91
Mallon, John 13
Manning, Georgina 71, 103
Mansergh, Nicholas 1, 19, 43
Maume, Patrick 68, 82, 106
Meleady, Dermot 4, 13, 15, 105–6
Milner, Alfred 17–18
Mitchel, John 23
Mohr, Thomas 89
Monypenny, W.F. 109
Moore, Colonel Maurice 59
Moran, D.P. 108, 110
Morley, John 35, 37, 106
Mother and Child Scheme 100
Mulcahy, Richard 98
Mulvagh, Conor 55, 81
Murphy, Cliona 73
Murphy, William Martin 18

Nannetti, J.P. 5
National Centre Party 77, 83, 94, 97
National Convention of Parnellites (1891) 39
National Guard 97
National League 37, 63, 86
National Volunteers 57, 59
nationalism 12–14, 16–17, 19, 55, 57, 77, 110
    constitutional 20, 26, 42–3, 45–9, 68, 80
    militant 49
    northern 77–9, 84
Nationalist Party (Northern Ireland) 8, 85–6
Nationality 76
neutrality 83–4
New Departure 3, 12, 21, 27, 30–1
Northern Ireland 8, 50–1, 77–8, 85 *see also* Stormont
    civil rights movement 86
    peace process 106
Northern Ireland Protocol 9
Nugent, John Dillon 77–8

O'Brien, Conor Cruise 4
O'Brien, Francis Cruise 19, 30, 32–3
O'Brien, R. Barry 34, 36

O'Brien, William 4, 12–13, 15, 41, 56, 66, 75, 79, 107
O'Connell, Daniel 4, 14, 20, 31, 47–8
O'Connor, T.P. 16, 22, 34, 54, 77
O'Connor Power, John 34
O'Day, Alan 21
O'Donnell, Frank Hugh 25
O'Donnell, Tom 81–2
O'Duffy, Eoin 83–4, 96–7
O'Farrelly, Agnes 67
Ógra Fianna Fáil 105
O'Higgins, Kevin 81–2
O'Kelly, J.J. 13
Oldham, Charles 66
O'Malley, William 82
O'Mara, James 76
O'Neill, Patrick 78
O'Shea, Katharine 2, 36
Ostrogorski, Moisei 85

Pankhurst, Christabel 66, 68, 70
Parliament Act (1911) 16
Parnell, Charles Stewart 1–2, 7, 11–12, 15, 20–1, 24–5, 28–9, 45, 48, 52, 85, 105–6 *see also* Redmond, John
    death and funeral 12, 39–40
    manifesto 38
    monument 32, 41–3
    speeches 34–5, 106
Parnellism 24–5, 30, 41, 46, 105–7
Parnellite split 12–13, 32, 35–8, 41, 51, 75
    anti-Parnellites 12, 40
    Parnellites: 12, 40; National Convention 39
partition 7, 17–18, 45, 47, 50–2, 77, 85, 111
Pašeta, Senia 3, 62–3
Pearse, Margaret Mary 96, 101
Phoenix Park murders 106
Pigott, Richard 14
Pigs and Bacon Bill (1937) 98
Plunkett, Count George 18
Plunkett, Sir Horace 13, 15, 19, 77, 106
Primrose, Archibald (Earl of Rosebery) 16
Primrose League 62
prisoner releases 19
Prisoners' (Temporary Discharge for Ill-Health) Act (1913) (Cat and Mouse Act) 71
Property Defence Association 15
proportional representation 77, 85
Protestantism 21
Protestants 24–6, 35, 46, 105
    Ulster 21, 26, 31, 35
Provisional Government 89

Ranch War 108
Read, Charles 22
Recess Committee 13, 106
Redmond, Bridget 3, 9, 84, 88–104
Redmond, John 105–13

and Fenian amnesty campaigns 13, 15, 106, 108
background 1, 12, 46
and Carson 44–52
Catholicism 4, 7, 46, 49
character 33–4, 36, 38, 42, 48, 52
death: 91; centenary of 45
early career 12
funeral 1
and Home Rule 11–13, 15–18, 21, 25–31, 39–43, 44, 108
influences: Butt 26, 28–31; Parnell 12, 32–43, 46, 106
and imperialism 4–5, 11, 19, 20, 27–8, 43–5, 48–9
and the IPP 25–6, 40–1, 53–61, 107
and the Irish Convention 17–19
MP for New Ross 1–2, 33
MP for Waterford 2, 40, 92
nationalism 49, 53
opposition to women's suffrage 63–7, 69–73
and partition 18, 50–2
speeches 28–9, 32, 34–40, 43, 62–3, 70, 108; Woodenbridge 34, 56
support for the First World War 18, 54–8
travels: 5; Australia and New Zealand 28, 43; USA 30, 43
Redmond, Johanna 36
Redmond, John Edward (Redmond's uncle) 1
Redmond (née Hoey), Mary 1, 105
Redmond, Capt. William Archer 1, 9, 28, 33–4, 71, 76–7, 79, 81–2, 87, 88, 91–3
Redmond, Willie 5, 12, 63, 65, 69, 71, 105
Redmondism 3, 7–9, 53–4, 75, 80, 86, 91–2, 95, 99, 105–13
  neo-Redmondism 84
Redmond-Howard, Louis 44–5
Reform Act (1884) 6
Regan, John M. 81
Representation of the People Act (1918) 89
Representation of the People Bill (1913) 71, 73
Republic of Ireland Bill (1948) 99–100
republicanism 12, 106, 109
Reynolds, Mary 94, 96, 100
Rice, Bridget Mary 100
Rosebery, Earl of (Archibald Primrose) 16, 47
Rover, Constance 65–6
Runciman, Walter 70
Russell, George (Æ) 19
Russell, T.W. 34

Saint-Gaudens, Augustus 32
Salmond, Alex 45–6
Scotland 9, 108–9
Scott, Andrew MacCullum 80
Scottish nationalism 109
Second World War 84
separatism 29, 31, 43, 45, 48–9, 106, 112

Sexton, Thomas 37
shared sovereignty 51
Sheehy, David 71
Sheehy (Kettle), Mary 65, 82
Sheehy Skeffington, Frank 64, 66–7
Sheehy Skeffington, Hanna 63–5, 67–8, 100
Shepherd, John 80
Sinn Féin 8, 18–19, 42, 51, 60–1, 63, 74–81, 83–6, 89, 92
Smith, F.E. 109
Snowden, Philip 68–9
Social Democratic and Labour Party 86
Spender, Harold 106
Stead, W.T. 34, 36
Stewart, Joseph 86
Stopford Green, Alice 19
Stormont 79, 84–87
Sullivan, A.M. 33–4, 111
Sullivan, T.D. 14

Tenant Right League 22
Thorney, David 20
Tone, Wolfe 13, 42
Town Tenants Act (1906) 42
Townend, Paul 5
trade unionism 5
Trimble, David 112

Ulster crisis 21, 75
Ulster question 35–6, 43
Ulster Unionists 18, 22, 55, 62, 109
Ulster Volunteer Force (UVF) 70
Ulster Volunteers 18, 54–5
Ulster Women's Unionist Council 62
unionism 12, 14, 16–17, 26, 40–1, 44, 48–51, 110
Unionist Party 25, 75, 78, 80–1
United Ireland 14, 26
United Ireland Party *see* Fine Gael
United Irish League (UIL) 15, 41–2, 57, 63–4, 75, 79, 85, 107, 110
  Young Ireland Branch (YIBs) 63–4
United Irish movement 26
United Kingdom 47, 85
united kingdoms 47–9, 52
USA 85
  and the First World War 18–19
  fundraising in 18

Valiulis, Maryann Gialanella 90
Varley, Tony 79
Vincent, John 15

War Office 56, 58–9
Ward, Margaret 101
Waterford Pig Dealers' Association 93
Waterford Women's Nationalist Association 92–3
Webb, Deborah 67
Wheatley, Michael 76, 81, 109–10

White, Terence de Vere 20, 25
White, Vincent 92, 94–5
Wilson, Henry *see* Clarke, Tom
Wilson, Woodrow 19
Windle, Sir Bertram 18
women, political participation 3, 88–91, 100–4
    see also Redmond, Bridget
Women Graduates' Association (WGA) 101–2
Women's Liberal Federation 62
women's rights 89–90, 101
Women's Social and Political Union (WSPU) 64, 66, 69–71
women's suffrage movement 2–3, 5, 8, 62–73, 89
Wyndham, George 17
Wyndham Act (1903) 41, 107
Wyse-Power, Jennie 71–2, 82–3